Children's Novels
and the Movies

UNGAR FILM LIBRARY
SELECTED LISTING

Children's Novels and the Movies

Edited by Douglas Street

WITH HALFTONE ILLUSTRATIONS

FREDERICK UNGAR PUBLISHING CO.
New York

Copyright © 1983 by Frederick Ungar Publishing Co., Inc.
Printed in the United States of America

Design by Marsha Picker

Library of Congress Cataloging in Publication Data
Main entry under title:

Children's novels and the movies.

  Bibliography: p.
  Includes index.
  1. Children's literature—Film and video adaptations.
I. Street, Douglas.
PN1997.85.C44   1983   791.43'75   83-14816
ISBN 0-8044-2840-9
ISBN 0-8044-6883-4 (pbk.)

For Jack and Marjorie Street

Contents

ACKNOWLEDGMENTS I wish to thank David Greene for initially steering me to this project, and Tom Jordan and David Mucci of Texas A&M for providing resources and assistance in several film matters. William G. Catron of Mattel, Inc., must also be recognized for his aid and information. My gratitude goes to Thomas Erskine and James Welsh of *Literature/Film Quarterly* for allowing Carol Billman's article to be reprinted here. To Billie Street goes my appreciation for her optimism and understanding during the hectic stages of preparation. A special thanks must be given to Stanley Hochman of Frederick Ungar for his guidance, support and patience throughout the course of this undertaking. And lastly, but by no means least, my warmest thanks to all the contributors, without whose expertise and interest in the subject, this volume could not have been executed.

PHOTO CREDITS Unless otherwise noted, photos are courtesy of Collectors Book Store, Hollywood, California.

Introduction

No screen writer faces a more difficult task than the translation of a classic from the printed word into celluloid, and when
the classic is for children, the difficulty is increased because
many generations have read and loved that book.
     —Florence Ryerson & Edgar Allan Woolf

Transferring any literary work to the screen can at times be a
no-win proposition. And, as the adapters of *The Wizard of Oz*
attest above, "when the classic is for children, the difficulty is
increased because many generations have read and loved that
book."

CHILDREN'S NOVELS . . .

The immortal works of childhood seem to conjure up memories
and emotional attachments which transcend the tactile world
of the novel itself. Adults and children alike are quite posses-
sive and vociferous about their favorites and to tamper with
these memories through the objective medium of the movies is
to invite a reaction by and large inconceivable in any other art.
Indeed the business of filmmaking for the child audience includes more variables than movies primarily intended for
adults; if the film has a literary counterpart, that movie's multifaceted nature adds further complications.

To better understand this hybrid and hence the scope and
concerns of this volume, we must first come to terms with what
is to be meant by "children's" fiction. While most readers will
readily accept the designation as fittingly applied to, for instance, *Pinocchio*, *Wizard of Oz*, or *Charlotte's Web*, some may
balk at including *The Hobbit* or *Watership Down*, fantasies
equally at home in the university library and on the young
person's bookshelf. In addition, books such as *Little Women*,

Tom Brown's Schooldays, Kim, and *Hero Ain't Nothin' But A Sandwich* might better be seen as intended for adolescents rather than children. To a great extent concepts of what can legitimately be considered "suitable for children" are directly contingent upon personal biases concerning what a child is, likes, needs, and is capable of understanding and enjoying— conclusions often arrived at without direct juvenile contact.

For the purposes of our discussions the children's novel shall be classified as a full-length fictional creation fitting into one or more of three particular categories. A book may qualify as a children's book if it is judged to be clearly and unabashedly conceived specifically for a child audience. *Alice's Adventures in Wonderland, The Wonderful Wizard of Oz,* or *Pippi Longstocking* for example, contain fun and fantasy clearly woven into the narrative to ensnare the imaginations and accolades of the young.

The second group of children's novels is composed of works written primarily for the pleasure of the authors themselves. Such books are characterized by a highly personal commitment to narrative structure, setting and personality development; the writer more often than not is totally immersed in the fictional reality of the creation, frequently weaving the tale from the inside out. Fantasists such as J. R. R. Tolkien and Richard Adams shun strict categorization of their works. In a televised response to a reviewer who asked if his *Watership Down* was intended for children, Adams said: "There's no such thing as a children's book and [*Watership Down*] is not a children's book—it's a book. If children read it and like it, that's fine. If [adults] read it and like it, that's fine."

The third category of children's novel includes those seminal works that were originally the official property of adults but have over the years been adapted for and energetically adopted by young readers. For example, this volume's Filmography includes works by Defoe, Swift and Dickens that through time and transformation have become undeniable cornerstones in the foundation of the literature of childhood, and have provided inspiration to generations of filmmakers. "If children read it and enjoy it, that's fine." Enjoyment is the key; a work need only be sufficiently enjoyed by the young to make them usurp it for themselves.

A children's novel then is simply one repeatedly read and enjoyed by children. If not written particularly for them it does contain features that will allow it to become part of their world. And when the children's novel becomes the "classic" children's novel, it means that acceptance and longevity have made it a highlight of the genre.

But classic or no the children's novel has both in the critical and the popular arenas been long maligned. Too often it is seen as of pseudo-literary nature, inherently inferior to "real" (that is, adult) writing. Equally often, children's novels are considered as no more than literary "training wheels," educational tools for the classroom development of reading skills.

A parallel stigma was incurred in the cinema when the family film gave way to the post-World War II, Disney-dominated "children's movie" (a label implying the same sort of inferiority and superficiality). It seemed inconceivable that an intelligent adult, *sans* child, would choose to see a "children's movie" for his or her own personal pleasure. Natalie Babbit (whose own *Tuck Everlasting* was adapted for the screen in 1976) has complained that our society tends to view:

> . . . a ladder of life with only two rungs; the bottom rung reserved for children and the top for adults, . . . And while as adults we allow ourselves certain diversities, children are pressed all together into one vast single child who squats on that bottom rung like a chimpanzee, cute and clever, perhaps, but still only an imitation of humanity. . . . This schism we have created is clearly visible in the vast majority of books we produce for our children, and accounts for the palpable undertone of apology we can discern so often in the words, 'I write for children.'[1]

That the novel for the child audience is necessarily trite and superficially constructed is a misconception debunked as long ago as 1865 by the appearance of Lewis Carroll's *Alice's Adventures in Wonderland,* which invokes a marvelously complex world of nonsense and nonsequiturs in a multileveled construct of slapstick humor, ingenious wordplay, and cerebral insight.

[1]Natalie Babbitt, "How Can We Write Children's Books If We Don't Know Anything About Children?" *Publishers Weekly* 200 (July 1971), p. 65.

More current offerings like Norton Juster's 1961 *Phantom Tollbooth* successfully continue this sophisticated tradition. Monosyllables and sugarcoating do not guarantee the appreciation of the child audience. As *Charlotte's Web* creator, E. B. White, noted in "On Writing for Children": "Anybody who shifts gears when he writes for children is likely to wind up stripping his gears. . . . Anyone who writes *down* to children is simply wasting his time. You have to write up, not down. Children are demanding."[2] Currently acclaimed fiction for children reinforces the validity of this approach. As Paul Heins noted in his still timely August 1970 *Horn Book* article, "Coming To Terms With Criticism":

> Children's literature is a part of general literature; and even at the risk of overemphasizing the notion of branches, children's literature may be said to be a branch on the tree of literature. There have been authors like Stevenson, Mark Twain, and Kipling who in the past have written for both children and adults, as well as more recent writers like Thurber, C. S. Lewis, and E. B. White. . . . If children's literature is a part of all literature, then the criticism of children's literature becomes a part of the criticism of all literature. A children's book deserves to be probed as much as an adult book. . . . Not for the purpose of what is often called "dry" analysis, but for the joy of discovering the skill of the author. (pp. 370–371)

This argument is equally applicable to the world of the film. C. S. Lewis takes Heins's thinking one step further: "I am almost inclined to set it up as a canon that a children's story which is enjoyed only by children is a bad children's story. The good ones last."[3]

Lewis's canon for fiction is equally fitting to the appreciation of film, and Pauline Kael seems to echo it in saying: "I can't think of a single *good* 'children's' picture that intelligent adults can't enjoy, and I see no reason why we should not re-

[2]E. B. White, "On Writing for Children," in *Children and Literature: Views and Reviews*, ed. Virginia Haviland (Glenview, IL: Scott, Foresman, 1973), p. 140.

[3]C. S. Lewis, "On Three Ways of Writing for Children," *Horn Book Magazine* 39 (October 1963), p. 461.

spect our children at least as much as we respect ourselves."[4] Adult enthusiasm for films such as *Wizard of Oz, Adventures of Robin Hood,* or *E.T.: The Extra-Terrestrial* bear her out. The schism in viewing tastes, like that in literary tastes, is more coincidence than actuality. "Before Disney began to dominate this market," reflects Kael in *Kiss Kiss Bang Bang,* "it used to be assumed that good adventure movies could be enjoyed by adults and children; it was only after adventure movies and domestic comedies were reduced to formulas and silliness that this split developed between what *you* could enjoy and what you had to take your children to." And the truth is that many film and fiction classics have been carried along on the equally supportive and discerning shoulders of children and adults.

... AND THE MOVIES

Fiction and film, though distinct arts, have many points of kinship. For example, film has decided narrative qualities, and literature often freely borrows from film the equivalents of ellipsis, establishing and tracking shots, the long shot and the close-up. These standard cinematic techniques are to be found in the work of several accomplished writers. However, though these techniques are related, the transformation of the writer's visual language into the filmmaker's language of vision requires essential alterations of the original.

Like it or not, partisans of both mediums must realize that film and literature are, as George Bluestone sums up, "different aesthetic genera, as different from each other as ballet is from architecture." The craft of fiction is no more sacred because of its longer history than is film because of its greater audience accessibility. To discuss filmic realization in terms of literal transposition from page to celluloid is by and large an impossibility. There will always be literary purists howling over the slightest of screen deviations from the page demanded by the inherent differences in the media; however, literal reconstructions may appear even less like the originals than free adaptations. When one uproots a home, transports it to a

---

[4]Pauline Kael, "Movies for Young Children," *Kiss Kiss Bang Bang* (Boston: Little, Brown, 1968), p. 179.

new site, and sets it on a new foundation, though it may appear unchanged, its very transference has altered it. Outside it has a different spatial relationship with its new surroundings; inside, changes in situation, solar exposure, and view, noticeably alter the feel or long-established character of each component. A Victorian house that looks quite proper among its own kind may when transplanted to a modern setting appear antique and out of place unless changes are made to acclimatize it to its new surroundings. Administered intelligently and judiciously, such changes enhance its original attraction and contemporary value.

The same is true of a literary piece translated onto celluloid. Ultimate success is dependent upon the perceptive preservation of original feeling and attraction in harmony with requirements necessitated by the new, cinematic setting. Eugene Vale, in *The Technique of Screenplay Writing* (1972), concludes that it is not feasible to merely delete or rearrange the material nor to attempt photographic transpositions of entire novelistic scenes. "Since the physical characteristics of the different forms have different requirements, the very same scene may be inexpressive, if it is not properly integrated into another form. The smooth continuity may be completely disrupted by false transformation, one which does not go back to the facts of the material."

The screenwriter's initial step in reworking the fiction is to take the novel and return its multifaceted nature to the basic elements from which the novelist's ultimate creation blossomed. Only in this way can the fiction writer's product survive the change of medium. Director Lewis Milestone called this procedure a return to the "seed" of the creation: "If you want to produce a rose you will not take the flower and put it into the earth. . . . Instead you will take the seed and stick it into the soil. From it will grow another rose."

When applied particularly to children's fiction and the films from it, the faithful transplanting and cultivating of these "seeds" is crucial. While concept and technique are of utmost importance, as Maureen Gaffney contends, "translations of children's literature into visual media are more affected by the filmmaker's (or director's) attitude toward children, than by any other consideration."[5] The controversy over the artistry and suitability of the Disney product, for example, testifies to the truth of Gaffney's assertion. In her now famous 1965 *Horn Book* article, "Walt Disney Accused," Frances Clarke Sayers (like others after her) assails the animator for his lack of consideration for both the literary original from which he adapted so freely, and for his child audience to which he pandered for financial gain. Where Milestone sought to take the literary seed and cultivate it into a fresh blossom, say these children's critics, Disney shunned such a process as too time-consuming; he was content to take pictures and blueprints of such to his technicians for the manufacture of a paint and celluloid imitation—dazzling yet often lifeless.

The name and aura of Walt Disney have so pervaded this film market that the casual moviegoer thinks him synonymous with it. But, while one cannot deny the Disney popular impact—particularly within the realm of animation and its technology—his studio's novelistic reworkings, from the 1940 *Pinocchio* to its current releases, account for less than one-fifth of the total representation in the genre; and of those features, few have been notable or influential.

The history of the cinematic adaptation of the children's novel is closely intertwined with the overall history of the movie industry, and some of cinema's first reels drew on books for the young. By the close of our century's second decade, while movies were still in their infancy, the neophyte filmgoer had already been treated to at least seven screen versions of Charles Dickens's *Christmas Carol* (five released before 1915 alone!), four helpings of *Alice in Wonderland* beginning with Cecil Hepworth's 1903 print, three *Robinson Crusoe*s, and three *David Copperfield*s. In addition, there were two adaptations each of Dickens's *Oliver Twist* and *Pickwick Papers,* Mark Twain's *Tom Sawyer* and *Prince and the Pauper,* and Stevenson's *Treasure Island.* To these must be added seven solo releases, ranging from *Little Women* to *20,000 Leagues Under The Sea.* Similarly, one cannot talk of the dawn of the animated feature without noting *Gulliver*s and *Pinocchio*s

---

[5]Maureen Gaffney, "Point of View and Tone in Film Adaptation," *Children's Literature,* Vol. 9 (New Haven: Yale Press, 1981), p. 124.

adapted as early as 1911. It is somehow fitting that the motion-picture industry in its own youth should turn for inspiration and development to the substantial literature of childhood.[6]

This volume commences in moviedom's high-strung adolescence and closely follows its subsequent maturation into the respected artform it has become. Readers encounter here a literary heritage spanning over a century and a quarter and a film heritage of nearly fifty years. Products of children's literature's "Golden Age" are shown recast in films from Hollywood's golden era: Norman McLeod's *Alice in Wonderland* (1933), George Cukor's *Little Women* (1933), and Victor Fleming's *Treasure Island* (1934), each examined alongside later filmed versions. Lavish escapism and cautious realism characterize the two competing tendencies operating in the pre-World War II cinema (see MGM's *Wizard of Oz* [1939] and RKO's *Tom Brown* [1940], respectively), while the sensibility and light-heartedness of the postwar forties appear harbingers for the fifties' television age. The Disney mark in animation, set in the 1940 *Pinocchio,* gives way to his postwar, television decade; his initial live-action adventure, the 1950 *Treasure Island,* begins the trend toward the marriage of television concepts with backlot cinematic production that was to be a Disney trademark from the late-fifties until his death.

Movie treatments from the 1960s and 1970s are seen here to diverge into distinct yet interrelated camps. One finds a return to the high-budget musical spectacular—*Willy Wonka* (1971), *Chitty Chitty Bang Bang* (1968), *The Little Prince* (1974), etc. Simultaneously emerges the unpretentious yet lyrical, low-budget high-quality personal creations—*The Railway Children* (1972), *Island of the Blue Dolphins* (1964), *Sounder* (1972). Enriching these tendencies are remakes of the old classics, *Alice* (1972), *Treasure Island* (1972), *Little Women* (1978), *Kidnapped* (1971), and the 1980 *Little Lord Fauntleroy.* Seemingly with the death of Disney, this same period after a twenty-year lull sparked rejuvenated experimentation in the full-length animated feature. Such inspired activity produced

[6]For a brief history of these filmed adaptations the reader is directed to my, "An Overview of Filmic Adaptation of Children's Fiction," *Children's Literature Quarterly* 7 (Fall 1982).

Charlotte's Web (1973), *The Hobbit* (1977), *Watership Down* (1978), and *The Lion, the Witch and the Wardrobe* (1979).

Since the infant days of the movies it has been repeatedly shown that the classic children's novel, judiciously adapted and perceptively filmed, can achieve new glory in the celluloid medium. The timelessness and imaginative richness of those truly great literary works attracts filmmakers decades apart. Reading Roderick McGillis's analysis of the 1933 and 1972 *Alice* films, Perry Nodelman's insights into *Treasure Island* 1934, 1950, and 1972, or Phyllis Bixler's account of *Little Lord Fauntleroy* from Freddie Bartholomew to Ricky Schroder, one sees these novels showing a worth and an immediacy as viable in 1930, 1950 or 1980, as when they greeted their first readers in the last century.

In exploring the nuances of cinematic adaptation, the contributors to this volume had to confront several aspects of the medium and its adaptive behavior. Many a classic, for instance, has that timelessness allowing it to transcend the generations, yet when filmed it may likely develop a contemporaneousness that locks it into a specific era, unequivocally separating it from other kindred treatments. Though the Lord Fauntleroys brought together in the Bixler essay are cut from the same 1880s literary cloth, cinematically they nevertheless show the nearly forty-five years separating them; "the 1936 adaptation exaggerated the sentimentality and melodrama in Burnett's book, while the 1980 version shows a greater concern for psychological and social realism." Lucien Agosta in discussing the cinematic adaptation of the 1857 *Tom Brown's Schooldays,* notes that the 1940 film was steeped in messages of steadfastness for Britain's World War II audience, and therefore concludes that such works indeed exemplify "the common assertion that films reflect the psychological realities of the cultures which make and view them."

Just as period effects the adaptation, so too may a cinematic translation be endowed with the unmistakable personal vision or style of its director or producer. This is particularly true of Disney films, and those discussed in this volume exhibit the indelible print of the iron-willed Burbank cartoonist. Directorial vision and input often account for the difference between a motion-picture classic and a mediocre movie. Disney was periodically able to pull off this miracle, as were others in the industry. Carol Gay notes in her article that because of George Cukor's instincts as director his 1933 *Little Women* is still the truest to the book and a classic in its own right. There is also an *auteur* quality to the film version of *The Railway Children,* which Lionel Jeffries produced, wrote and directed as an exceptionally personal offering for the moviegoer. The film was, as Keith Odom notes, Jeffries's visual paean to a remembered childhood in England.

Through his work in *Island of the Blue Dolphins, Sounder,* and other films, producer Robert Radnitz makes clear his concern for creating the distinctive Radnitz feature. In his 1964 *Horn Book* article, he relates his excitement upon first reading *Island of the Blue Dolphins,* though he realized it contained all of the prerequisites for a good film, he was equally aware that a screen version of O'Dell's work presented enormous difficulty. "Mr. O'Dell's novel is basically an intimate monologue. It also has a certain mystique about it. Everyone, child or adult, who reads the book, feels that it is *his.* . . . How can a personal experience be translated into film?" Similar pitfalls, notes Roderick McGillis, await those attempting translation of Lewis Carroll's *Alice* books:

> No matter how "filmic" the *Alice* books appear, . . . the books depend heavily on verbal play. True, some advantage for the filmmaker resides here in that voice and comic dialogue transfer well to the sound cinema, yet any advantage is undercut by two disadvantages: verbal ingenuity is basic to *Alice,* but the cinema is not fundamentally verbal; the film viewer *looks for* action to counterpoint dialogue and character to provide subtlety to conversations.

As Tom Jordan concludes in reference to the successfully conceived *Watership Down* (1978): "Since the plot is rarely the reason for a book's success, the film is left with the impossible task of explaining to its audience why the book was significant when the film has almost no devices to make the explanation. . . . Even if a picture is worth a thousand words, a film cannot compress a major novel into ninety minutes."

Contributors have included views and misgivings of

novelists faced with the decision as to whether or not to allow their creations to be filmed. Gene Hardy presents Tolkien's vehement objection to anyone's "Disneyfying" his characters. Marilyn Apseloff reiterates E. B. White's insistence that any *Charlotte's Web* adaptation must not "violate 'the spirit and meaning of the story.' " To circumvent this potential trauma, several novelists attempted the screen translation themselves. Despite this, such films as *Pippi Longstocking* (1969), *Willy Wonka and the Chocolate Factory* (1971), and *Hero Ain't Nothin' But A Sandwich* (1978) still show a marked alteration of the authors' original approach, style, and thematic concerns. In her article on *Pippi Longstocking* as a novel and a film, Harriette Andreadis concludes that novelist Astrid Lindgren in turning scriptwriter "flattened the characters, enhanced the sexism, degraded the humor, emphasized conventionality and materialism, and used visually surprising and spectacular material in the screenplay; the result is a pallid and charmless reflection of the uniqueness of the original."

To the usual problems of theory, process, and authorship must be added the special obstacles faced by filmmakers and writers adapting stories to the musical form. Faithfulness of characterization and narrative are sometimes impossible to achieve when primary consideration must be given to choreography, lyrics, and musical scoring. As will be seen in the discussions of *Pinocchio, The Hobbit, Charlotte's Web* and *Watership Down*, animated films are faced with special problems that may sink a film adaptation despite technical and artistic wizardry.

Any investigation of such an all inclusive artform as film sets the stage for deeper inquiry. The reader while absorbing filmic considerations should remember that this volume offers a representative spectrum of the history of children's literature, from the Victorian Age to the Space Age. In ranging from *Tom Brown* to *Hero Ain't Nothin' But A Sandwich,* these collected studies consider a myriad of approaches and types within the development of fiction for children. They additionally focus on changing concepts of the child, as seen in children's literature from *Tom Brown* to *Hero,* from *Little Women* to *Pippi Longstocking.*

In any attempt at a detailed survey of a relatively unexplored artistic form, some selection process must be arbitrarily effected. In this first major collection of critical essays devoted exclusively to the children's novel and its motion picture counterparts the number of essays was limited to allow for the more ample development of each. Inevitably, a few favorites had to be omitted. It might, for example, have been profitable to focus on the 1940 and 1960 film versions of *Swiss Family Robinson*, to compare Alan Holubar's silent *20,000 Leagues Under The Sea* with Disney's 1954 version, or to analyze the film translations of Mary Norton's *The Borrowers*, Kipling's *Jungle Book*, or Juster's *Phantom Tollbooth*.

As an editor, I have tried to avoid overloading this collection with proponents of one discipline to the exclusion of another. Emphasis has been placed on contributors comfortable with both children's fiction and film studies. With the exception of Carol Billman's *Wizard of Oz* examination, all the essays were especially prepared for this volume.

—*Douglas Street*

Pride and Pugilism:
The Film Versions of *Tom Brown*

LUCIEN L. AGOSTA

On the eve of Tom Brown's departure for Rugby, his father the Squire elects to keep his parting advice short, providing Tom with an aphorism or two which he "could keep in his head ready for use."[1] Thomas Hughes's preparation of his son Maurice for Rugby was a good deal more prolix: it grew into *Tom Brown's Schooldays,* published in April 1857 to an enthusiastic reception at home and abroad. Its bewildered author could only find it "odd how it suits so many different folk"[2] as the novel ran into six English and two American editions during its first year. Since then, it has never been out of print. Its continuing popularity accounts for three film versions—one in 1940, directed by Robert Stevenson; another in 1951, directed by Gordon Parry; and a third, the BBC/Masterpiece Theatre five-episode serial, aired during the 1970s. In addition, *Tom Brown's Schooldays* has inspired a recent series of popular novels by George Macdonald Fraser chronicling the fortunes of Tom Brown's erstwhile persecutor, Harry Flashman, following his expulsion from Rugby.

The continuing popularity of the novel probably does not lie in its episodic, loosely knit plot structure which begins with a very young Tom comfortable in a nest of Browns at home in

---

[1]Thomas Hughes, *Tom Brown's Schooldays,* ed. by H. C. Bradley and ill. by Hugh Thomson (Boston: Ginn, 1918), p. 77. Subsequent quotations, taken from this edition, are indicated in the text.

[2]Edward C. Mack and W.H.G. Armytage, *Thomas Hughes: The Life of the Author of Tom Brown's Schooldays* (London: Benn, 1952), p. 89.

the Berkshire Vale of the White Horse. The promising scion of a sturdy race of prosperous soldiers and country squires, Tom is sent to Rugby to become, as his father puts it, "a brave, helpful, truth-telling Englishman, and a gentleman, and a Christian" (p. 78). Bullied by Flashman—at times unmercifully—Tom survives and wins out. With his friend Scud East, he gets into all sorts of scrapes, earning a reputation for recklessness and irresponsibility. In order to stem his heedless rush towards expulsion, Dr. Arnold, the famous headmaster of Rugby, entrusts the timid Arthur to Tom's care. As Tom eases Arthur into the boy-world of Rugby, Arthur is instrumental in Tom's evolution into the mature, responsible man his father has sent him to Rugby to become.

Emerging from this plot are three paramount thematic concerns: the novel is first of all a *Bildungsroman* in its concern with the physical and moral development of its young hero. Second, the novel, written at the dawn of the great age of the British public school, sets out to describe and defend that institution. *Tom Brown's Schooldays* is the first true "school story," a subsequently popular fictional sub-genre which demonstrates, according to John Rowe Townsend, "a self-contained world in which boys—or girls—are full citizens" of a community only marginally controlled by adults.[3] Third, the novel expresses an even larger social concern in that Rugby is shown to be a training ground for those who will eventually govern the nation and build the empire.

Of these three thematic concerns, it is the successful delineation of Tom as a character and the skillful depiction of his developmental drama which accounts for the fact that *Tom Brown's Schooldays* still finds its way into the hands of the modern reader. Tom's pluck in fronting the tyranny of Flashman, his carelessness in allowing the candlesticks he is supposed to be cleaning to warp in the fireplace, and his moral struggles with the ethics of using "cribs" in the preparation of his lessons all help to portray Tom as a true-to-life boy whose adventures are universal. Tom's maturation into adulthood

[3]John Rowe Townsend, *Written for Children* (Philadelphia: Lippincott, 1975), p. 111.

mirrors—at least in its broad outline—that process by which most arrive at full majority after successfully negotiating the trials of childhood and adolescence.

If this universal theme does indeed explain the continuing popularity of *Tom Brown's Schooldays,* one might reasonably expect that the various film versions would center on this aspect of the novel. Instead, they reflect the political and social realities of their times and thus find their centers in the contemporary concerns of their audiences and directors. It has by now become a truism that, as George Bluestone insists, a novel and its film adaptation represent "different aesthetic genera, as different from each other as ballet is from architecture."[4] Certainly this is true of the film versions of *Tom Brown's Schooldays* which differ not only from the novel but also from each other.

The 1940 film version of the novel exemplifies the common assertion that films reflect the psychological realities of the cultures which make and view them. By 1940, France and England were already at war with Germany, which had previously bluffed its way into acquiring new territories. Though America was not yet at war, many Americans feared their country soon would be. *Tom Brown's Schooldays* is a fitting novel for film translation in such combative times. Though not included in the film, its ode to pugilism is famous: "After all," asks the narrator of the novel, "what would life be without fighting, I should like to know? . . . Everyone who is worth his salt has his enemies, who must be beaten, be they evil thoughts and habits in himself or spiritual wickednesses in high places, or Russians, or Border-ruffians, or Bill, Tom, or Harry, who will not let him live his life in quiet till he has thrashed them" (p. 312).

Tom Brown's Schooldays, then, would have had special relevance for a wartime Anglo-American audience and consequently for Robert Stevenson, an Englishman brought to Hollywood in 1939 by David O. Selznick. Though Stevenson was making *Tom Brown's Schooldays* in Hollywood, his con-

[4]George Bluestone, *Novels Into Film* (Berkeley: University of California Press, 1961), p. 5.

sciousness of a beleaguered England's plight is manifest throughout the film, beginning with the prologue, which stresses the great tradition of Rugby, "for hundreds of years a nursery of soldiers and statesmen, athletes and scholars." The implication is that Rugby, located "in the heart of England," is an institution worth defending and preserving, like the country for which Rugby is an emblem. The prologue then dissolves to a focus on Arnold's gravestone in Rugby Chapel. In a high long shot, Tom is shown making his way down the aisle as a treacly music swells in the background. After kneeling at Arnold's grave, a tearful Tom rises to meet East who offers Tom his hand and asks to be his friend again. After the boys agree that Arnold was "a great man," the scene immediately shifts to a flashback in which a blustery Squire Brown offers Arnold the headmastership of Rugby on behalf of the school's trustees. From this point on, it becomes apparent that the film will focus primarily on Arnold, chronicling his setting out to "change the face of education in England" and showing his initially unpopular procedure of expelling all "liars and cowards." The film then vindicates Arnold and his reforms and draws a sentimental picture of the headmaster in Tom's study fondly recalling all the boys whose names are carved on Tom's desk top. The film ends where it began with a dissolve to Arnold's gravestone followed by a superimposition of Tom and East shaking hands. In the film, then, Arnold assumes a prominence denied him in the novel, where he plays a largely behind-the-scenes role.

Why the changes in focus between novel and film? In the first place, Stevenson, with his eye apparently on the box office, was able to provide in the film's Arnold an appropriate acting vehicle for his countryman, Sir Cedric Hardwicke, knighted in 1934 and then popular among American audiences. The second reason is the more important: the primacy of Hardwicke's solemn, brooding Arnold in the film allows for the introduction of a generous dose of Churchillian wartime rhetoric. The first third of the film is structured around several key addresses delivered by Arnold at Rugby. His message is the same in each address: that "freedom demands reponsibility," that those who "may tomorrow govern a great nation" must "first learn to govern themselves," and that his aim at

Rugby is to produce "honest, courageous, God-fearing gentlemen," who will fight wrong where they find it.

The second third of the film, in its detailing of the resistance of Tom and his cohorts to Flashman's tyranny, serves as an *exemplum* of Arnold's pronouncements and offers, perhaps, an analogy for countries like Britain and America confronted with fascist aggression. Flashman smacks of the fascist, as is clear from Arnold's parting words to him after his expulsion: "There have been bullies in every school, in every community, in every nation. Sooner or later humble men will rise and throw them down." By the time of his expulsion, in fact, Flashman has lost most of his dictatorial power because of the revolution by the lower-form boys (or "fags"), a revolution which Stevenson rather overdoes. The swarthy, dark-curled Billy Halop—then nineteen and an earlier star of the "Dead End Kids"—plays Flashman like a relatively ineffectual street hood. He bullies a Tom (played by a sixteen-year-old Jimmy Lydon) and an East (played by a fifteen-year-old Freddie Bartholomew) who are only slightly smaller than he and only three or four years younger—a ratio of stature and age greatly different from the book. This peculiar casting may simply result from Stevenson's recognition that these actors were all still good box-office draws, but it is also possible that they were chosen *because* of their proximity in age and size. The implication is that the oppressed, though they face a formidable foe, can indeed engage in a successful resistance.

When the much admired sixth-form boy, Brooke, calls for an end to bullying, Tom refuses to fag for Flashman, who has no right to require fagging of him. Flashman consequently "roasts" Tom before an open fireplace and the fags then join with Tom in open rebellion against the bully. Their retaliation against Flashman and his followers, however, is excessive: they hit them and douse them with slops, shoot barrages of peas at them from behind cover, set Flashman's pants on fire (while he is wearing them!), and affix his furniture to the ceiling so that when he tries to detach chairs and desk they fly apart and he is doused with water from concealed buckets. Flashman is then shown smearing his face with a greased towel the fags provide him. This aggressive response of the fags in the film is very different from the effective, but passive resistance of the small boys in the novel.

Because the filmic Flashman's punishment seems so in excess of his crime, Stevenson comes close to producing in his later audience an effect opposite from the one he intends. If one begins to sympathize with Flashman, all is lost! Though the film never makes sympathy an inevitable response, it does prompt the viewer to ask if the easily routed Flashman was ever really so much a threat to the fags that they needed protection from him in the first place. And Flashman's travails do not end with a greased face. He is soon challenged to a fight by Tom who holds his own against him. During the fight East tries to rouse Tom by reminding him of the roasting he suffered at Flashman's hands and Arnold overhears him. Flashman, bested in a more-or-less equal fight, is subsequently expelled by Arnold for bullying and lying. This complete annihilation of the villain is characteristic of popular wartime films wherein an enemy, often shown to be less powerful than he initially seems, is unmercifully trounced.

Though the 1940 film, with the prominence it gives to the preaching of Arnold and to Tom's victory over Flashman, addresses itself primarily to a wartime audience, it nevertheless does not completely ignore the novel's central concern—the physical and moral development of Tom. Once Flashman has left Rugby, the final third of the film deals, in a series of ponderously contrived situations, with the lessons Tom—and East—must learn on their journey to maturity. The lessons are stock ones: Tom has to learn that he must not run away from his difficulties and that he must not pay back a wrong with a wrong; East must learn forgiveness.

The rift between Tom and East, alluded to in the first scenes, results from East's unfounded assumption that Tom has "peached" on Flashman about the roasting, thereby effecting Flashman's expulsion. East and his cohorts thus ostracize Tom, who then triumphs over his impulse to run from his difficulties. Tom pays East back by allowing him to bear the blame for a misdemeanor that Tom committed, hoping that East will be forced to "peach" on him and thus experience the same ostracism he has made Tom suffer. After Arnold finds out that

Tom was the culprit, he dubs Tom "a mean, despicable cow-ard." At this point, the distance the film has traveled from the novel's plot line and characterization of Tom becomes apparent. Though irresponsible, the novel's Tom could never have involved a friend in undeserved blame. This startling revision of Tom's character is justifiable only in a film which deals primarily with Arnold. Tom's treachery here serves to precipitate *Arnold's* crisis: Tom Brown "was to be the symbol of my success," laments the dispirited Arnold; "Now, he's the symbol of my failure. . . . He came to Rugby with every promise—and Rugby has made him a coward." As Arnold is leaving his study to expel Tom and then resign, Tom appears on the doorstep and confesses, saving Arnold from his sense of failure and vindicating his reforms. East, however, refuses to forgive Tom, and these two inseparable friends in the novel remain bitter enemies until their reconciliation over the grave of Arnold whose influence is pervasive even after death.

The emphasis of the 1940 film, however, is not on the lessons of courage and forgiveness Tom and East must learn. As a sign of this change from the novel, Arthur, the immediate instrument of Tom's moral regeneration, is omitted entirely, even though the film covers Tom's complete tenure at Rugby through the use of montage. Stevenson apparently judged that Tom's moral development was less thematically significant in the film than were the wartime allusions aimed at his 1940 audience.

In 1951, when the second film version of *Tom Brown's Schooldays* was released, the social climate in Britain had changed significantly. England had been so involved with America during the war that after victory was achieved British culture found itself enmeshed with the culture of its powerful overseas cousin. This meshing was nowhere more evident than in the British cinema, which had experienced its "golden age" during the war when the British film industry was producing the great wartime semidocumentaries and the British public was patronizing them in enormous numbers. Following the war, however, the British cinema was again so thoroughly dominated by Hollywood that in 1947 a 75 percent *ad valorem* tax was imposed on the box-office draws of American films. The government's drastic action was perhaps understandable. After all, according to John Russell Taylor's "Reflections on the Un-Englishness of English Films" (*Sight and Sound,* Spring 1974), "it is possible, oversimplifying a little but not really that much, to see the whole history of the British cinema in terms of its fluctuating relations with America and the American market."

During the postwar era, this struggling British film industry was producing fluently acted adaptations of British literary classics. So numerous were these film translations that Roy Armes, in *A Critical History of the British Cinema* (1978), characterized the "first ten or so years after the war" as "an age of adaptation" (p. 198). David Lean, for example, produced his brilliant *Great Expectations* in 1946 and *Oliver Twist* in 1947. Laurence Olivier produced and acted in films of Shakespeare's *Henry V* in 1945, *Hamlet* in 1948, and *Richard III* in 1956. It would be difficult, of course, to prove that these films and the many others like them were made in reaction to the pervasive American influence on postwar British culture, but the emphasis on these adaptations at least suggests an attempt by British directors to define a peculiarly *British* cinema. In this group of cinematic literary translations must be counted the 1951 remake of *Tom Brown's Schooldays,* directed by Gordon Parry.

The 1951 *Tom Brown's Schooldays* has certain features which allow one to see it as part of a movement to recall the distinctiveness of British culture. The film's prologue, for instance, announces the director's decidedly antiquarian interest in the public school, a uniquely British educational phenomenon. Rugby is thus recreated as a historical institution: the film, according to the prologue, is set against "the authentic background of Rugby School as it was in 1834, and follows closely the style, language and atmosphere of those ancient days." The prologue's concluding assertion that Rugby "is the birthplace of the game of Rugby . . . from which American football has developed" calls attention to the fact that parts of the pervasive American culture have distinctly British origins.

In addition, unlike the 1940 version, which starred the Americans Jimmy Lydon and Billy Halop and the Anglo-

American Freddie Bartholomew, this film employs British actors. John Howard Davies plays a slight, blond Tom to John Charlesworth's dark, more intense, certainly middle-class East. John Forrest plays Tom's foe Flashman as a nasal, dandified aristocrat. This casting thus introduces into the film that feature so frequent in British cultural artifacts and so clearly missing from the 1940 Americanized version of *Tom Brown's Schooldays*—the perennial social conflict between the aristocracy and the middle class. The choice of British actors, including Robert Newton as Arnold, helps to produce the film's peculiarly British flavor.

Its main purpose being the portrayal of life as it was lived in the nineteenth-century British public school, the film focuses not on Arnold but on Tom Brown, a representative British school boy. Greeted on his arrival at school by East, Tom is quickly introduced to the dominant power structures at Rugby. A "double government" is operative: though Tom will be required to adhere reasonably well to the dictates of the headmaster and teachers, he must scrupulously obey the largely separate code of behavior legislated by his peers. A series of short scenes chronicles Tom's introduction to both of these legitimate governing forces: he is shown successfully negotiating the mandatory quizzing by his classmates as to his age, lineage, former school affiliation, and athletic prowess. Next, he is taken to a class where the master informs him of the birchings that await his inevitable infractions of classroom laws. Tom's subsequent introduction to Rugby football is an auspicious one: Tom dashes from the sidelines to save a goal for his schoolhouse before having the wind knocked out of him in a mass tackle. Tom's demonstration of required "pluck" is duly noted by Brooke, the schoolhouse captain.

Up to this point, all indications are that Tom will thrive at Rugby, satisfying both masters and peers. But for Tom the usual two-pronged power structure is complicated by a third force, embodied by Flashman, whose dictates often contradict the dictates of the two legitimate governing forces. Following a few preliminary skirmishes with Flashman, Tom is introduced to Arnold, who conducts evening prayers. Arnold's reading of the Parable of the Sower (Luke 8:5–9) during prayers is not particularly subtle in intent: its allegorical application in the film is underlined by Parry through camera cuts to Flashman when Arnold reads of the seed falling among thorns and then to Tom when he reads of the seed falling on fertile ground to yield fruit a hundredfold. Arnold's reading of this parable frames an antagonism between Tom and Flashman which dominates the film. The novel, on the other hand, focuses on Tom's moral development and devotes only two of its eighteen chapters to Tom's difficulties with Flashman who is expelled before the close of the novel's first half. Two reasons may be offered for the film's emphasis on the struggle between Tom and Flashman. In the first place, Tom's gradual moral growth is difficult to chronicle in the time limitations of the film medium. In the second place, the didacticism of George Arthur's admonitions, so liberally scattered throughout the latter half of the novel, are clearly out of fashion for modern audiences. The film, consequently, ignores Tom's moral evolution.

Except for Flashman's bullying, the film's Tom, who exhibits no particular character flaws, is quite happily at home at Rugby. Scenes of typical boy-life at Rugby are interwoven with scenes of Flashman's various cruelties: blanket-tossings, beatings, and general bullying. So severe are Tom's first-day trials that he seeks refuge in Rugby Chapel where, weeping, he is seen by Arnold who silently forms the correct inference about Tom's presence there and is thus strengthened in his resolve to abolish bullying. This chapel scene is followed by an extensive montage, beginning with a shot of a happier Tom carving his name on a desk top. The shot dissolves to show the typical pursuits of the normal, healthy Rugby boy—swimming, batting at cricket, studying in his room, praying in chapel, roughhousing with his fellows, and fishing. The montage sequence is closed with Tom's putting the finishing touches on his carving and then adding the date 1834.

The film is thus governed by an effective interplay of idyll and catastrophe in following Tom's fortunes at Rugby. The preceding idyllic montage is in turn followed by the catastrophe of Tom's roasting, a crucial episode in that it explains and justifies Arnold's attempts at reform and it precipitates

Tom's stout allegiance to Arnold. Taken to the sickroom after his roasting, Tom is comforted by a solicitous Arnold who tells Tom that he is trying to stamp out such brutality. Though Tom cannot tell Arnold who has done this to him because of his adherence to the boy-code which forbids "peaching," he nevertheless forms at this point a strong bond of allegiance to Arnold and his gentlemanly code.

Arnold's reforms, then, extend not only to the form of school government administered by the masters, but also to the governing structures maintained by the boys among themselves. Arnold is incensed at Tom's roasting because it violates what he sees as an ideal code of justice which the boys are empowered to maintain among themselves. However, after promising to expel the culprit, Arnold is condemned by the Rugby masters for interfering with the *laissez-faire* system of boy-justice which has prevailed at Rugby for generations. The self-deprecatory way in which Arnold justifies his reforms makes him more human than the austere wartime Arnold of the 1940 film or the remote Arnold of the novel. His explanation, couched in the seed imagery of the film's initial parable, is marked by sensitivity and intelligence: "I allow for the possibility that I may be wrong, misguided, that things were better left as they were. All I have is the belief that I am right, the faith that the forces of good will ultimately triumph over the forces of evil. I believe in that boy Brown. I have faith that in him I may see my principles and theories take seed and come to life and grow."

After this scene, the boys leave for vacation, and the first half of the film ends. On his return to Rugby, Tom finds that a frightened, stuttering George Arthur has been entrusted to his care—not, as in the book, because Tom needs taming, but instead because the Doctor has seen Tom weeping in the chapel on his first day and thus recognizes him as a sensitive boy who will help another sensitive boy adjust to the rigors of Rugby. When Flashman intrudes in Tom's study, twisting Arthur's ear and demanding that Arthur become his personal fag, the second half of the film begins to mirror the first. Tom recognizes that Arthur, if unaided, will have to undergo the same tortures that he had had to endure at Flashman's hands on his first arrival. Here the reformation of the boy-code at Rugby School actually begins: Tom, the seed of Arnold's ideals now having taken root in him, openly resists Flashman's tyranny. When Tom and East best Flashman in a fight, Flashman vows revenge.

Flashman's final confrontation with Tom, East, and Arthur precipitates the film's climax. Tom and East, followed into the countryside on a game of "Hare and Hounds" by the frail Arthur, happen on a fight between Ned Taylor, a local farmer, and Flashman, who has been paying ungentlemanly attention to a local milkmaid. Knocked by Ned into Barby Weir, Flashman is saved from drowning in the turbulent waters by Tom and East. Arthur, reaching out to help Flashman up the bank, falls in and Flashman abandons the three boys, who barely save themselves. Coming in after locking-up, Tom and East are reprimanded and Arthur is sent by Arnold to the sickroom with chills and a fever.

The climax of the film involves the resolution of three concurrent tensions resulting from the episode at Barby Weir. In the first place, Arthur's health declines dangerously. Asked by Arnold to pray for Arthur's recovery, East confesses to Tom that he cannot because of the inefficacy of his previous prayers for the return of his mother, who had abandoned him as a child. Tom, however, persuades East to try once more. The second tension, then, involves East's crisis of faith, which is resolved with Arthur's eventual recovery. The third tension is more complex, involving a test of Arnold's system of justice at Rugby. Tom and East are incriminated by Flashman's version of the happenings at Barby Weir. Flashman tells Arnold that he had had to rescue Tom, East, and Arthur, who landed in the weir because Tom and East were teasing Arthur by pretending to throw him in. Though Tom and East deny Flashman's story, they refuse to "peach" on him about his fight with Ned. Their adherence to one of the central tenets of the boy-code at Rugby places them in the power of a villain who subverts the code of justice Arnold encourages the boys to govern themselves by. Flashman, in fact, uses this honor code to enhance his own dishonorable position wherever possible. But Arnold is in control, separating the wheat from the thorns: he produces Ned

Taylor who confesses all to Flashman's horrified denials. Justice is summary: Flashman is expelled in spite of his wealthy connections and family influence, ending the external obstacle to Tom's full and happy participation in Rugby life. The 1951 film version of *Tom Brown's Schooldays* ends on the playing field where a healthy Arthur cheers for the play of Tom and East who, at game's end, run off field toward the camera. As East flags, Tom runs past him, stops to turn and wave, and then runs toward Rugby School framed in the film's parting long shot. This final shot reminds the viewers that the film, as its prologue announces, is primarily concerned with a nostalgic recreation of nineteenth-century public school life. But this parochial intention is expanded by the film's more universal themes. Arthur's struggle with physical illness and his victory over death, East's wrestling with doubt and despair during his search for faith, Tom's strategies for dealing with inequity and social tyranny as exercised by Flashman and his henchmen, and the Rugby schoolboys' attempts, with the help of Arnold, to create a just political order in the microcosm of the public school are all matters which, in individual ways, concern every human being. The 1951 *Tom Brown's Schooldays*, in presenting these universal concerns in a peculiarly British way, must thus be accounted a successful *British* film in an era when the British cinema was suffering from a crisis of identity.

The most recent film adaptation of *Tom Brown's Schooldays*, the BBC/Masterpiece Theatre's five-episode series, was aired during the early 70s, but is now available only for television broadcasting. This latest film adaptation, with its very favorable presentation of the nineteenth-century public school as defined by Arnold, seems a strange anachronism in an era which also saw Lindsay Anderson's production of *If . . .* (1968) and the publication of George Macdonald Fraser's novels, purportedly drawn from the "recently discovered" Flashman papers." *If . . .*, produced during a time of student revolutions on college campuses across the country, deals with a violent rebellion of public school boys against established order. In Fraser's novels, Flashman—an amoral, albeit charming, opportunist and adventurer—makes his way through a nineteenth-century Europe racked with political and social upheavals, as were

Europe and America during the turbulent 1960s and early 1970s. Fraser's cynical and anarchic Flashman and the main character of Anderson's film may thus be seen as spokesmen, if not exactly heroes, for those recent times. Perhaps the BBC film adaptation of *Tom Brown's Schooldays*—so strikingly different in tenor and tone from Anderson's film and Fraser's novels—was produced in reaction to a prevalent cynicism manifested in Fraser's Flashman and Anderson's *If.* . . . If this is so, the BBC production, like the two films of *Tom Brown's Schooldays* which preceded it, may be seen as a product of its time, made for an era which had lost, but nevertheless still longed for Tom Brown's innocent idealism and Arnold's firm sense of moral purpose and direction.

Novelty and Roman Cement:
Two Versions of *Alice*

RODERICK McGILLIS

Filmmakers of the last eighty years have sensed a rich source of material in literature, and debate over adaptation with its attendant issue of the relationship between cinema and literature will continue. One thing, however, is certain: since the verbal language of literature differs from the visual language of film, literary scholars too often like to think that the adaptation of a fiction into film is a reduction: by picturing character or setting film imagines for us what the writer had asked us to imagine. The logic here states that a picture is less imaginative than a verbal description. Tell this to a painter or a cinema director! Or imagine telling it to Lewis Carroll, photographer, writer, logician, and mathematician, whose books *Alice's Adventures in Wonderland* (1865) and *Through the Looking Glass* (1871) have been filmed more than fifteen times.

Whatever Lewis Carroll would have replied, we can be sure his imagination was both visual and verbal: his seven-year-old character Alice probably speaks for him when she asks: "What is the use of a book . . . without pictures or conversations?" Carroll's two wonderland fantasies contain both. The conversations, we can guess, were there from the famous "golden afternoon" on July 4, 1862, when Carroll first told the story of wonderland to the three Liddell sisters, and the pictures were drawn first by Carroll himself for the manuscript version of *Alice's Adventures under Ground* which he prepared for Alice Liddell in 1864 (this was later published by MacMillan in 1886). When Carroll published *Alice's Adventures in Wonder-*

land in 1865, he employed (and he was a trying employer) John Tenniel to illustrate the story. Tenniel's illustrations for the two *Alice* books have exerted a powerful influence on later illustrators (see the range of Tenniel influenced illustrations in Graham Ovenden, ed., *The Illustrators of Alice,* 1972), and on the many film versions of Carroll's books. (I suspect that only Jonathan Miller's 1966 production for the BBC departs significantly from a Tenniel-oriented visual style). In short, these illustrations have largely supplied the descriptive element of the stories, freeing Carroll to get on with his conversations. The Carroll/Tenniel collaboration results in books tempting to filmmakers because they appeal not only to the ear, but also to the eye. They appear to have everything the cinema could wish: songs, conversations, visual spectacle, scenic episodes, special effects, interiors, exteriors, conflict, and a range of emotions. Little wonder that there are so many film versions of *Alice*, the first appearing in 1903 only five years after Carroll's death.

What Carroll would have thought of these versions of his stories is conjecture. He seems to have been pleased with the stage version of *Alice* in 1866. But, as Carroll points out in his witty tale, "Novelty and Romancement," danger awaits he who too quickly and unreflectively sees romancement where there is only roman cement.

Literature and film are different. No matter how "filmic" the *Alice* books appear, they present serious obstacles to the filmmaker. First, there are two books, each with a different governing metaphor and a different tone. The chess metaphor of *Through the Looking Glass* provides a deterministic framework that is missing in the free-fall world of *Wonderland.* The tone of *Through the Looking Glass* is autumnal in contrast to *Wonderland's* summer atmosphere. There are no sympathetic characters in *Wonderland,* at least in comparison with the Gnat and the White Knight of *Looking Glass.* Ontological uncertainty is more threatening in *Looking Glass.* Despite such differences, commentators from the time of Empson's essay (1935) until recently invariably discussed the two books as one, and film adaptors have also felt the necessity or desire to piece together episodes from both. To do so, however, inevitably destroys the unity and thematic clarity of each book. Although both books deal with the problem of growing up, *Wonderland* sentimentalizes its theme in a way unavailable to Carroll seven years later. The danger of solipsism that resides in *Wonderland* becomes the one reality of *Looking Glass*. Most film versions in combining the two *Alice* books forego a coherent theme; they break down into loosely related episodes that must work singly or not at all. None captures the thematic strength of the *Alice* books.

Second, the *Alice* books depend heavily on verbal play. True, some advantage for the filmmaker resides here in that voice and comic dialogue transfer well to the sound cinema, yet any advantage is undercut by two disadvantages: verbal ingenuity is not basic to *Alice,* but the cinema is not fundamentally verbal; the filmviewer *looks for* action to counterpoint dialogue, and character to provide subtlety to conversations. Many of Alice's encounters involve little action and even less interaction. Perhaps Alice's word, "conversations," misleads since there are few, if any, conversations, in the sense of give and take, in the *Alice* books. There are no characters in the usual novelistic sense. Most often the creatures (including Alice) speak to themselves. When they do speak to others they seek to promote themselves or to order others about; they can be truculent, aggressive, and frightening. Are they funny—or nasty? What is a filmmaker to do? Accent the mad quality of Carroll's nonsense, or play it for the zaniness?

And what of Alice? Film versions invariably fall for Carroll's loving, gentle, courteous, and trustful innocent. Recently commentators have discerned a more "realistic" child galumphing through the Wonderland and Looking Glass worlds, but this seven-year-old "monster" has rarely shown through the sweet and even-tempered Alice of the movies, which resolutely attempt to speak to the child audience (the appeal to adults comes in the choice of "stars" to play the various characters). But this may have to do with Alice's maturity: in the books she is seven (*Wonderland*) and seven-and-a-half (*Looking Glass*). Except for Disney's 1951 Alice, film Alices are always in their teens (or older).

A third difficulty for the filmmaker is an extension of the

second: much of Carroll's fun with language, most apparent in his use of parody, directs our attention to literature. Carroll's books are about books; he is clearly conscious of literary tradition. On the most obvious level, the *Alice* books (especially *Wonderland*) have fun with the tradition of children's literature as it has developed from the early eighteenth century. Carroll refers to his books as fairy tales, and while his books differ greatly from the stories we associate with Grimm and Andersen, they are free of the didacticism of most literature for children up to the 1860s. By categorizing his work as fairy tale, Carroll implicitly argues for an interior view of literature, the closed verbal space. Fairy tales speak to us through other fairy tales: the *Alice* books speak to us by way of romance forms, especially of the internalized sort found in Romantic poetry. The myth of the child as innocent, as an entelechy rather than a beginning, is at the heart of the *Alice* books, and the heart has a murmur. The *Alice* books disturb the adult reader who refuses to accept the fun of a decentered world because of the tension between Romantic myth and Freudian romance. Once again: how are the movies to translate this double-sided book? What usually happens is that adaptors opt for the Romantic myth of the clear, unclouded brow.

The question the filmmaker must ask, then, is: "Shall I attempt to remain faithful to the books or shall I use them as raw material for a film that must be a film first and adaptation second?" The two films I wish now to discuss choose differently. Norman McLeod's 1933 film, *Alice in Wonderland* (Paramount), succeeds because of its insistence on novelty; William Sterling's lavish *Alice's Adventures in Wonderland* (British, 1972) reaches for romancement and finds roman cement. Both films take their visual styles from Tenniel, although the British version is more rigorous in pursuing this beyond costume and into set designs. The moral is: the more there is of Tenniel, the less there is of interest. William Cameron Menzies's designs for *Alice in Wonderland* have nothing obvious to do with Tenniel or Carroll, yet they are interesting and significant. In contrast, the designs for *Alice's Adventures in Wonderland* by Michael Stringer are meticulously faithful to Tenniel, noting his use of fox gloves, fountains, ivy, and buck teeth. Despite this, they fail to reflect anything meaningful, partly because of heavy-handed and unimaginative extrapolations from Tenniel: hideous rocks with faces and seaweed moustaches that form a background to the Lobster Quadrille, labyrinthine forests that lack atmosphere while offering confusion, swamp mist over muddy water and lily pads that form the pool of tears, the Duchess's kitchen chaotic with broken china and unpleasantly unhygienic with food-splattered walls, and an orange, purple, and puce field of mushrooms. Really, this is all curiously flat.

The whole film is flat: rarely have so many possibilities come to such a jejune result. Lacking in sound and fury (abundant in the books), this film still signifies nothing. Filmed in 70mm, *Alice's Adventures in Wonderland* is a large screen spectacular sporting its lavish sets and a cast consisting of many of England's most prestigious actors and celebrities: Flora Robson (Queen of Hearts), Ralph Richardson (Caterpillar), Michael Hordern (Mock Turtle), Peter Sellers (March Hare), Dudley Moore (Dormouse), Spike Milligan (Gryphon). (Alice is played by Fiona Fullerton.) William Sterling, who wrote as well as directed this musical version of *Alice*, has set out to honor an English classic, presenting it as resplendantly as he can. He clearly wishes to remain faithful to Carroll/ Tenniel, and to this end the screenplay focuses on *Wonderland*, including only one episode from *Looking Glass*, Tweedledee's and Tweedledum's battle (more about this later). Strangely, he also wishes to idealize Wonderland, perhaps taking his idyllic opening and closing from the sentimental ending of Carroll's *Alice's Adventures in Wonderland.*

Sterling's film version of *Alice* begins with a soft focus shot of a river amid lush banks. It is a bright mid-summer's day. In fact, what we see is described in the final poem in *Through the Looking Glass*:

> A boat, beneath a sunny sky
> Lingering onward dreamily
> In an evening of July—

The camera glides closer to the boat and we see two dark-jacketed, white-trousered young men with three beautiful young ladies. This is an afternoon flirtation, although we are to take it as a faithful rendering of the "golden afternoon" of July 4, 1862 when Carroll, Duckworth, and the three Liddell children boated on the Isis. The tone is wrong; the rhythm is wrong. The film moves here in response to the prefatory poem of *Wonderland*: "Full leisurely we glide." In the book, the reader waits only until the third sentence before the White Rabbit appears in waistcoat fussing out loud about being late; in the movie, a remarkably poised and articulate (he does not stammer) Dodgson rows to shore where the five youthful boaters lounge on the grass, and the girls encourage Dodgson to continue his story of Alice. (Hywel Bennet plays Duckworth who rests against a tree and says nothing during the entire film.) One of his audience, Alice, becomes drowsy, bored with the story meant for her. Watching a white rabbit in the bushes, she falls asleep and the dream begins.

As the five sat amid the trees, they played with cards which now rise up and flutter fantastically to signal the move from romantic reality to romantic dream. Alice sees the White Rabbit (Michael Crawford), now dressed as Tenniel pictures him, and she pursues him into a natural tunnel which goes on interminably with mazy turns. Sterling has missed the point of Alice's fall down the rabbit hole; in the book, it represents, among other things, Alice falling into sleep completed with the sudden "thump! thump!" as she lands "upon a heap of sticks and dry leaves." The significance of the labyrinthine tunnel escapes me, but once Alice does fall down the hole we return to familiar territory including the sticks and dry leaves. As in the book, Alice soon finds herself in a long hall lined with doors. This is gray in the film. A curtain covers one door, the small one. Generally, this scene follows the action of the book; however, the screenplay includes such logical, but inane, statements as Alice's "Oh, I am small again" after she has fanned herself with the Rabbit's kid gloves. And then there is the music; Alice here sings the first song of the movie, "Curiouser and Curiouser."

After completing her song, Alice finds she is sitting in a pool of water (her tears). This covers her ankles and knees; she shrinks and swims. The pool now resembles a murky swamp, and the mouse who appears on cue gives Alice a lecture on crying as the two of them climb ashore where Tenniel's creatures await the Caucus Race.

The race over, comfits passed round, Alice with her thimble proceeds to the White Rabbit's house which she enters, as in the book, to fetch a pair of gloves for the Rabbit. She cannot, however, resist drinking from "a little glass bottle that stood near the looking glass." What follows is close to the book: the broken cucumber frame and the booting of Bill up the chimney. Bill the Lizard presents us with one of the film's few sexual images (another bizarre one is the clear outline of Dodgson's underwear visible beneath his white trousers). The book, as we have heard often enough, is full of them, and this particular episode sustains several sexual readings. The curious thing about Sterling's depiction of the scene is that it sustains no sexual reading, yet it contains a grotesque sexual image. As Bill shoots out the chimney "like a sky-rocket" his long phallic tail detaches from his body and when we see him surrounded by anxious creatures he is holding his detached tail in his hands. What else can a rejected lizard do? The implication is unpleasant, but more important, it is pointless. Tastelessness can be served with piquancy, but here the attempt at slapstick is bland.

Lapses in taste occur elsewhere, most egregiously in the Duchess's kitchen. In the book, this scene parodies a genre convention: the epic journey to Hades. It is also one of the most nightmarish sequences, one of the few times Alice experiences "terror." Sterling senses this, and he directs the scene accordingly. The Duchess vigorously bounces a baby as she recites "Speak roughly to your little boy," and the baby cries in discomfort and confusion. Since genuine cries from a baby must unsettle some unspirited viewers, the sound track has been lowered; the baby's screams are audible, but only just. Worse, however, is the white spittle that appears dribbling from the baby's mouth. The violence of the scene—dishes and kitchen utensils thrown by the Cook pelt baby, Duchess, and Alice—is harmless, but the treatment of the child is unpleasant. And again, where is the point in all this? This scene is a good example of the filmmaker's failure to consider his audience. Who is this picture for? Rather than think in terms of a child or adult audience, Sterling has attempted to remain faithful to Carroll's text, without grasping its meaning.

Sterling's *Alice's Adventures in Wonderland* has good intentions, but no sensitivity to or understanding of Carroll's book. What happens in the Duchess's kitchen captures the surface action of the book, little else. Since the nightmare atmosphere is not consistent, when it does appear it signifies nothing. Perhaps the central moment in the book occurs in this same chapter: Alice's conversation with the Cheshire Cat after she has left the kitchen and dropped the baby (now a pig). This is absent from the film. The film contains no talk of madness. We do not see a grin without a cat, yet later in the royal garden we are asked to accept the cat's head without its body. The cat's appearance is gratuitous; we have no sense of his motives or his character since we have never heard him speak. In the book he is ahead of everyone else; here he is simply a head. What this reveals is inconsistency. Without an understanding of the book's coherence, even the most sincere effort at faithfulness must break down.

Also inconsistent is the inclusion in the film of one sequence from *Through the Looking Glass*: the battle between Tweedledum and Tweedledee. My guess is that Sterling thinks this scene is less disturbing, less like nightmare, than the sequence it replaces, the scene in which Alice nibbles a mushroom, shrinks until her chin bangs her feet, nibbles again, and grows so long that a pigeon takes her for a "serpent," screaming the word at her. Instead of this, we have the childish antics of Tweedledum and Tweedledee as they prepare to fight over a broken rattle. The scene is mercifully brief, most of it devoted to the coming of the crow. The monstrous crow allows for the special effects people to do their stuff.

Unfortunately, the film's special effects are undistinguished. The crow is impressive, but the distorted lenses and awkward angles of the trial scene, and the stop-action camera during the Lobster Quadrille irritate rather than enliven or illuminate. There are, in fact, few interesting effects in the picture. For whatever reason, the director has chosen intimacy rather than technical virtuosity as the basis of his film. Virtually every shot is a close-up or medium shot. The masked faces of Peter Sellers, Dudley Moore and company hover over the audience pleading with us to see through the make-up. The impression one has is of teeth and cavernous nostrils. Why we must see giant nostrils breathing from the expanse of a 70mm image eludes me. Little in the film warrants the wide screen, and the intimacy and intensity of the close-up are simply out of place in a movie without characters.

There is a lesson here. It is, as George Bluestone says, "fruitless to say that film A is better or worse than novel B" (*Novels Into Film*, 1971, pp. 5–6), but it is fair to say that William Sterling's *Alice's Adventures in Wonderland* neither conveys the fun of Lewis Carroll's fantasy nor succeeds as a film.

The triumph of Norman McLeod's *Alice in Wonderland* is that it is a successful film. The *Newsweek* review of the film (December 30, 1933, p. 30) reflects a typical difficulty viewers have with film adaptation: "The screen version of *Alice in Wonderland* is not likely to please either lovers of Lewis Carroll's famous book or those who like their cinema straight." Agreed: those who merely wish to "see" the fantasy they have loved to read must inevitably be disappointed. But what does "straight" cinema mean? If by straight, the writer means a film that adheres to the fictional realism of Dreiser and Hemingway or the filmic realism of von Stroheim's *Greed* (1924), or Wellman's *Public Enemy* (1931) then he is right. But in another sense, he is wrong. This *is* straight cinema; it is a film about film, as much as it is an adaptation of Carroll's book. Rather than weakening the film as an adaptation, this aesthetic dimension neatly turns the book's synchronism into filmic terms. *Alice in Wonderland* is about filmic reality, or what has often been referred to as the "reel" world, and this dimension places it firmly in the Romantic tradition of works of art that speak about the imagination's situation as mediator between what Frank McConnell calls "the warring alternatives of reality and dream" (*The Spoken Seen*, Baltimore, 1975, p. 43). The film follows the Romantic enterprise of creating a language to contain these alternatives.

The screenplay by Joseph L. Mankiewicz and William

Cameron Menzies uses scenes from both *Wonderland* and *Looking Glass,* skillfully fitting these together. An example of the skill is the opening sequence. After the credits, which take the form of a book whose pages have pictures of the various characters and the actors who play the roles, we see the exterior of a grand Georgian house on a snowy afternoon. Fade-in to a fireplace, a warm room with Victorian furniture and bric-a-brac. Alice and her governess, Miss Simpson, sit on either side of the fire, Miss Simpson tatting and Alice restlessly reading with Dinah the cat on her lap. This is the beginning of *Looking Glass* with Miss Simpson thrown in. As the scene proceeds, Alice gets up and wanders about the room, looking for a moment out the window where she sees a white rabbit hopping about the croquet set that is visible on the snow-covered lawn. This blending of the two books continues: Alice passes through the mirror and finds the chess pieces "down in the hearth among the cinders"; but when she floats from the house she meets the White Rabbit, follows him, and falls down the hole. Given the dream premise, all of this is plausible.

But Miss Simpson is new, a creation of Mankiewicz and Menzies. In terms of causality, she informs us how tedious a life Alice must lead when closeted indoors with her governess: Miss Simpson is an inversion of Alice's sister at the end of Carroll's *Wonderland.* However we interpret her, she announces a departure from the book, a departure extended as Alice makes her round of the room. First, Alice gazes at a picture of Uncle Gilbert and his wife that hangs to the left of the fireplace. She wonders what it must be like to hang there year after year; to Alice, the picture represents the real Uncle Gilbert. Uncle Gilbert, who does not appear in either of Carroll's *Alice* books, is a key to the meaning of this film, and we will meet him briefly again. Now, we follow Alice as she plays desultorily with her father's chess set, knocking over the White Queen and remarking, "She never does look where she's going." To this, Miss Simpson says, "Are you sure that is true?" Miss Simpson disapproves of fantasy, and her unsympathetic question moves Alice to the settee where the breakfast tray rests. Alice puts the two halves of a hardboiled egg back together, she notices the rabbit out the window, she wanders on and fingers a lampshade with roses on it. Before returning to her chair, she watches the gold fish in the aquarium.

The point, of course, is that in her dream Alice will perceive all these things fantastically; the rationale for the dream events recalls the end of *Wonderland* where "the rattling teacups . . . change to tinkling sheep-bells, and the Queen's shrill cries to the voice of the shepherd boy . . ." But coming at the beginning rather than the end, this explanation for the dream suggests that the real room might not be as restrictive as Miss Simpson would like Alice to believe. In short, the *telos* is different here than in *Wonderland*. Conventional reality demands close inspection; it does not simply domesticate our dreams. Uncle Gilbert makes this clear when we see him again in the Looking Glass room. When Alice makes her way through the mirror (an effect well done; the director's eye for detail from Tenniel's two illustrations of this action is sharp) she naturally sees Uncle Gilbert and his wife from behind. His trousers are patched.

Uncle Gilbert looks so real that Alice reaches out to touch him. He turns around and speaks, leaving Alice with this remark: "After all, it is only the front of a picture that counts, really." Reely? In the case of the film, this is certainly true; there is no way of getting behind the scenes or the screens. In short, Uncle Gilbert warns us to look closely at what the picture shows. Visuals in film replace the literary voice. In the *Alice* books, much of the meaning derives from authorial voice, the ironic voice that gently pokes fun at Alice; the puckish voice that subverts as well as inverts; the playful voice that delights in puns; the literary voice whose misprison is free of anxiety; and the philosophic voice with its serious existential questioning. Not all of this appears on screen, but Carroll's puns have their visual counterparts, and his confusion of dream and reality, or his more unsettling vision of the artificiality of reality also find expression in filmic language.

The Wonderland of the film is the creation of William Cameron Menzies (the film credits cite Robert Odell as set designer, but anyone familiar with Menzies's work as a set designer for films such as *The Thief of Bagdad*—both the 1926 and 1940 versions—*Things To Come* (1936), *The Maze* (1952), and *Invaders from Mars* (1954) must credit him with influence on *Alice*). What he does in *Alice in Wonderland* is provide a guide to modern art: the Tweedledum and Tweedledee forest sets are expressionistic (note the drawing of a monster on the rock behind Tweedledee during "The Walrus and the Carpenter" recitation); the apocalyptic banquet scene with its talking pudding and walking leg of mutton is surrealistic; the acorns, grasses, and toadstools by the pool of tears are Pre-Raphaelite; the painted sea and landscape backdrop to the Gryphon/Mock Turtle scene reflects American poster art; the forest through which all the king's horses and all the king's men advance is symbolist; and the animation of the Walrus and Carpenter song is familiar cartoon art. Hollywood here displays not only special effects, but also its influences from the visual arts.

As Carroll parodies earlier children's literature and as Tenniel parodies earlier artistic movements, McLeod's film parodies Hollywood itself. Perhaps the best sequence is that with the White Knight. Played by Gary Cooper in a marvelous performance, the White Knight nicely winks at the Virginian. Here the questing hero shows up as a rattlepated knight who means well, but who cannot stay on his horse for longer than sixty seconds at a stretch. The Knight, looking exactly as Tenniel pictures him but sounding like Gary Cooper, rides through the most gaudy set of the film: Christmas tree balls hang from trees; a cockatoo appears in the foreground on a perch; a giant hand stands fingers up in the middle distance; and a huge artificially lit candle rises in the rear. Hanging from a tree and clearly visible near the knight while he chats with Alice are a toy horse, a toy elephant, and a doll. These might reflect a child's mind, but more likely they reflect a Hollywood exuberance unchecked by good taste. What really matters is the front of the picture, and here the picture's style or lack of it is the subject. The knight collects the oddest things—a little deal box, a beehive, a mousetrap, anklets, a dish for plum-cake, old vegetables, a bellows—and so does the set in which he acts his part.

Fun is the intention. Cooper and other Paramount stars

and character actors (Cary Grant, W. C. Fields, Roscoe Ates, Sterling Holloway, Jack Oakey, Edward Everett Horton, Alison Skipworth) enjoy their roles. The set designers have fun turning trees into ceramic bottles, umbrellas, chandeliers, and coat-trees. The cinematographer uses dissolves, fade-ins, cross-cutting, montage—the gamut of shots. Everyone has fun. When the Cheshire Cat fades leaving radiant eyes and a grin, he says to Alice: "Don't you wish you could do this?" Hollywood can make all wishes come true, at least in the reel world. Dream and reality are not alternatives here, Hollywood is not simply displaying its dream factory for depression-weary viewers; a filmic language is presented that reminds us rather, that both dream and reality are contained in it. The real/reel world is language.

The conclusion to all this is simple: of the two films the one that works best is the least faithful, the most complex, and the most spirited. Both films sense the importance of "spirit," and they attempt to display it by concentrating on Wonderland's inhabitants rather than on Alice (played by Charlotte Henry). The creatures of Alice's imagination are what will interest children's eyes, and both films know this. Film, however, is action as well as portraiture, and the action of Sterling's *Alice's Adventure in Wonderland* is strained and strangely languid. Neither child nor adult will find much fun here. McLeod's version is enjoyable, a film meant for children, yet offering something extra for adults willing to pay. E. M. Forster once said that fantasy asks us to pay something extra; if we are generous with these two films *Alice in Wonderland* will reward us with novelty, *Alice's Adventures in Wonderland* will repay us with roman cement.

Little Women at the Movies

CAROL GAY

There have been two major film versions of Louisa May Alcott's *Little Women,* George Cukor's in 1933 and Mervyn LeRoy's in 1948. Both films are important not only for what they reveal about themselves and the times in which they appeared, but also for what they reveal about the book and its position and worth in both children's literature and American literature as a whole.

Little Women has been controversial from its publication in 1868 to the present, controversial in the wide range of critical and popular opinion that surrounds it and in the critical assessments that have been made of it. Indeed, as the major work of its author, it reflects the fortunes of Alcott's reputation as a writer of books for children and adults. A January 8, 1898, article called "Books That Separate Children from Their Parents" in the *New York Times Saturday Review of Books and Art* quoted an extremely indignant mother as saying: "I am sorry to be obliged to be sorry that Miss Alcott ever wrote." The main ground of her attack was that Alcott had failed to write a book that would appeal to all ages of readers. Although not too many people are sorry that Louisa May Alcott ever took up writing, most critics have ignored her except for passing mention as a children's author, still a term of denigration in most contexts. Alexander Cowie in his *Rise of the American Novel* (1951) relegates *Little Women* to a footnote, categorizing it as a "domestic novel," and Carl Van Doren passes over *Little Women's* depiction of the home side of the Civil War to commend William DeForest's treatment of the Civil War in *Miss Ravenel's Conversion from Secession to Loyalty* (1867) as "coldly truthful in its descriptions of battles and camps, crisp and pointed in its dialogue, penetrating, if not oversubtle, in its character analysis, sensible in its plot and in its general temper," concluding that it is "still almost as convincing as it was once precocious."

The problem is: whom does it convince? Who ever picks it up except the most dedicated student of American literature? Yet everything that Van Doren says about *Miss Ravenel's Conversion* can be said about *Little Women*—except that *Little Women* is still being avidly read. Perhaps the readership and circulation figures of *Little Women* have been telling a tale long before feminist criticism started pointing out that war is not the only major theme of importance to humankind as opposed to mankind and that books dealing with war or the male initiation theme are not the only books that ought to be included in the canon of mainstream American literature. A glance at Alma Payne's 1980 Alcott bibliography indicates that to that date there have been only three years since Alcott started writing in 1855 that she did not provoke some commentary—complimentary, derogatory or analytical—in print. Payne herself refers to *Little Women* as "a puzzling and persevering classic."

Almost from the beginning of its interesting and successful publishing history there have been attempts to dramatize, first on the stage, then in the movies, and then in television, Alcott's tale of the growing up of Jo March and her sisters. Although there is yet no bibliographical study of the stage dramatizations and performances for both adult and child audiences, there is enough information to indicate a steady interest in giving dramatic form to Alcott's lengthy work, so that F. B. Sanborn, a friend of the Alcotts and the biographer of Thoreau and Emerson, can refer in a 1912 *Independent* article to "the representation of Miss Alcott's 'Little Women' as a drama, in theaters from Buffalo westward amid applause and appreciation . . ." As early as November 11, 1918, the *New York Times* headlined: " 'Little Women' shown on Screen/The Strand presents Brady's Motion-Picture Version of Louisa M. Alcott's Book," and noted that producer William A. Brady and director Harley Knowles had done an excellent job of capturing the atmosphere of New England in the 1860s. Katherine Cornell was starred in a London stage version in 1919, and in 1931 a review in *Commonweal* indicated that Brady was still interested in reviving *Little Women* as a stage vehicle. In 1945 George Jean Nathan called a 1944 production of Marion DeForrest's version of *Little Women* one of the better revivals of this play. Television versions in 1958, 1973, and 1978, also suggest the staying power of the book as a dramatic vehicle.

Some of this no doubt can be explained by what F. B. Sanborn referred to as a "tribute to the dramatic element in her gifted nature," and some of it can be explained as Kate Ellis does in "Life with Marmee: Three Versions" in *The Classic American Novel and the Movies* (1977) when she says it is "not surprising that, in the aftermath of wars or depressions, books and films idealizing the domestic sphere should find an especially receptive mass market." Ellis perceptively indicates that the "ideal" presented by Alcott in 1868 was a relatively new one for the times, articulated and popularized by such educators and writers for children as Jacob Abbott, by Louisa's own father, Bronson, and by Louisa herself. It advocated "teaching by example rather than severity," and it both "reflects the democratic spirit stirring in the larger society, and . . . at the same time preserve[s] the moral pre-eminence of Father." However, in this context the struggle of the March girls toward self-realization and, in two cases, toward financial independence—which is the main thrust of Alcott's novel—is reduced in the film versions to fit in with the conventions of their own times which in both cases were not as liberating as Alcott's. As Ellis indicates, though in the book Jo becomes a strong economic factor in the affairs of the March family, this is not the case in either the 1933 or 1949 film versions. Ellis comments: "In the 1930's . . . feminism was perceived to have run its course and died. By 1949 there was a strong backlash against the idea of women working outside the home at all." Further, the strong characters of the girls, especially Jo—a strong mix of the "maternal" and the "masculine"—could not be portrayed in either 1933 or 1949, periods when the girl child's role was firmly fixed and there was no way to cope with the complexity of the Jo that Alcott presented.

And the character is indeed complex, in ways, perhaps that

Louisa herself may not have even been aware of, but in many ways also that Louisa was aware of and that even the latter half of the twentieth century has not yet been able to accept or depict. Obviously, some of the elements in *Little Women* are not complex but merely contradictory, the title for instance. As feminists attacking Alcott for her lack of feminism do not hesitate to point out, even the title is denigrating. Father looks on the girls as his "little" women, a term feminists feel is not only descriptive of their diminutive stature but of their diminutive worth as well. And many, reading the book superficially, have seen in Jo's struggle to overcome her temper and become a "lady" and in her giving up her writing in order to become a wife, Alcott's giving in to the conventional submissive female role. And instead of complexity some other elements of the book merely reflect the confusion of Alcott's coming to terms with her own role as a woman. Martha Saxton in *Louisa May: A Modern Biography of Louisa May Alcott* (1977) calls *Little Women* "a regression for Louisa as artist and woman" and a "reversion to adolescent morality." And much has been said of Louisa's ineptness as a writer and her lack of intellect as a thinker. We are not dealing with a *Hamlet* here, or even a *Huckleberry Finn*.

But complexity there is. A complexity of enough texture for version after version to retell the story in its own terms and for its own times without exhausting the book's possibilities or even successfully capturing all of what the book does indeed say. The latest attempt is the four-hour 1978 television production directed by David Lowell Rich in which Alcott's feminist propensities are dwelled on and emphasized so that Jo, played by Susan Dey, becomes totally liberated; while nursing Laurie back to health, she not only disrobes him but stays all night with him, finally crawling into bed and lying side by side with him in the morning hours, totally perverting the maternal impulse that Jo exhibits so strongly in the book. Aunt March, played by Greer Garson, is not only crusty and outspoken but becomes a militant feminist recounting to Jo a cautionary tale about her own youthful love, implying that the one saving grace to her life was her wisdom in consummating that love before her young man was killed. Even though David Victor, the producer, feels that television offered him an opportunity that previous film versions lacked and that he could therefore "do it correctly for the first time" (as he said in a September 28, 1978 *New York Times* article), many would doubt that he has indeed accomplished that feat.

It is George Cukor who perhaps comes closest to this for three reasons. First, perhaps, is Cukor's respect for the novel. In *On Cukor* (1972) Gavin Lambert gives us Cukor's initial reaction to *Little Women*:

> When Selznick wanted me to do *Little Women*, I hadn't read the book. (Kate Hepburn once accused me of never having finished it, which is a lie.) Of course I'd heard of it all my life, but it was a story that little girls read, like *Elsie Dinsmore*. When I came to read it, I was startled. It's not sentimental or saccharine, but very strong-minded, full of character, and a wonderful picture of New England family life. It's full of that admirable New England sternness, about sacrifice and austerity.

His description of his reaction as "startled" is interesting and somewhat typical perhaps. The novel and its movie versions have become so much a part of our cultural milieu that like *Huckleberry Finn* it is one of those books that we all come to with a great many preconceptions and that we all "know" even if we have not read it. It therefore often startles. (Suzanne Clauser, who wrote the 1978 teleplay, said for instance that she discovered Alcott was "a much more gutsy writer than I had thought.") At any rate, Cukor admired the book and his own version of it was "his favorite" movie among those for which he is remembered: *A Star Is Born*, *Dinner at Eight*, *Adam's Rib*, *Born Yesterday*, and *The Philadelphia Story*. His respect for it shows through in his successful depiction of the times in setting and atmosphere, his careful copying of the Alcott house, for instance, and his meticulous attention to the novel's Civil War context. As interesting as it is unusual is the fact that both Cukor's film and Mervyn LeRoy's later version were written by the same screen writers: Sara Y. Mason and Victor Heerman. Andrew Solt joins Mason and Heerman in the credits for the LeRoy production, presumably to bring things up to date. Viewing both films gives one the impression that the directors are using basically the same screenplay with few but distinct changes in dialogue, thematic focus and emphasis. A look at these differences will illustrate the second reason for the success of the earlier version. Cukor's version opens in a commissary where Marmee and other townswomen are gathering and preparing supplies for their husbands, fathers, and sons on the battlefields or in the camps. The grimness of the war and its impact on the homefront is illustrated quickly as Marmee finds an overcoat for an old man who has lost three sons in the war and who needs the coat so he can reach a fourth son now wounded and dying. This brief opening scene establishes the film in the context of the Civil War, a context that is never allowed to be frivolous or forgotten as it is in the LeRoy production where the only use of it is to offer Laurie's tutor the opportunity to show up in a handsome uniform. The fear that so quickly overpowers the happy family scene when the telegram arrives with news of Mr. March is never too far from the March household and helps give both the book and the 1933 film a sense of realism. This reality is further deepened by the actual depiction of the poverty of the Hummels and of the death of Beth (both of which are omitted by LeRoy), and is missing altogether from superficial considerations of the book. Alcott's realism is in large part responsible for the staying quality and worth of the novel. It is perhaps marred—a better word might be masked—by the brash and mocking tone of the narrator (not Jo and not necessarily Louisa either) and by what we would call the blatant didacticism that is everywhere in the book:

> That was a very happy breakfast, though they didn't get any of it; and when they went away, leaving comfort behind, I think there were not in all the city four merrier people than the hungry little girls who gave away their breakfasts and contended themselves with bread and milk on Christmas morning.
> "That's loving our neighbor better than ourselves, and I like it," said Meg, as they set out their presents, while their mother was upstairs collecting clothes for the poor Hummels.[1]

[1]*Little Women* (Boston: Little Brown, 1968), p. 16. All subsequent references noted in the text.

The twentieth century doesn't quite know how to react to passages like this. Though they sound sentimental and pious, they are the gist of the book's reality—for part of what every reader of *Little Women* brings to the book is a knowledge of the Alcott myth which emphasizes that Elizabeth Alcott died in March 1858 because she had contracted scarlet fever from a family that Mrs. Alcott was helping. Loving one's neighbor better than one's self indeed has serious consequences. Thus one of the most pious incidents in the book, and one of the book's most sentimental, Beth's death, is real and gives the book its realistic underpinning. Louisa doesn't sentimentalize it either in style or focus: but we do. Only recently have we thought death an appropriate subject for children's novels, and it is certainly something we avoid dealing with or even talking about in our own lives. But it is the central turning point in the book, and it is Jo's struggle to come to terms with the ugly fact of her innocent sister's death that brings her to maturity: "And while learning this hard lesson,/My great loss becomes my gain."

This focusing on the March girls' struggle to grow up and become moral, responsible adults (as opposed to finding mates or becoming financially independent) is established by Cukor when, after placing the action in its Civil War context, he switches to three brief vignettes which establish the characters of each of the three oldest daughters individually and thus indicate that the struggle to grow and develop is a major theme, as it is indeed in Alcott's novel. The 1949 version opens directly in the March living room with the girls in a group during a rehearsal of Jo's melodrama, which not only sets the tone of hilarity and cuteness governing the whole production but which focuses on the girls as a unit rather than as individuals and blurs—indeed obliterates, the self-discipline and moral pain of growing up.

The latter quality comes through more in Cukor's version because of his conscious retension of the episodic quality of the book. Cukor confirms this: "The script was very right, too, and did something quite original for the time. It wasn't slicked up. The construction was very loose, very episodic, like the novel. No plottiness. Things happen, but they're not all tied together. (The later version made the mistake of slicking it up.)" The result of "slicking it up" tends to force the emphasis on the girls' adventures on the pathway to finding husbands. Alcott does what many nineteenth-century women novelists do—she allows her heroine to marry, but only after she has liberated herself from conventional notions of the female role and is capable of becoming a true "helpmate," a partner to her husband rather than a submissive toy.

Of course it is Katharine Hepburn as Jo who is one of the most obvious contributing factors to the integrity of the 1933 *Little Women*. LeRoy's Jo, June Allyson, indicated her tomboy qualities, important in any interpretation in which Jo is seen as having such peculiarly "masculine" qualities as ambition, pride, spirit, and intelligence, but she brought little else to the role. (Her films, on the whole, have actually epitomized the whole artistic failure and moral vapidity of the popular films of the 40s and 50s.) Hepburn, however, was able to bring more to the film than either her unquestioned acting ability or the stamp of the tomboy or brash, outspoken female found in so many of her early films. She brought a sexual ambiguity that, like Alcott's, is not quite androgynous. In other words, she brought to the role a personality and even a physical appearance that seemed to be a perfect, almost inevitable, match of Jo's. But part of that personal character that fits the role so perfectly is not only the right sexual ambience, the right liberated stance, but a moral integrity that everyone assigns to Hepburn. She's become almost a dinosaur in the 80s with her rigid self-discipline and sturdy uprightness. She still seems to believe that one should strain toward perfection even though it's a losing battle. In part, this is what Alcott's book is about:

> Now, if she had been the heroine of a moral storybook, she ought at this period of her life to have become quite saintly, renounced the world, and gone about doing good in a mortified bonnet, with tracts in her pocket. But, you see, Jo wasn't a heroine; she was only a struggling human girl, like hundreds of others, and she just acted out her nature, being sad, cross, listless, or energetic, as the mood suggested. It's highly virtuous to say we'll be good, but we can't do it all at once, and it takes a long pull all together, before some of us even get our feet set in the right way. Jo had got so far, she was learning to

do her duty, and to feel unhappy if she did not; but to do it cheerfully—ah, that was another thing! She had often said she wanted to do something splendid, no matter how hard; now she had her wish, for what could be more beautiful than to devote her life to father and mother, trying to make home as happy to them as they had to her? And, if difficulties were necessary to increase the splendor of the effort, what could be harder for a restless, ambitious girl than to give up her own hopes, plans, and desires, and cheerfully live for others? (p. 393)

This is what *Little Women* is about, whether we in the twentieth century, who are embarrassed by such a staunchly moral stand, like it or not. And this is the quality that Hepburn is largely able to transmit to the viewer of Cukor's film. Jo's goal is not to become financially independent or to be a great writer but to help others. Indeed, she wanted to be a teacher, and further a nurturer, a mother. As Jo "earnestly" tells us:

"Just understand that this isn't a new idea of mine, but a long-cherished plan. Before my Fritz came, I used to think how, when I'd made my fortune, and no one needed me at home, I'd hire a big house, and pick up some poor, forlorn little lads, who hadn't any mothers, and take care of them, and make life jolly for them before it was too late. I see so many going to ruin for want of help at the right minute; I love so to do anything for them; I seem to feel their wants, and sympathize with their troubles, and, I should *so* like to be a mother to them!" (p. 436)

Her writing was a means to an end, first to helping her parents, then to founding a school. Of course it is Aunt March's bequeathing her Plumfield that "makes her fortune" and enables her to carry out her goals, but it is Jo's steady persistence in her progress as a moral pilgrim that enables her to become strong, independent, and so sure of her own individuality that she is able to offer it to Bhaer and to others without fear of submerging it—and it is this that Alcott focuses on. Although the 1949 film never even approaches this vision of the book and Cukor's version blurs it by allowing Jo to turn to jelly at the sight of Professor Bhaer and loll shamelessly against the piano and against the bannister in almost physically impossible attitudes, it is *this* dimension that Hepburn brings to the film, and that gives it its essential integrity.

Strangely enough, though we are able to respond to Alcott's feminist qualities because they find answering chords within us, we find it difficult to cope with the other thread of the book: its depiction of growing up as a moral struggle with oneself and with the world—in Alcott's terms, a *Pilgrim's Progress*. Ellis, for instance, identifies this theme, but sees Alcott as simply making use of an "exemplary tradition of her predecessors," rather as though Alcott would be afraid to break into a tract for women's rights without paying at least lip service to the Puritan tradition that preceded her. However, the book's underlying moral stance is one of its strengths rather than one of its weaknesses. And it is certainly consistent with Alcott's Transcendental upbringing. The main thrust of American Transcendentalism—whether it is Bronson Alcott, Ralph Waldo Emerson, Henry David Thoreau, or Louisa May Alcott—is the admonition to inquire what it is that life is all about, to make one's own choices, and to pursue the vision of life that God would vouchsafe to one who did these things. The emphasis from *Nature,* to *Walden,* to *Little Women* is always eminently moral.

LeRoy ignores, or doesn't see, this aspect of *Little Women.* Using almost the same screenplay, every adjustment he makes emphasizes the sexual prurience and the gross dishonesty that overwhelm his production: the opulence of the sets distorts and makes ludicrous the book's emphasis on the family's genteel poverty, and he loses all sense of the firm grounding in New England by having his Concord resemble an Oz populated by pretty people. Peter Lawford's Laurie, for example, never suggests that character's struggle to develop his own sense of individuality against his grandfather's strength; he becomes simply "the boyfriend," more sexual than Jo or Louisa could ever deal with. In addition, Mary Pickford is a beauteous and never aging Marmee, and Elizabeth Taylor is an alarmingly buxom Amy.

I hesitate to even mention the technicolor rainbow that unashamedly envelops the March home in the final scene. Just as telling in its betrayal of the spirit and theme of the book is the final gathering of the March family after Amy and Laurie return from Paris. All are there—Aunt March, Father March, Marmee, Meg's babies and husband—and in the book and in Cukor's film it is one of those scenes that communicate warmth and joy with the touch of wry humor that the narrator maintains throughout the book. But in the LeRoy film, the scene is joyless. The movement of the characters about the room is constant but to no point. There is a petulance and complaining quality to the scene that seems to epitomize the end result of a family which has not subjected itself to the intense struggle of self-discipline that can bring its rewards, a family that is unsure of its values, indeed that has none.

The LeRoy production, then, is the hackwork that many have seen in the Alcott novel. It reinterprets the work for its times but fails to recognize any of the basic integrity or complexity of Alcott's work. Cukor's is also tied to its time both in theme and in technical aptitude, but in its recognition of the basic worth of the book it transmits some of the qualities that make the novel a true classic in American literature, not just in children's literature. Alcott did, indeed, accomplish "something splendid." As Twain said of Wagner's music—that it's not as bad as it sounds—Miss Alcott's novel is much better than it reads.

Mouseketeer in the Center Ring

RUTH K. MacDONALD

James Otis Kaler's *Toby Tyler; or, Ten Weeks with a Circus* (1881) investigates the dark underside of nineteenth-century circus life and its runaway boys—the abusive and conniving behavior of the circus bosses, the exhausting schedule of performing and then moving on to the next town without any rest in between, the grotesque, although sometimes kindly, people who perform under the big tent. Though Kaler's Toby is an orphan in a country group home where he feels unloved, life with his surrogate parents, Uncle Daniel and Aunt Olive, is better than the rough treatment he receives at the hands of his circus employers, Job Lord and Mr. Castle, the villains of the story. Kaler's message, a rather sentimental one, is that home is best, even if that home is characterized by chores, churchgoing, and criticism about one's gargantuan appetite.

One suspects, however, that Kaler's book succeeded not because of its overt message that the circus life is a miserable one, but rather because of the natural attraction of circus life to children. Though Toby is brutally treated as a peanut vender's assistant and whipped as he is being trained as a bareback performer, though his pet monkey is shot in one of the most pathetic scenes in the book, children, and adults who remember the book, notice and remember only the scenes of bright circus life.

When Disney Studios took on the project of making the book into a film, the screenwriters were wise to ignore Kaler's message—subverted by the attractiveness of its subject—and to make a film only loosely based on the original, which was often horrifying in its brutality and bathetic in its sentiment.

The Disney staff traded heavily on its success with a circus theme in *Dumbo* (1941). But the animated Disney films that had followed *Dumbo* were costly and the financial rewards insufficient, and so the studio turned to live action films that could be turned into short series for the Sunday night Disney television show, and could also be paired with other Disney films to make a complete evening's entertainment at a movie house. Such an arrangement allowed the studio to control the distribution of all Disney films. The aim of the live action films was neither fidelity to the original text when a classic was adapted, nor artistic excellence, but rather box-office receipts. For the most part, such films were artistically mediocre, safe in that they took no chances that might offend the audience or challenge the limits of film artistry. Disney saw himself as appealing to "Main Street" Americans, the conservative middle class who wished to protect their children from vulgar language, and who subscribed to patriotic and work ethic values. The Disney version of *Toby Tyler* (1960) is no exception to Disney's philosophy.

The circus theme was popular at the time, not only because of *Dumbo* but also because of a television series loosely based on the Kaler novel, *Circus Boy* (not a Disney production). Furthermore, Disney had a likely candidate for Toby on his *Mickey Mouse Club* show: Kevin Corcoran, an appealing young tyke who was already recognizable as Moochie, a mischievous but ingenuous boy in a series featured on the television show. Kaler's Toby is described as fat, gluttonous, and often as conniving as that of his taskmasters. Kevin Corcoran is a more appealing type, with large blue eyes, younger than Kaler's original, and the character he plays is more wholesomely innocent, i.e., without Kaler's originality of language and slang dialogue.

Disney also played on an American penchant for monkeys in films. Though the Kaler's novel featured a monkey who was Toby's best friend in the circus, the original Mr. Stubbs was described as old, mangy, and melancholic. Such a pathetic, morose character would not do for a cleaned-up Disney version, so the studios substituted a chimpanzee who was more human and therefore more visually attractive than a sickly monkey. The chimp gets into sufficient mischief to jeopardize Toby's

Tom Brown's Schooldays, 1951: Tom (John Howard Davies), right, is challenged by the bully Flashman (John Forrest), center, while young East (John Charlesworth) receives a collaring.

Alice in Wonderland, 1933: Alice (Charlotte Henry) finds things becoming curiouser and curiouser.

Alice's Adventures in Wonderland, 1972: The Gryphon (Spike Milligan) and Alice (Fiona Fullerton) listen to the tale of the Mock Turtle (Michael Hordern).

Little Women, 1933: The March women gather in song. From left: Amy (Joan Bennett), Marmee (Spring Byington), Beth (Jean Parker), Meg (Frances Dee) and Jo (Katherine Hepburn).

Treasure Island, 1934: Long John Silver (Wallace Beery) introduces young Jim Hawkins (Jackie Cooper) to his new shipmates.

Little Lord Fauntleroy, 1936: Dick the bootblack (Mickey Rooney) tries to understand the good fortune awaiting Cedric (Freddie Bartholomew) as the new Lord Fauntleroy.

Kidnapped, 1971: Davie (Lawrence Douglas), Catriona (Vivien Heilbron) and Alan Breck (Michael Caine) find more casualties of the Highlanders' rebellion.

The Wizard of Oz, 1939: publicity still. From left: the Cowardly Lion (Bert Lahr), the Tin Man (Jack Haley), Dorothy (Judy Garland), the Wizard (Frank Morgan), the Scarecrow (Ray Bolger) and Toto.

Kim, 1951: the young Kim (Dean Stockwell) learns another lesson from the Teshoo Lama (Paul Lukas).

The Railway Children, 1971: Peter (Gary Warren), Bobbie (Jenny Agutter) and Phyllis (Sally Thomsett).

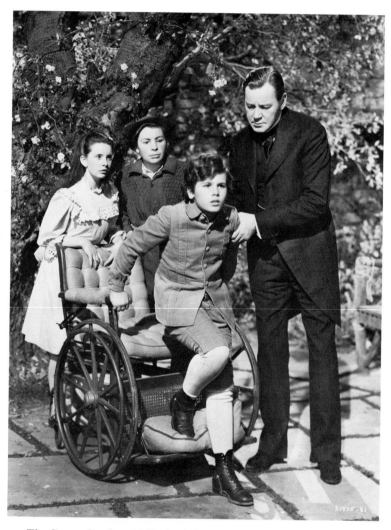

The Secret Garden, 1949: Archibald Craven (Herbert Marshall) helps his invalid son Colin (Dean Stockwell) take his first steps, as Mary (Margaret O'Brien) and Dickon (Brian Roper) watch.

The Hobbit, 1977: Bilbo Boggins (left) and Gollum trade riddles in the dark. (*Illustration copyright 1977, Rankin/Bass Productions, Inc.*)

The Little Prince, 1974: The newly tamed Fox (Gene Wilder)
dances with his Little Prince (Steven Warner).

Pippi Longstocking, 1969: Pippi (Inger Nilsson) finds living alone lots of fun.

Island of the Blue Dolphins, 1964: Rontu watches as Karana (Celia Kaye) befriends an otter.

Charlotte's Web, 1973: Charlotte the spider spells out a "terrific" message for Wilbur the pig and his excited friends: Mrs. Goose, Templeton the rat and Fern Arable.

Willy Wonka and the Chocolate Factory, 1971: Willy Wonka (Gene Wilder) churns up more chocolate. In background: Mike Teavee (Paris Themmen), Charlie Bucket (Peter Ostrum), Grandpa Joe (Jack Albertson).

Chitty Chitty Bang Bang, 1968: Caractacus Pott (Dick Van Dyke) departs with passengers Truly Scrumptious (Sally Ann Howes) and children Jemima (Heather Ripley) and Jeremy (Adrian Hall), for another exotic excursion aboard Chitty Chitty Bang Bang.

From the Mixed-Up Files of Mrs. Basil E. Frankweiler, 1973:
Mrs. Frankweiler (Ingrid Bergman) and Claudia Kincaid (Sally
Prager). (*Courtesy Museum of Modern Art, Film Stills Archive*)

Sounder, 1972: David Lee Morgan (Kevin Hooks) visits his father (Paul Winfield) in jail.

safety and well-being with the circus, but the Disney Toby remains loyal to him. Disney here appealed to every boy's fantasy to have a chimp of his own.

For the rest of the cast, the studio chose character actors with broad, expressive faces, recognizable from other Disney productions but not closely tied to any particular character in them and not "names" in the Disney studio. The faces and acting styles reflect the studio's earlier interest in cartoon-like characters, for the actors themselves are like caricatures: few lines, blemishes, or other facial marks, broad rather than subtle facial characteristics, bodies which are extreme but yet avoiding the grotesques more typical of Kaler's sideshow freaks—for example, the fat lady and skeleton man who befriend Toby. The film characters resort to expressive language of the down-home variety, meaningful but not offensive epithets such as "don't you try to bear grease me" and "you lily-livered skunk," authentically American, not very original, but laughable clichés in context.

It is obvious that the movie was made on a slim budget; Disney goes in for effects only to save money. Even the circus acts are rather scarce, with only a quick shot of trapeze artists flying from bar to bar and then landing in the net below, a weightlifting scene, a few elephants, monkeys, and large cats, a calliope, and of course Toby's bareback riding. The scenes showing Toby in performance are more extensive, but they do not require much clever photography or many stand-in stuntpersons.

Disney Studios even stinted on the music for the movie; whereas "When You Wish Upon A Star" or "Hi-Ho, Hi Ho" became popular tunes as a result of Disney animated features, *Toby Tyler* does not even have a song with a complete stanza of words. "Biddle Dee Dee" is sung in snatches, almost under the breath, by both Ben and Toby; it is never sung out loud, all the way through, by either of them. It is not a recurring theme song, but rather an odd line of tune here and there; "my way of thinkin' it's not so bad" and "away we go" characterize the almost unheard lyrics. While the job of providing musical background falls mostly to the circus band—particularly brassy, brilliant, and typical in their red uniforms—the fact

that Disney should have stinted on a theme song indicates a
certain lack of care about the film's design.

Though Kaler's circus is dingy and inhospitable, Disney's
presentation of "Sam Castle's All-American Circus" is painted
a patriotic red, white, and blue. Vivid, physically attractive
and inexpensive, it remains neat and clean even during un-
loading and packing up; large and extraordinarily sanitary
animals abound in the small circus. There is no attempt to make
the circus look real; grime and graffiti are banished, and the
neatly pressed uniforms and costumes—red, white, and blue, of
course—remain bandbox new throughout. Toby has a number
of them, including a vender's military jacket and hat, and a
bareback rider's cape, tights, and satin tunic and sash.

There are lions, tigers, elephants, and especially clowns—
not in Kaler's novel—but none of the grime and grotesques
which the original features. The presence of the clowns is particularly significant, for it indicates the Disney purpose in producing the film: to provide good, clean fun of a distinctly
"American" variety—lots of laughs, especially of the pratfall
type, set in an attractive environment.

In the novel, Toby's special friend who tries unsuccessfully
to protect him from abuse, is Sam Treat, the Human Skeleton,
who is married to the show's Fat Lady. Eager not to offend, the
studio substituted a Sam Treat who is a clown with a family of
trained dogs. It is he who gives Toby a friendly ear and firmly
but kindly trains him in the art of bareback horsemanship. The
clown is an attractive protector rather than a sideshow curiosity. He is also skilled in veterinary medicine, so that he can
treat the chimp whenever the latter gets into trouble. His love
of animals makes him all the more attractive.

Toby is further protected by Ben Carter, a roustabout in
the original, but a weightlifter as well in the film. Disney's Ben
is more brusk and abrupt with Toby than Kaler's original, but
he is good-hearted nonetheless, and he gives Toby good advice
about lying, hard work, respect for one's employer, and sticking to a job once started. All of these accepted values of American life play no part in the original but are added by Disney to
ennoble circus life.

Given the Disney Studio's known propensity for handling a

literary property with some disdain for the original story line, it is surprising how close the movie stays to the book. Once the physical violence, consisting of rubber canes and misapplied horsewhips, is eliminated, the movie follows the novel in incident until the very end. Toby is seduced away from home with promises of the good life by concessionaire Harry Tupper, Disney's cleaned-up, clean shaven, smoothtalking version of Kaler's more malevolent Job Lord. Tupper controls Toby only by a few angry looks and tweeks of the ear rather than by caning him. As in the novel, there is an accident with a circus wagon during which Toby rescues the chimp on the loose and is rewarded with his exclusive care. Toby learns to be a bareback rider as a partner to Jeanette, a young circus regular, and is a success at his debut, as he is in the novel. His guardians, smalltown farmer folk Dan and Olive, have called him a "millstone around" their necks, as Toby reports, and his feelings are so hurt and his eyes so dazzled by the circus that he is more than willing to follow the circus when it leaves town.

But the motivations for the characters are considerably different, leading to an ending that has a totally different effect from Kaler's. During his time with the circus (the ten weeks is not mentioned, and the passage of time in the film is unclear), he writes home and intends to return to Daniel and Olive as soon as he has enough money to prove that he is no burden to them. Indeed the film Toby is justified in running away since they have been so heartless in emphasizing his expense to them. Life at the circus is hard, but Toby is a favorite of both Sam Treat and Ben Carter, and eventually of the circus owner and ringmaster Sam Castle, all of whom mitigate the loneliness that the novel's Toby feels so deeply. The film Toby's only motivation for running away from the circus is the discovery of a letter (courtesy of the chimp who picks Tupper's pockets for the withheld mail) from Olive telling him that Uncle Daniel is overworked back at the farm and that they need him. The film's Toby does not have to learn the lesson, as the novel's does, that home is best. In the film, Toby runs away, chimp in tow, but Tupper, mindful of the cut of Toby's earnings that he gets while Toby is a performing star, finds him and brings him back to the circus, where Olive and Dan, reconciled to Toby's fame and his wandering life, are pleased with the friends he has made and gladly own him as their real son. There is, therefore, no lecture about the virtues of home and the perils of running away. Though in this failed escape the chimp is shot by a hunter, as he is in the book, he does not die; it later becomes clear that he is only slightly wounded ("bullet only ventillated his hide a little," as Sam Treat reports), and in the grand finale he is able to join Toby in center ring in the bareback riding routine.

Indeed, it is this ending that most clearly shows Disney's subversion of Kaler's theme and his failure to substitute anything but a stereotyped vision of the pleasures of circus life. Sandwiching Toby's attempted escape, Stubbs's shooting, and Toby's return to find Olive and Dan waiting for him at the circus are two long sequences of Toby performing in the ring. The first scene shows Jeanette and Toby performing as a duo, compatible "like ham and beans," as Sam Castle says. They stand on trotting horses, jump through hoops, and jump onto the back of the same running horse. The sequence validates Toby's success as a circus performer, and it satisfies the American fantasy of being a star and a success in show business.

The second scene, which closes the movie, shows Toby performing solo (at least until Mr. Stubbs mischievously jumps on his back, to Toby's surprise and the crowd's delight), this time riding on a chair balanced on its two back legs, which are in turn balanced on the horse's back. Though this feat is accomplished by the gimmick, obvious even to the least perceptive viewer, of a platform on the horse's back specially made to hold the chair steady, it is meant to demonstrate Toby's proficiency as a performer in his own right, capable of "a feat of horsemanship and balance seldom witnessed in the sawdust ring," as it is described by ringmaster Sam Castle.

More importantly, it also shows the approval that Toby has gained from Olive and Dan, who are in the audience, from Sam Castle, and from Harry Tupper, who automatically turns from vending bad peanuts, and from a new runaway boy whom Tupper has seduced away from home to take Toby's place as vender's helper. At the end of the film, the issue of Toby's staying with the circus is not resolved, but his guardians clearly

approve of such a life—as does the audience. From an unwanted boy, a "millstone around" the necks of his guardians,
he has turned into a famous, wealthy, admired, talented boy
who has more than enough protection and attention. There are
those who would see Toby as an autobiographical comment on
Disney's conception of his own life; but the rags-to-riches
success story is a potent enough stereotype in American culture to be evocative without that parallel.

These two circus scenes are longer than any others in the
movie, and have as their main purpose entertainment rather
than investigation or resolution of plot and thematic issues. In
the first of the two, Ben, Toby's oversized protector, is shown in
the ring lifting two ponies by means of a bar over his shoulders.
Ben's talent as a circus performer does not come from Kaler's
novel, nor is it important to the film. It is simply there to
present yet another circus spectacle. There is also a procession
of elephants that does little more than provide atmosphere and
additional spectacle.

Finally, the film does not confront the issues of Toby's discomfort back on the farm, the drawbacks of circus life, or the
realistic fate of young boys who run away from home to join
such a life. Instead, Disney plays on the stereotypical American boy's dream of joining the circus and becoming a star. The
movie opens with a title "Once upon a time when the circus
came to town, it was the biggest day of the year"; the fairy tale
formula is realized with the inevitable happy ending. Disney
also plays on that nostalgia for the supposedly happier life of
smalltown America which has passed into idealized history.
The panoramic scenery shown as the circus travels by night
out of one town into another is of a pastoral and idealized
smalltown America—a church steeple and a cluster of neat
homes nestled in a distant valley—reminiscent of a Currier
and Ives landscape. It is clearly not real but simply a backdrop
on which the images of the live actors are superimposed. However, the viewer is rather inclined to accept them uncritically,
since they too are part of that stereotypical American fantasy
of the good life of the circus, moving from one clean, attractive
small town to another to provide the one speculator event of
rural life each year.

Unlike Kaler's novel, Disney's film clearly implies that the circus is a grand life of excitement, travel, and friendly people where a child can make his fame and fortune and even have a chimp for a pet. Appealing to America's nostalgia for its rural past, the Disney version of *Toby Tyler* is all surface, no artistry, and no problems.

Pinocchio—From Picaro to Pipsqueak

DOUGLAS STREET

Since its 1881 debut in Rome's *Giornale dei Bambini,* "bambini" around the world have continuously and vociferously embraced Carlo Collodi's rough and tumble *Adventures of Pinocchio.* The episodic scenarios of this pine picaro from Tuscany seem as vibrant today as when originally fashioned. And just as readers have been captivated by the trials and tribulations of the puppet desirous of humanity, so too have filmmakers, eager to explore the story's cinematic possibilities and box-office potential, labored industriously to transform the woodenhead's "dolce vita" into a moving picture saga. Practitioners of the animated medium in particular have been especially captivated by Collodi's vision.

One of the earliest European experiments in film animation drew its inspiration from Collodi's novel. Pinocchio's countryman Cesare Antamoro felt the marionette the perfect vehicle for his fledgling 1911 animated project, and while it never reached completion it did serve as prototype to cinematic animators in Italy and the United States for the next thirty years. In 1936, Raoul Verdini, photography director Carlo Bachini, and their Cartoni Animati Italiani Roma (CAIR) completed a professedly faithful filmic retelling premiered as a sixty-minute, black-and-white animated feature. However, a desire on the part of Verdini and CAIR to experiment with new processes developed abroad and reshoot this sophisticated version in color, led to the 1936 offering being shelved; full attention was given over to an ambitious color *Pinocchio,* envisioned by Verdini for a 1940 Italian release. War in Europe made

47

completing the film on schedule improbable, and the new *L'Avventuri Di Pinocchio* received its death blow when in February of that year Walt Disney's *Pinocchio* was released. Though lacking the integrity of narrative adhered to by the Romans, this animated version has since been acclaimed by film experts as Disney's animation masterpiece. The CAIR project was abandoned. Over forty years later the American's creation remains artistically arresting—a paragon of animation technology and a vintage Disney in approach, style and content.

All of the animated features released before Disney's death, and most noticeably the pre-1950 offerings, were indelibly marked with his perfectionist traits. Disney succeeded in directly influencing *every* film project; nothing developed without his unrelenting personal approval. Frequently months of writing and drawing, and hundreds of feet of completed footage were scrapped by a Disney veto and his insistence on beginning afresh with improved angles or concepts. In discussing "the Disney touch" in his *The Art of Walt Disney* (1973), Christopher Finch elaborates on two of the most visible elements of the vintage releases:

> Disney's training in the field of cartoon shorts had taught him how to tell a story without wasting a single foot of film. There is nothing in *Snow White* [nor in *Pinocchio*] that does not contribute either to developing character or to moving plot. . . . Yet this does not lead to a feeling of spareness, because crammed into this framework is a profusion of detail that is almost overwhelming. (p. 197)

This mania for plot economy resulted in constant criticism of the filmmaker's repeated "telescoping" of narrative structural elements to better enhance cinematic priorities. For Disney, the devices of fiction—literary subplotting, peripheral characterization, narrative nuance, etc.—were easily dispensed with. For this reason, for recognizable similarity to original plotlines, the fairy tale adaptations fair best. The simpler, more linear, more cinematic the original tale, the less the filmmaker felt obliged to delete. The multileveled narratives exemplified by *Pinocchio* suffered unmercifully under this animator's direction.

Disney's passion for transforming complex narratives into simplistic screenplays was in direct contrast to his insistence on seemingly endless artistic frill. In *Pinocchio,* for example, where original storylines were matter-of-factly trimmed to the bones, weeks of artistic effort were directed into the meticulously extravagant rendering of naturalistic detail on such inconsequential scenic elements as the wood shavings and the briefly showcased music-box figures among the clutter of Geppetto's workshop, and the marionettes and background paraphernalia in the Stromboli shots. Disney even spent thousands to airbrush a single miniscule highlight on each finished cel to enhance in his mind the appearance of Figaro the Kitten—the audience never notices most of this artistry, but Disney would never let the work be released without it.

The complete character development of every Disney screen creation was yet another mark of the master. As Paul Hollister, writing for *The Atlantic Monthly* (December, 1940), about "Walt Disney: Genius at Work" asserts: "Article I of the Disney constitution stipulates that every possible element of a picture shall be not a mere pictorial representation of a character or an element of scenary, but an individual, with clearly defined characterstics" (p. 691). Because of this, viewers reflecting on past Disney features may remember the seven dwarfs more distinctly than Snow White, Gus-Gus the mouse more than Cinderella, and Cleo, Figaro and Jiminy Cricket more vividly than their wooden companion. The primary means for conveying both plot and character was always visual.

By his own admission, Disney read little. He was oriented pictorially—integrity of literary adaptation simply never was a factor as long as his visual integrity was fostered and maintained; in this he was uncompromising.

[Disney Studios] was a very harsh place to work in . . . but harsh with every kind of advantage, [relates Shamus Culhane in Leonard Maltin's *Of Mice and Magic*, 1980]. Even in those days a movieola . . . cost twelve hundred bucks or something, but everyone had one. You could shoot stuff over as long as you wanted. . . . The marvelous thing about the studio . . . was that you could work all day the whole eight hours, and at the end of the day look at what you did and put it in the wastepaper basket with no compunction. Nobody would ask you why you did it; they would ask you if you *didn't*.

As *Pinocchio* epitomized this process, it is understandable that Disney once (as Maltin relates) conceded that "*Pinocchio* might have lacked *Snow White's* heart appeal, but technically and artistically it was superior." It is true that though a success with its audience, it has never matched the commercial appeal of *Snow White* and several lesser studio releases. It is also understandable, given these elemental features of the Disney product—lean plot, meticulous visual characterization, lavish and extravagant artistic complexity—why this motion picture is simultaneously considered an adaptational travesty and a cinematic masterpiece.

According to *Newsweek's* "Pinocchio à la Disney" (February 19, 1940), the idea for the feature starring Italy's marionette hero came from members of the studio staff, not from the boss. "Disney had never read Carlo Collodi's world-famous story. . . . Several members of his staff knew the legend, however, and Disney was impressed by their enthusiasm for the wayward little puppet." From the beginning, as Disney was wont to do, the narrative was relegated to second position behind the utilization and sophistication of elevated animation technology. This film would make extensive use of the newly developed multiplane camera. First used in the 1937 short "The Old Mill," this camera allowed the animated frame to take on a reality through depth and perspective closely approximating that in live footage. Collodi's tale, with its village scenes, nightscapes, seascapes and the like seemed well suited for multiplane experimentation. From the outset however, Collodi's saga proved difficult for the animators to "Disney-fy"; after six months of initial activity the boss finally called the project to a halt, completely scrapped work already completed, put the animators on other assignments, and commenced to reevaluate his character and narrative concepts.

As in other studio adaptations, in *Pinocchio* every visual

nuance was exploited for personality and character screen appeal. However, the novel's psychological shifts, changes in conscience, and picaresque peculiarities could not be left unchecked. Good and evil had to be, in the film, simplistically discernible; complex personalities had to devolve into black-and-white caricatures. This film had to conform to the already established code of propriety and ethics demanded by Disney.

When the project was resurrected, the chiaroscuro personalities of Pinocchio and father Geppetto were washed into excessive blissfulness and kindheartedness, respectively. Disney clearly allied these "good-guys" with his made up Figaro the Kitten and Cleo the Goldfish, and his made-over Jiminy Cricket. The Blue Fairy assumed a "Fairy Godmother" persona as mitigator against the evil Stromboli, the sinister Fox and Cat, the delinquent Lampwick, the satanic Coachman and the carnivorous whale. What evolves on the screen—but is absent from the novel—is an ominously didactic tone: the audience is forcefully advised to be good to their families, work diligently without complaint, and tread the path of righteousness if they intend to reap life's rewards; to forsake, question or ignore such maxims ends in humiliation, tragedy or death. In direct contention with the central theme of its European model, this approach gives no credence to character enlightenment nor repentence as alternative means for salvation.

After the good and evil were clearly delineated, the major point of studio contention apparently centered on the essential character of Pinocchio himself. Should he be portrayed as a living puppet or as a naïve little boy? Disney took the position that his character had to project the appealing qualities of a little boy while remaining a wooden marionette. An examination of the literary classic shows what caused the animators such consternation. As is immediately apparent to all familiar with Collodi's narrative, this Tuscan woodenhead bears little resemblance in physique or temperament to Disney's Burbank *burratino*. The same holds true for the majority of Collodi's creations. Collodi's wooden hero is a picaro—Disney's is a pipsqueak.

Long before Geppetto finishes his creation Collodi establishes his hero as a selfish, mocking personality:

After choosing the name for his Marionette, Geppetto set seriously to work to make . . . his eyes. Fancy his surprise when he
noticed that these eyes moved and stared fixedly at him. Geppetto, seeing this, felt insulted. . .

After the eyes, Geppetto made the nose, which began to
stretch as soon as finished. . . . Poor Geppetto kept cutting
it . . . but the more he cut, the longer grew that imperti-
nent nose. . . . Next he made the mouth. No sooner was it finished than it began to laugh and poke fun at him. . . . The
mouth stopped laughing, but it stuck out a long tongue. . . . The
legs and feet still had to be made. As soon as they were done
Geppetto felt a sharp kick on the tip of his nose. "I deserve
it!" he said to himself. "I should have thought of this before I
made him. Now it's too late!"[1]

Pinocchio goes on a continuous rampage that consumes nearly
half the narrative. Initial episodes establish his impudence as
being responsible for the imprisonment of Geppetto and the
killing of the Talking Cricket. Sorrow and remorse come hard
on the heels of calamity (as when he incinerates his feet or
when he is left to hang), but new moral lapses send him reeling
once more. It is evident that for this character to receive reward in the end, he must be taken through a rigorous process of
purgation and education—the beginnings of which are necessarily self-initiated. In this world, character shifts are expected
and repentance encouraged. Pinocchio's upward path begins
while he is in the belly of the Shark (Collodi allows for the hero
to literally and figuratively climb from the depths into the
light). Clever and courageous, he escapes with his father: "You
can climb on my shoulders and I, who am a fine swimmer, will
carry you safely to the shore" (p. 203). The puppet is as good as
his boast; his father is saved, yet the purification is not complete. Pinocchio must do penance by strenuous, selfless service
to his ailing father and the hospitalized Fairy; such work, done
in the presence of old adversaries, purges the puppet of past
transgressions and assures his long sought transformation into
a real boy. "Bravo, Pinocchio! In reward for your kind heart, I
forgive you for all your old mischief. Boys who love and take

[1]*Pinocchio,* tr. by C. Della Chiesa (New York: Collier Books, 1972 pp.
10–11). All subsequent references noted in the text.

good care of their parents when they are old and sick deserve praise even though they may not be held up as models of obedience and good behavior" (p. 218).

As developed by Collodi, the Italian marionette is a headstrong pivotal figure, vibrant, active, powerful and charismatic. The narrative action is initiated by him, for him, and because of him. He never sinks to the simplicity of his cinematic alter ego, the childish pipsqueak pushed around by a streetwise cricket.

Interestingly enough, this peripheral moralistic character in the novel mutates into a singing and dancing major figure in the Disney version, usurping all individuality, importance and screen appeal of the picture's erstwhile namesake. This insect guides the viewers through the story, "clarifies" moral issues through song and slogan, and when possible keeps the puppet on the proper course; with the aplomb of a Brooklyn bouncer he moves adversity aside so his infantile charge may pass through. Jiminy gets the songs and the dialogue, plus focus in every shot in which he appears—Pinocchio gets the title only. In fact Jiminy Cricket so dominated the screen that Disney featured him—*sans* Pinocchio—in the 1947 release *Fun and Fancy Free,* from whence the cricket went on to star in several Disney educational films and television segments, becoming ultimately a recognized spokesperson for the Disney organization. Ironically, a termite nearly starred in the 1940 film: "Because Pinocchio was a wooden puppet, a termite seemed at first indicated for the job. Then someone reminded Disney that Collodi's story had a Talking Cricket who occasionally served as the puppet's alter ego . . . thus a cricket was elected." (*Newsweek,* February 19, 1940)

Two other character alterations must be mentioned. Nowhere in the novel does one experience the kindly little Arthur Shields-esque woodcarver blessed for his goodness with the getting of a supernatural son. The true Geppetto is a Pantelone who, while not of an evil nature, is prone to tantrums and fits of temper. "Geppetto looks like a good man," says a neighbor early on, "but with boys he's a real tyrant. If we leave that poor Marionette in his hands he may tear him to pieces!" (p. 14). Collodi's narrative focuses on the transformation of the puppet into a responsible and loving son, but a secondary theme is Geppetto's change from a crusty bachelor and cantankerous artist into a humane, appreciative, and loving father. It must be remembered that in the novel Pinocchio's initial animation is not Geppetto's divine reward for a kind heart; when the puppet comes to life he represents an unwanted sliver in the hand of an already sour Geppetto. Obstacles must be surmounted and lessons learned by both parties before rewards may be reaped. It is in this perspective that Collodi is strongest and his tale most universal. Disney, unable to mix qualities, whitewashes his character, as he does Pinocchio's, until, laments Christopher Finch, "Geppetto is the least interesting of the main characters. He is asked to function on a single, fundamentally sentimental emotional level, thus presenting the animator [and the audience] with very little challenge."

Though the animator failed to capture the essence of Collodi's Tuscan woodcarver, he made amends with the incredible leviathan Monstro the Whale. This creation swallows whole Collodi's lethargic, asthma-afflicted Shark from which the novel's heroes make a clever yet uninspired escape. The multiplane shots down the creature's belly, and the wild and riveting pursuit footage epitomize the Disney mastery of the medium. With minute attention paid to perspective, this whale appears so large and threatening, filling as he does most of every frame, that the viewer is forced to fear for the well-being of any creature near. And when he rears and charges the fleeing twosome (a chase scene as effective as any Hollywood has yet produced) he instills the film with something *Snow White* did not have—terror. The plunging, surging spectacle of Monstro the Whale as created in *Pinocchio,* is visually terrifying. Such a cathartic episode exemplifies Disney's use of the medium to enhance the narrative—similar impact eludes Collodi.

To plot and character deviations must be allied a third departure from the original tale. In order to turn this tale into the desired 1930s American parable, the need was felt to significantly alter and commercialize Carlo Collodi's episodes in the alternately translated Land of Toys/Land of the Boobies, a world of idle fun, games and constant entertainment with no school for distraction. Collodi's playland wherein "Boys who stop studying and turn their backs upon books and schools and teachers, in order to give all their time to nonsense and pleasure, sooner or later come to grief" becomes in screen translation the debauched "Pleasure Island" inhabited by beings seemingly conceived as crosses between the "Dead End Kids" and mutants from H. G. Wells's *The Island of Doctor Moreau*. Collodi's boys are living out the ultimate childhood fantasy—escaping to a schoolless land of neverending fun and camaraderie; while Collodi shows that the end results of such behavior are personally destructive, the fun itself is not. Lack of education and guidance leads in the novel to childish play and idleness; for Disney such behavior leads to a corruption of morals, wantonness and vice, gluttony, fighting, and eventually disfiguration and death. The scenes of happy boys riding bicycles, playing marbles, going to puppet theaters, and the like, are replaced with shots of young delinquents carousing in poolrooms, roaming the streets, smashing windows, burning books, and loitering in "Tobacco Lane" smoking, and conversing like B-movie hoods. Disney's moral vision seems straight from Bosch's "Garden of Earthly Delights"—Collodi's, out of Disneyland.

The movie's layout artists, notably Gustav Tenggren, Ken Anderson, Charles Philippi and Hugh Hennesy, have reinforced such visions through meticulously executed island panoramas recognizably influenced by the gaieties and gayways of San Francisco's Treasure Island ("Treasure" became "Pleasure") and its 1939 World's Fair. Just as noticeable is the Alcatraz influence dominating artistic renderings of the Pleasure Island's exterior walls. When Pinocchio and his cricket cohort go over the wall and into the sea, they recreate yet another prison break from "The Rock," as searchlights explode into light, sirens scream, bloodhounds howl, and rifles blast; the screen erupts in a frenzy of fear and excitement, paralyzing the audience while the heroes make good their harrowing escape. No such drama is afforded the novel's hero, as Pinocchio in full donkey metamorphosis, is led sorrowfully away and sold to a circus.

Given the filmmaker's heightened sense of the cinematic

and the dramatic, while the scenic recreations plumb the depths of moral decay in direct opposition to Collodi's vision, the animated scenarios rivet the viewers and initiate in them a truly Aristotelian catharsis. Disney's film so manipulates its viewers' senses and emotions for maximum impact that, though the interpretations, concepts, and thematic-narrative devices are diametrically opposed to the essence of the original, they are, ultimately, cinematically outstanding.

The overriding difference then in the two *Pinocchio*'s does not fundamentally emanate from the film versus fiction dichotomy, but rather from a difference in cultural indoctrinations. The real Pinocchio, like the real Collodi (born Carlo Lorenzini), is undeniably Italian, and specifically Tuscan; the film's adaptation emanates from an ambitious, poorly read cartoonist steeped in the values of breadbasket America and nurtured by the dreams of a California cartoon empire. The former exudes character and scenic traditions of the Commedia dell' Arte, of Harlequin, Pantelone and Brighella—the latter, pure Horatio Alger. Two more disparate influences could not be found. To achieve an entertaining filmic adaptation of this harlequin's escapade, at once true to the novelistic intent and the cinematic mode, a director would necessarily need to revel in the Tuscan milieu of the novel and its creator, and develop sufficient cinematic expertise to recreate this necessarily episodic, somewhat improvisatory Italian adventure. It could be said that *Pinocchio* the novel is better fitted to the cinematic world of Federico Fellini than to that of Disney. In the film tradition of *La Strada* and *La Dolce Vita,* Pinocchio's harlequinade is every bit as powerful of those of Zampanò and Marcello, respectively. Fellini's cinematic style exemplified by those films—the series of self-contained episodes or vignettes which seem disconnected but which when taken as a whole provide a myriad of situational viewpoints and a complete motion picture experience—is the celluloid cousin of Collodi's narrative structure. Collodi's *Pinocchio can* be transferred successfully to the screen, but only by one comfortable enough with its tradition and its conventions to embrace its richness intelligently.

Susan Gannon, writing on the observation of the novel's

centennial, correctly recognizes that "Pinocchio's story shows how a puppet—an instrument designed to be manipulated by others—can become a powerful independent source of life." Such occurrences come about not because Pinocchio has proven to be faithful and obedient to authority, but "because he respects both the spirit of the moral code of his 'parents' and his own inner obligation to his real self."[2] It is this quality which has given Collodi's woodenhead life for a century and will ensure it immortality. It is this same combination of free spirit and respectful obligation that Fellini instills in both Zampanò and Marcello, and that is instrumental in their screen successes. This aspect eluded Disney—though his charge blithely sings, "I've got no strings to tie me down," the moviegoer sees otherwise. Had the master cartoonist matched the insight of Fellini with his own artistic genius, maybe his *Pinocchio* too could have bid for immortality as both a landmark of animation *and* an adaptational masterpiece.

[2]"Pinocchio: The first hundred years," *Children's Literature Quarterly* 6 (Winter 1981/1982), p. 7.

Searching for *Treasure Island*

PERRY NODELMAN

Treasure Island was my favorite book when I was young. Or so I've always believed—for when I sat down to reread it as an adult I found I was reading it for the first time. The pirate I'd loved, the one with the parrot on his shoulder and the evil glint in his one open eye, was Robert Newton's Long John Silver; it was the Disney film of *Treasure Island* (1950) I'd been recalling with such pleasure.

Now that I've really read *Treasure Island,* I still admire it. In it, Robert Louis Stevenson not only sets up the conflicts that govern all adventure stories; he cleverly refuses to resolve them, so that *Treasure Island* never tells us how to think about anything that happens in it. More exactly, it insists that we think two opposite things at once.

The older Jim who tells the story of his youthful adventures is a hypocritical, sanctimonious, and decidedly undeserving recipient of ill-gotten gains. He believes that pirates are thoughtless and unhygienic, and that people like his younger self who seek adventure are just plain foolish. Since Jim learned these very proper attitudes on his own adventurous treasure hunt, we shouldn't be surprised that he ends up speaking of the place they happened as "that accursed island."[1] But we can doubt his honesty when he insists that "from the first look onward, I hated the very thought of Treasure Island" (p. 83). In fact, he clearly enjoys not just the first sight but much that follows it. For readers thrilled by the events the older Jim describes with such distaste, the younger Jim's un-

[1] *Treasure Island* (New York: New American Library, 1965), p. 212. All further references are to this edition.

deniably less sensible attitudes ring truer. At the beginning, bored by his quiet life at home, he has "sea dreams and the most charming anticipations of strange islands and adventures" (p. 48). And later, his enthusiastically unthinking actions undermine his older self's priggish caution both by causing all the excitement and by eventually saving the day. For readers, *Treasure Island* is the "delightful dream" (p. 53) Jim expected because it allows us both to realize why we shouldn't lust after our own adventures and to nevertheless enjoy Jim's; to both hate Long John Silver and to enjoy him for exactly the same reason—his charming self-indulgence; to both understand the usefulness of Jim's thoughtlessness and to see how dangerous it is; to both enjoy the exciting danger of the island and to be thankful for the boring safety of our own ordinary lives.

Almost everyone who talks about *Treasure Island* sees it as a combination of something and its opposite. But whatever the terms of the oppositions, the distinguishing quality of *Treasure Island* is that it doesn't resolve them, doesn't come down on one side or the other, doesn't even compromise. And that happens because of the vast difference in attitude between the Jim who tells the story and the Jim the story happens to; it is a trick of narrative technique that makes us come away from the novel feeling only the same delicious ambivalence we've felt all along.

Films cannot easily duplicate such a technique. According to Seymour Chatman, in films "the dominant mode is presentational, not assertive. A film doesn't say, 'This *is* the state of affairs,' it merely shows you that state of affairs. . . . The camera depicts but does not describe."[2] Unless they resort to the clumsiness of a voice-over narration, films cannot easily imply an ironic attitude to the things they show. So I wondered if a film that contained the same events as *Treasure Island* could capture its ambivalence.

MGM's 1934 version has none of it. Under Victor Fleming's direction Jackie Cooper's Jim Hawkins and Wallace Beery's Long John Silver are unambiguous caricatures of boyish inno-

[2] "What Novels Can Do That Films Can't," in *Critical Inquiry,* Autumn 1980, p. 128.

cence and unattractive evil. Imperviously innocent, Cooper's Jim perceives a charm in Beery's charmless Silver invisible to everyone else, including the audience. The film has it both ways: it asks us both to despise Silver and to admire Jim's ability not to notice how despicable Silver is. Neither Jim's innocence nor Silver's evil is the least bit ambiguous.

But Cooper's Jim is clearly better off in his innocence of Silver's evil than we are in our mature knowledge of it. Jackie Cooper, the ultimate cute, blonde, gnome-faced kid, makes Jim so insufferably loveable that we know we have to admire his determined blindness to the truth. The lighting helps him; he never appears without an angelic halo around his head. Johnny Lee Mathin's script helps him too, by asking him to squeak "Bless my soul" or "Upon my soul" every time something surprises him—and he is a surprisable child. But it's not just his cuteness that makes him adorable. He is an orphan; his father is already dead as the film begins, and he seems to seek the father he lacks in Silver. At one point, he endearingly asks Long John if he'd like to come and live with him, and soulfully adds, "We'll always be mates, won't we?" After discovering Silver's treachery he suffers terribly, and milks our sympathy even more terribly. And in an overlong sequence at the end of the film, he allows Silver to sweet-talk him into letting him escape, tries to talk Silver out of being wicked, and dissolves into tears yet once more when he discovers that Silver is trying to make off with part of the boodle. "You promised you wouldn't," he says, but he ends up offering Silver the money so he won't starve.

Only the hardest-hearted of moviegoers could fail to be won over by all this cute innocence; finally, the film implies that even Silver, Beery's charmless malevolent Silver, has been won over too. Disarmed as sentimental music swells and Jim cries, he gives the poor kid his parrot and promises that someday they'll go dig for treasure again. This is not the sagacious Silver of the novel, who sees something of his own talent for evil in Jim and says, "Ah, you that's young—you and me might have done a power of good together!" (p. 175). But then, this terminally ingenuous heart-wringer is not the Jim of the novel either.

But Cooper's Jim does have a boyish courage that belies his

adorable softheartedness, an astonishing resilience in the face of terror. It is *his* idea to search Billy Bones's body; later, his theft of the ship is a deliberate act, not the accident it is in the novel. He is playing a game of heroism. When Jim does that in the novel, he quickly discovers the ugly side of such adventures; after he shoots Hands, he feels "sick, faint, and terrified" (p. 162). But Jackie Cooper's Jim feels none of that. Satisfied at a job well done, he leaves the ship loudly singing "Yo ho ho" as he heads for the stockade; while he condemns Silver for being so violent, he seems to feel neither guilt nor revulsion for his own murders. This Jim is not an ambivalent mixture of innocent tenderheartedness innocently blind to the meaning both of his own actions and those of others; he is merely sometimes tender and sometimes not, and he leaves Treasure Island as blind as he was at the start.

This film so depends on adoration of Jim's innocence, his vulnerability, his childishness, that it totally distorts the story to support it. What attracts Cooper's Jim to Silver isn't Silver's evil, nor Silver's dismissal of civilized values—the enticingly dangerous things that attract Jim in the novel. Instead, it is a nonexistent niceness in Silver that he refuses to stop believing in. Since the whole point of the film is that Jim constantly misreads Silver, Wallace Beery doesn't have to be attractive; and with his eyes constantly tucked up under his eyebrows, he is anything but.

The script supports his one-sided interpretation by continually making Silver obviously bad, and Jim oblivious to his badness, so that the worse Silver gets, the more we are supposed to admire Jim's obtuseness. Furthermore, the forces of good are as ineffectual and as boring as Stevenson himself depicted them, but without that manly courage that grudgingly allows us to admire them in the novel. Finally, Fleming's *Treasure Island* turns into just another cute story about a nice kid and a nasty man, tricked out in the standard pseudo-gusto of MGM in its heyday—silly jokes about sharks and parrots that bite, Merrie Olde England country dancing and jollity, pirates suddenly dropping everything piratical in order to sing lustily in unison—a story devoid of taste and deficient of meaning, but with a heart as big as all Hollywood.

John Hough's 1972 *Treasure Island,* with Kim Burfield as

Jim and a gargantuan Orson Welles as Long John, is just the opposite: it has no heart at all. No matter what dirty trouble he gets into, Kim Burfield's hair is always just as squeaky clean and as angelically backlit as Jackie Cooper's was. But that made Cooper a hero; in this laundered version, not even the pirates are dirty.

Orson Welles does sweat a little. But considering his bulk, that's not surprising; his performance gives no evidence that he's exerting himself much. Wearing a strangely Gaugain-ish straw hat, he mumbles his way incomprehensibly through scene after weary scene; and he bulks so large and moves so rarely that he seems more like a cathedral with laryngitis than a pirate. It's no wonder that Jim's response to this Long John is so vague—there really isn't anything for him to respond to.

However, the feelings of the characters in this version are rarely clear. The film often downplays or eliminates moments that might reveal emotional conflict or suggest strong feelings. Billy Bones *gives* Jim his map, so there's no question of corpse-robbing; and although we see Silver get a crewman drunk and then push him over the side of the ship, we aren't allowed to believe he drowns; we see his body lying on some convenient mid-Atlantic shore as the ship pulls away behind him. Later, as soon as he reaches the island Jim runs off from the pirates, not on impulse but as part of a cold-blooded plan, for he has arranged to meet his friends at the stockade. This Jim is so well-organized that he seems devoid of the sense of play and disregard for consequence that govern Jim in the novel. His capture of the ship is no fluke, but a deliberate action, explained to Ben Gunn in advance; unlike the novel's Jim, he feels no revulsion for his deeds, and unlike Jackie Cooper's Jim, he doesn't even enjoy them. He calmly shoots Hands, tranquilly steers the ship, and reveals nothing but determination and a boring, inhuman competence.

Even when Jim might be feeling something, this film doesn't make it clear. He rarely speaks. His attachment to Silver is taken for granted, and they hardly talk alone together until the final third of the film; and then, Jim merely listens while Orson Welles's Silver incoherently mumbles lengthy explanations of the situation in scene after fragmented scene, as the Wolf Mankowitz–O.W. Jeeves screenplay descends into chaos. Earlier, Jim tries to explain the situation to Ben Gunn in another unwieldy patch of exposition; but since he's hardly opened his mouth until then, the fact that he can speak more than three words in a row is so astonishing that it's hard to pay attention to what he actually says. Without knowledge of what Jim feels, we have nothing but Kim Burfield's boyishly pretty face; and while the priggish words of the older Jim in a voice-over narration are admirably close to the novel, they make little sense without the balance of a younger Jim's enthusiasm and involvement. We begin to suspect that maybe the older Jim is right, that maybe pirates aren't so exciting after all.

In fact, under John Hough's direction, this film is so dead that we have no other choice. Like many British TV versions of great classics, its careful and ostentatious craftsmanship constantly leeches away excitement. When Jim hides and watches Silver kill a sailor, we see a close-up of the pirate's knife covered with blood, then a falling body; but we don't see the wounding or the wound, and the composition is so careful and the blood so jewel-like that the scene is more pretty than scary. Again and again the dark bodies of actors form interesting shapes against lighter backgrounds, and again and again actors appear in the background framed by interesting objects in the foreground; again and again shots from below establish the presence of ceilings and the solidity of the sets. The film stars its backgrounds, and the nostalgic yellow light it bathes them in turns them into museum pieces, pretty but lifeless artifacts of another time; you can feel the presence of an invisible rope to keep you out of the display. Similarly, the island itself is travelogue country; it's hard to remember that the dark silhouettes moving through these postcards while lush music plays aren't traveling salesmen on a guided tour, but pirates.

Beyond arranging themselves into interesting compositions, the characters in this film seem to have no other function than to disturb the peaceful nostalgia of ye olde Admiral Benbow or the peaceful solitude of beautiful Treasure Island; finally, we have to agree with the words of the older Jim on the soundtrack. Pirates *are* disgusting, adventure *is* overrated, and there's no place like home—particularly if you're fortunate enough to get as good a decorator as Mrs. Hawkins found for the Benbow.

Though neither of these two films capture the ambivalence of Stevenson's novel, interestingly enough, they distort it in opposite directions. The 1934 film tells the story from the viewpoint of the younger Jim; it admires both the good fun and the blindness of innocence without the qualifications of maturity. While the 1972 film accepts and proclaims the priggish "mature" vision of the older Jim, it lacks good fun altogether. Obviously, then, either of these unqualified viewpoints can be depicted on the screen; but is a combination that allows the two to mutually qualify each other possible?

In some ways, the Byron Haskin directed Disney version I remembered so fondly is the least accurate but most satisfying of the three. It introduces a pistol that Long John gives Jim, and makes it central to the plot. Jim's mother never appears, nor does any other evidence of quiet domesticity. The film opens with a bang, as a vile-looking fellow arrives at the inn to hand Billy Bones the black spot—and we don't find out exactly who Bones is or what a black spot means. From that point on, exciting event follows exciting event at an ever-increasing pace; the last third of the film, which covers at least the last half of the novel, is a crescendo of hectic—though not always meaningful—action. The film sacrifices exposition for action, atmosphere for drama—and in doing so, paradoxically, is a surprisingly accurate rendering of the novel; what I enjoyed in this film as a child isn't much different from what I've come to admire as an adult in the novel it was based on.

Scene after scene takes place in near darkness, with brightly lit faces expressing strong emotions or silhouetted figures moving fast, but rarely seen from a distance. Except for two montages, one to establish the boistrous charm of a Bristol suffering a population explosion and the other to evoke the romance of a full-rigged ship at sea, scenery is almost nonexistent. The Admiral Benbow is there, and so are the ship and the stockade; but we almost always see them behind emotion-wrought faces and fast-moving bodies. They register as tight, dark places where exciting things happen, not as museum pieces. Even the treasure hunt focuses on the pirates, not the exciting terrain they cross; Long John leads Jim tied on a rope, and that makes us more interested in what Jim feels than in palm trees.

The camera is always nervous, always creating tension. Few shots last more than two or three seconds, and in exciting moments, we see faces expressing emotion from many different angles, so that we become more interested in reactions to action than in the action itself. Even in the stockade battle, the emphasis is less on the fighting and more on the way Jim and Long John respond to it. In avoiding exposition and emphasizing action, this film might easily have lost the ambivalence of the novel. But it doesn't do that; by focussing on reactions to action rather than on action for its own sake, it makes us realize the ambiguity of Jim's situation. We don't need an older Jim to tell us how painful all this excitement is, for we see it and feel it ourselves.

The film makes us think carefully about Jim's enthusiasm for adventure. At the beginning, Jim's dealings with Bones show him to be competent, assured, even mature beyond his age; and Bobby Driscoll has none of the Hollywood cuteness of the other two Jims, only a cool, boyish seriousness. Jim picks up his excitement from the squire, a fat, aging man whose boyish enthusiasm is silly enough for Jim's adoption of it to seem a little regressive. When Jim arrives in Bristol and sees a sailor, he apes his walk just as he aped the squire's enthusiasm, while music on the sound track picks up and cutifies the sailor's whistling. Once more Jim's enthusiasm for the sea makes him a little ridiculous. He is clearly ripe for temptation by Silver, and we have been carefully prepared to have an ambivalent attitude toward what tempts him.

The temptation occupies the middle third of the film, as we see Silver cleverly use Jim's boyish (and by now suspicious) love of adventure to manipulate him. When Jim doubts Silver's honesty after he sees Black Dog in Silver's inn, Silver wins Jim over by offering him a gun, in case he ever sees the villain again. "You mean to keep?" says Jim, with lust in his eyes; flattered by the gift and caught up in the thrill of adventure, he forgets his qualms. Paradoxically, Silver plays on Jim's childish innocence by pretending to treat him like a man.

While the ship is at sea, the film carefully focuses on how Silver enmeshes Jim even more deeply in evil. When the first mate finds a gun on George Merry and demands all the weapons on board, Jim mourns the fact he'll have to give up his own—the one Silver gave him, the symbol of his manhood. But Silver again pretends to treat Jim like the adult Jim thinks the gun makes him, and appeals to his friendship: Silver will be blamed if it's found out that Jim had the gun in the first place. Jim keeps it; Silver has cleverly used Jim's love of adventure to turn him into a liar.

Next he turns him into a thief, and an accomplice to murder. He talks Jim into stealing rum, in order to make a plum duff to "sweeten" Mr. Arrow, and that leads to the drunken Arrow being washed overboard in a storm. By now Jim sees himself as a man amongst men in the midst of a manly adventure. But having seen Silver use his charm and a boy's love of adventure to manipulate Jim outrageously, we know how ingenuous Jim has been.

After Jim discovers Silver's villainy, he reverts to a childish disdain for Silver's immorality. Asked by the forces of good to play along with Silver and pretend to still be his friend, Jim shows clear distaste. When Silver uses Jim as a hostage in the longboat, but insists he wouldn't harm a hair of his head, Jim tells him he's a liar; he escapes mostly because he can't stand being with him. Soon after, he tells Ben Gunn, "I *hate* John Silver"; and his self-righteous hatred continues almost until the end. But the film still cleverly keeps its ambivalence, for Jim still seems ingenuous; he has forgotten what Robert Newton's performance makes crystal clear, that Long John Silver *is* charming: clever, energetic, far more alive and more interesting than anyone else around. When Jim admires Silver, we saw more than he did; when Jim does not admire Silver, we still see more than he does.

In the last sequence, Jim finally admits his own ambivalence about Silver, and about the life of adventure he represents. Jim has been genuinely terrified by his encounter with Israel Hands on the ship, and clearly disgusted by his own murder of Hands; the film leaves no doubt that Jim's striking of the Skull and Crossbones after that grisly scene is a decision against adventure. But finally, Jim *does* help Silver get off the very beach he cleverly grounded him on, and as he makes a small, tentative wave at Silver rowing off into the void in a tiny boat, he reveals a highly ambiguous love for him.

Before that, Bobby Driscoll's small, competent perform-ance reveals little in the way of confusion in Jim's feelings for Silver. But it doesn't have to; Robert Newton's Long John Silver is so rich, so detailed, so monumentally right, that it expresses all the ambiguity the film needs. For the last hundred years, the one-legged Silver with a parrot on his shoulder has been everybody's idea of a pirate; for the last thirty years, Robert Newton in a three-cornered hat, one eye popping and one eye squinting, his mouth half-smiling and half-sneering as he deliciously growls "Arrrrh, me'arties," has been everybody's idea of Long John Silver. It's not surprising that Newton's TV series based on this character was so success-ful, or that I remembered his performance so clearly so many years after seeing it.

The film both allows Newton his bravura performance and depends on it. Everything focuses on it. We watch in admira-tion as Long John flatters Jim, in horror as Jim falls for the flattery. The ship sequence deals exclusively with Silver's fas-cinating ambiguity—his need to control the inevitably unruly pirates, but his cleverness in doing it; his sneaky manipulation of Jim, and the despicable way he maneuvers Arrow into drowning himself; the sanctimonious hypocrisy of his loud "Arrrr-men" at Arrow's funeral. During the stockade fight, the camera returns again and again from the action to Silver, who stands off by himself and bloodthirstily shouts, "Board 'em, you swabs!" and "Cut the Cap'n down!"—remarks that sum up both the ugliness and the excitement of violence. Finally, Silver joins the fight for the first time as his men retreat and he coolly takes aim and shoots Smollett.

But before that, this film shows a key moment of the novel the other two versions leave out: the one-legged Silver un-graciously maneuvered into sitting down for a parley by the Squire, and then left to get up by himself, even though he first made it clear he would need assistance. While Silver acts vil-lainously in this sequence, we can't help but feel some sympathy for him. Later, scriptwriter Lawrence Edward Watkin has Silver take the map from an unconscious Jim *before* he saves him from the other pirates; and in the end he cannot shoot Jim, even though it will save his own life and even though he tries to do it. On the other hand, he *does* try to escape, with a vicious lack of concern for the health and safety of others, including Jim; and his brutal temper flares as he not only guns down his colleagues in the empty treasure pit, but malevolently throws his crutch at them.

All these actions engender complex reactions. Once Newton appears on the screen, the film is mostly about Silver, secondarily about Jim's response to Silver, and only about the other characters in a minor way. Finally, it is our own ambivalence about Silver, created by Newton's powerful characterization and the attention the film pays to it, that replaces the conflict in the novel between the younger Jim's enthusiasm and the older Jim's disapproval. A brilliant performance and a careful focussing of attention toward it do much the same thing in the film as Stevenson's clever narrative technique does in the novel.

I wasn't the only child who loved this film in the early fifties. Encouraged by its success (and by the relative cheapness of shooting movies in England), the Disney studios made a series of similar live-action films: *Robin Hood* (1952), *The Sword and the Rose* (1954), *Rob Roy* (1953). In *The Disney Version* (1969), Richard Schickel accepts *Time*'s judgment that "they were all amazingly good in the same way. Each struck exactly the right note of wonder and make-believe. The mood of them all was lithesome, modest. Nobody was trying to make a great picture."

I can confirm that for one child, sitting in the dark on a Saturday afternoon in the early fifties, Disney's *Treasure Island* did indeed strike exactly the right note—and struck it so profoundly that I never forgot it, and recalled reading a book I'd never opened. *Time* went on to say that each of these films was "just what a children's classic is supposed to be, a breath of healthy air blown in from the meadows of far away and long ago." For me, seeing this wonderful film again thirty years later was a breath of healthy air blown in from the far away and long ago meadows of my own childhood.

Continuity and Change
in Popular Entertainment

PHYLLIS BIXLER

For almost a century and through a variety of media, Frances Hodgson Burnett's *Little Lord Fauntleroy* has been kept alive in the popular imagination. A tale of a disinherited American boy who wins the heart of his irascible English grandfather and regains his English title and fortune, it was originally published in 1885 in *St. Nicholas,* a magazine for children. It soon became an international bestseller and a long-running play, and Reginald Birch's illustrations for the book set a children's fashion in velvet suits with lace collars. This sartorial splendor as well as Burnett's idealized portraits of an innocent child and self-sacrificing mother eventually made Little Lord Fauntleroy a byword for "sissy," and the romance itself a synonym for excessive sentimentality. None of this, however, kept early filmmakers from recognizing that the book's fairy-tale plot and wide title recognition made it a natural for adaptation in this new medium.

In 1914, a British company made a film which, according to the *New York Times* (June 23, 1914) followed "very closely the original story." In 1921, audiences marveled as Mary Pickford, playing both mother and child, kissed a miniature version of herself on the silent screen. In 1936, David O. Selznick found in Burnett's story justification for displaying a panoply of Hollywood stars besides young Freddie Bartholomew. Finally, in 1980, Norman Rosemont took a moppet trained in television commercials, Ricky Schroder, added the prestige of Sir Alec Guinness, and wrapped them in scenes of British grandeur as an early Christmas present for CBS television viewers.

The durability and adaptability of *Little Lord Fauntleroy*

can be accounted for largely by its roots in popular formulas which never seem to go out of date. Burnett had often, especially in her ladies' magazine fiction, reworked the Cinderella formula: a worthy but fortuneless lass wins the love of a young man of wealth and superior social status and is rewarded by marriage to him. To adapt this formula for children, Burnett simply changed the protagonist to a winsome child, the suitor to an aristocratic relative, and the reward to being reunited with one's family. As a person who had lived in both England and America, Burnett could enhance the appeal of this rags-to-riches formula by adding a confrontation of American democratic and British aristocratic values, without denigrating either. Despite the combination of fairy-tale plot and idealized real world setting so often used in popular entertainment, one should not underrate Burnett's skills as a writer. Many readers aware of the book's sentimentality nevertheless get involved in the story and admit surprise that Cedric does not cloy more often. His reputation as a sissy is belied in a number of places in Burnett's text: he early wins a footrace with his friends, for example, and he later fearlessly undertakes his first pony ride.

Burnett was not really interested in realistic character portrayal in her romance, however. She balances idealized characters like Cedric and his mother with characters verging on caricature. Here, Burnett owed much to one of her favorites, Charles Dickens, whose hand can be seen especially in her commoners. Also like Dickens, Burnett laced her story with melodrama and relied on coincidence to effect a denouement. The virtue and innate nobility of Cedric and his mother are emphasized by the appearance of a mendacious virago who claims that her son is the rightful heir. The woman turns out to be the runaway aunt of Cedric's friend, Dick, an American bootblack; he and a groceryman come to England to expose her and to participate in the family reunion which concludes the book. Undoubtedly, therefore, *Little Lord Fauntleroy* has seemed inviting to twentieth-century film producers for some of the same reasons that Dickens's novels have. Interestingly enough, two years before he made *Little Lord Fauntleroy*, in fact, Selznick offered *David Copperfield*. Almost simultaneously with his 1980 production of *Little Lord Fauntleroy*,

Norman Rosemont filmed *The Tale of Two Cities,* also for television.

In explaining why he chose to film these works as well as, earlier, *The Count of Monte Cristo* (1975), *The Man in the Iron Mask* (1977), and *Les Miserables* (1978), Rosemont said that "the writers of the classics were all much better storytellers than we are today" (*New York Times,* November 23, 1980). As a fiction writer, of course, Burnett never matched Dickens; her human sympathy and social vision were never as broad or deep. But like Dickens she excelled as a storyteller—even her most condescending critics usually granted her that. The importance of story in making a book adaptable for film is suggested also by former stage actor and producer John Cromwell, who directed the 1936 film: "There are very few plays in their original form which lend themselves to the motion picture. . . . In most plays the story is static. . . . A screen story must flow, it must tell its story through the eye."[1] A comparison of Burnett's stage adaptation of *Little Lord Fauntleroy* with her romance and its film adaptations supports Cromwell's assertions. Without a roving narrator or camera to show Cedric in a variety of situations and backgrounds—sitting in Mr. Hobbes's grocery store, talking with sailors on the ship, approaching Dorincourt castle in a carriage, being dwarfed by its armor-draped walls—much of the best of *Little Lord Fauntleroy,* its story, is gone. Burnett apparently recognized the cinema potential of her fiction before she died. In 1913 she negotiated film rights to this and some of her other books; she considered writing an original story for film; and at age seventy-two she broke her retirement from public events to attend the premier of Mary Pickford's *Little Lord Fauntleroy.*

The adaptability of Burnett's romance for film is argued also by a closer look at the 1936 and 1980 versions; screenwriters accustomed to movies based on books felt little need to cut or add to Burnett's story. As would be expected, however, the films did modify certain characterizations, and emphasized or

[1] "The Voice Behind the Megaphone," originally in *We Make the Movies,* ed. Nancy Naumburg (New York, 1937), reprinted in *Hollywood Directors 1914–1940,* ed. Richard Koszarski (New York: Oxford University Press, 1976), p. 302.

played down certain scenes and themes to fit the stars and the presumed tastes of audiences at the time the films were made. The 1936 adaptation exaggerated the sentimentality and melodrama in Burnett's book, while the 1980 version showed a greater concern for psychological and social realism.

Little Lord Fauntleroy undoubtedly appealed to David O. Selznick partially because its settings in New York City and on a wealthy country estate in England during the 1880s allowed him to express the love for lavish period productions for which he would become famous—*David Copperfield* (1934), *Gone With the Wind* (1939), and *Rebecca* (1940). He probably also considered Burnett's romance a natural vehicle for Freddie Bartholomew, who had come from England to play David Copperfield. As a foil for Bartholomew's slight build and British manner, Selznick chose Mickey Rooney to play the bootblack Dick. Capitalizing on Rooney's fame, stocky build, and streetwise American demeanor, Selznick considerably enlarged the role Dick has in Burnett's book. To his child stars Selznick added a distinguished cast of adults. Seasoned on the London stage before coming to Hollywood to stride the screen as a grand old Britisher, C. Aubrey Smith painted the earl's character with a broad brush—glowering beneath his busy eyebrows and dropping his monacle to register surprise. Frequently rubbing his bald head when agitated, tubby Guy Kibbee as the groceryman captured an appropriately Dickensian flavor as did Jessie Ralph in her brief appearances as the applewoman. Also typecast was Dolores Costello Barrymore as Burnett's morally meticulous and sweet-tempered "Dearest." Costello Barrymore's fragile blonde beauty had often made her the innocent victim in silent screen melodramas before she made the transition to sound film.

Selznick also chose a screenwriter well qualified to interpret the romantic sentiment and Anglo-American theme in Burnett's book. Hugh Walpole was well known among American Anglophiles for his many romances about upper-middle-class English life, often with historical settings. He had coauthored the screenplay for *David Copperfield* and was now alone responsible for *Little Lord Fauntleroy*. The American director John Cromwell had in 1930 put on film Mark Twain's paeon to boyhood, *Tom Sawyer*.

The decision to confront rather than avoid the sentimentality in *Little Lord Fauntleroy* is suggested by Cromwell's later comments about adapting for film a similarly "antiquated, nostalgic story," *The Prisoner of Zenda* (1937). "Our problem was either to tell it realistically as well as possible, to tell it with our tongue in our cheeks, or to endeavor to create a period in which our story would seem credible. The first two methods would obviously not stand up today" (*op. cit.*). To increase the distance between Burnett's fairy tale and the life of a Depression audience, Selznick created an atmosphere that was idealized as well as historical. In the opening scenes, Cedric is seen in the New York streets struggling to ride a new bicycle with an oversized front wheel and then visiting Mr. Hobbes in his carefully detailed, old-fashioned grocery. Even less than Burnett's text does this film demonstrates the supposed poverty of Cedric and his mother. When they host the earl's lawyer, their dining table glitters with crystal, and Mrs. Errol changes her subdued but elegant clothes in almost every scene. When the story moves to England, many carriage rides allow park-like vistas and the exteriors of estate lodge, mansion, and church; and Selznick was equally lavish with a variety of interiors.

The emphasis on exotic spectacle is congruent with the spirit and much of the original appeal of Burnett's book. Though its story was chronologically contemporary with its late-nineteenth-century readers, it appealed to a nostalgic pre-industrial fantasy about how a responsible British aristocracy could enjoy its wealth happily at peace with loyal servants, appreciative tenants, and village neighbors. It was a fantasy shared by many Americans as well as Englishmen in an era when newspapers were celebrating marriages between the daughters of wealthy American industrialists and the sons of down-at-the-heels British families of title. Burnett herself would try to recapture this fantasy by renting a country estate in Kent; and she recreated it in two bestselling romances for adults: *The Shuttle* (1907) and *T. Tembarom* (1913).

Selznick's lavish production appropriately captures Burnett's nostalgic fantasy, but the film's handling of the story itself exaggerates the book's sentimentality. This is apparent in the film's lighting and camera work as well as in extended dramatization of scenes only briefly described in the book. For example, the film considerably draws out Burnett's efficient description of Cedric's farewell to his American friends. In part, no doubt, these scenes were developed to display the talents of Mickey Rooney, Guy Kibbee, and Jessie Ralph, but they also capitalize on Freddie Bartholomew's ability to register glassy-eyed sorrow. While Burnett draws a curtain over Cedric's last night with his mother, the film shows them alone by the fire as Dearest tells Cedric she will not be going to the earl's mansion with him; Cedric cries, they embrace, and then they bow their heads out of the light into the darkness. Costello Barrymore's face is frequently lit so that her blonde curls become a halo, and chiaroscuro is used also to emphasize the earl's change from villain to loving grandfather. In his first appearance, the earl sits in a room lit only by a fire, allowing every twitch of C. Aubrey Smith's heavy mustache and eyebrows to be outlined. Later, the film shows him stroking the sleeping boy's head, after which the camera lingers on his gnarled hand beside the child's unlined face as the light fades.

The film thus heightens the book's melodrama as well as its sentimentality. Burnett keeps the rival claimants to the Fauntleroy title largely offstage, presenting them fully dramatized only once, and then briefly. The film, however, has two scenes in which the mother, played by Helen Flint, flaunts her dancehall finery and presumed victory before the earl. Also, Selznick makes her son the source of low humor. Played by Jackie Searle, who had been the insufferable Sid in Cromwell's *Tom Sawyer,* the boy first appears with his hair over his vacant eyes while he sucks a huge stick of licorice which has smeared his face. In the exposure scene, someone opens the boy's door abruptly and he falls into the room on his face. Selznick obviously intended to emphasize the contrast between the true and false inheritors, but the unfortunate effect was to call attention to the greatest strain on credibility in Burnett's plot, the coincidence that the perjured woman is the aunt of Cedric's American friend, Dick. Burnett wisely skipped lightly over these scenes and would not stoop to using a child victimized by his mother as the butt of cheap humor.

In the treatment of the most famous source of sentimentality in *Little Lord Fauntleroy,* its title character, Selznick's film both follows and deviates from Burnett's book. During the 1930s, Little Lord Fauntleroy's reputation as a sissy was still very much alive; there were probably a considerable number of men who unhappily remembered being dressed in velvet and lace by mothers who tried to make life more like fiction. Selznick's film pointedly avoids the infamous garb and does not bleach or curl Freddie Bartholomew's short, dark, hair— details approvingly noted by the *New York Times* reviewer (April 2, 1936). Like his mother, Cedric appears in an array of attractive clothes, but his pants are always long, never knickers; his costume lightly brushed tradition only at a party, where his white collar and cuffs have a miniscule edging of lace.

The film's dramatization is from the beginning concerned to deflect the popular sissy concept of Fauntleroy. He first appears brandishing a wooden sword and reading aloud from a book about Robin Hood. When he takes his bicycle into the street, he is followed by a group of street toughs who call him "Mama's boy." Cedric's verbal defense of his mother lands him fighting at the bottom of the heap where, joined by Mickey Rooney as Dick, he gives almost as good as he gets. Neither the sword nor the reference to *Robin Hood* are in Burnett's text, but they appropriately underscore her portrayal of Little Lord Fauntleroy as a hero whose innocent compassion for the lowly and despised as well as his own incorruptibility gain him victories among those with greater worldly advantages. However, by changing the footrace in Burnett's book to a streetfight—in which Cedric throws a handful of dirt in a boy's face—the opening scenes show an excessive embarrassment about Burnett's frankly idealized portrait of a child, especially since the film soon relaxes comfortably into a fairly faithful following of her characterization. Like Burnett's book, the film delights in Cedric's misspellings and misinterpretations of the words adults use, his ingenuous use of Dick's gaudy scarf in fine company, his beautiful body as he lies asleep.

With his delicate face and piping voice, twelve-year-old Freddie Bartholomew proved effective and convincing as the ten-year-old Fauntleroy—Burnett's hero was only seven, which probably makes some of his cute behavior more credible and palatable. Bartholomew's ability to vary the pitch of his voice and to register quick changes of facial expression were often used to good advantage, as when Cedric is prattling to the earl about the American Revolution and suddenly realizes he may be offending the earl. Bartholomew's performance as well as that of the rest of the cast suggests that the movie's tendency to cloy arises more from the screenwriting and film technique than the acting. Because of this sentimentality, the 1936 *Little Lord Fauntleroy* may now seem as much an "antiquated, nostalgic" period piece such as its director apparently considered Burnett's original. Selznick's lavish production, the quality of much of the acting, and the fairy-tale charm of Burnett's story, however, give the film a sustaining power to engage a sympathetic audience.

The general philosophy behind the 1980 television movie of *Little Lord Fauntleroy* agreed with that of Selznick's version. Like the 1936 director, the 1980 producer Norman Rosemont recognized that in this, as in the other romantic classics he filmed, "the problems ... are not immediate ... for an audience" and there is "a degree of escapism." "What I do," Rosemont said, "is stick as closely to the original as I can and make it as physically authentic as possible." Like Selznick, therefore, Rosemont stressed the geographical and social panorama in Burnett's book, but he was able to enhance the spectacle with color photography. The resulting film, however, deviates from Burnett's original and Selznick's film predecessor in a number of significant ways; many of these deviations can be traced to the presumed changes in audience taste since 1885 and 1936. Rosemont tones down rather than exaggerates the sentimentality and melodrama in Burnett's main plot. Far more than Selznick's, Rosemont's film stresses Burnett's social themes, the differences between American and British societies and the contrasts between rich and poor. Finally, the most striking deviation from Burnett and Selznick is in the portrayal of Dearest. Rosemont, screenwriter Blanche Hanalis, and director Jack Gold apparently felt that an audience in 1980 would find a sweet, self-sacrificing mother too passive; departing from their usual practice of staying close to the original, they invented an entire scene to underscore Mrs. Errol's spunk.

In filming *Little Lord Fauntleroy,* Rosemont was clearly as conscious of Selznick's predecessor as of Burnett's book. "When we take a classic book," he said, "we are not fighting the story—but the memory of how it was treated in the previous film." What people remembered about the 1936 version, he noted, was British actor Freddie Bartholomew. However, the story concerned "a kid from the Lower East Side of New York. So, we open our film with him playing in Hester Street . . . and then some twenty pages into the script we take him to England and the castle . . . What we do is point up the contrast and dramatize the difference in background and style of living."

Accordingly, Selznick's relatively sedate residential New York neighborhood becomes Rosemont's noisy market street teeming with life, and Cedric's home has homespun furnishings and the clutter of his mother's work as a seamstress. Rosemont uses for the earl's residence not a stately mansion, as Selznick had done, but a castle set on a hill. In making the latter change, Rosemont not only heightens the contrast between New York and Dorincourt but also stays closer to Burnett's description and the fairy-tale aura of her book.

Heightened British-American contrast was achieved through the casting of the earl and Cedric. Sir Alec Guinness easily lived up to his reputation for playing noble British eccentrics, as in *Kind Hearts and Coronets* (1949). And though Ricky Schroder, like Freddie Bartholomew, had previously proved his ability to cry on cue—in the 1979 sentimental box-office hit, *The Champ*—he was a thoroughly American boy. Indeed, with his blonde hair and freckles, his dialogue liberally loaded with New York street slang, and his awkward, pigeon-toed walk, Ricky Schroder resembles Mickey Rooney—whom Selznick had cast as the bootblack—as much as Bartholomew. The film's focus on the effective performances of Guinness and Schroder thus partially belies Rosemont's assertion that while earlier film versions of classics were "vehicles for stars," his were not. However, most of Rosemont's actors—Colin Blakely as Mr. Hobbes, Eric Porter as the earl's lawyer, Connie Booth as Mrs. Errol—would be more familiar to theater audiences than to the large moviegoing public; and Rosemont does not enlarge the roles of minor characters to accommodate the use of stars, as Selznick had done.

Since Rosemont had a less ethereal child in his title role, he could use more subtle ways to establish that Cedric is not a sissy, and he could even brave the infamous velvet knickers, satin sash, and white lace. Instead of throwing dirt in the face of a street tough, the 1980 Cedric talks knowingly about the dancers at the Rose and Garter in Hester Street—as in Selznick's film, this Cedric is several years older than Burnett's seven-year-old. On his first morning at Dorincourt, Cedric is asked to don his Little Lord Fauntleroy garb; gazing at himself in a mirror, he declares that he is glad his Hester Street friends cannot see him but that he will wear the clothes to please his grandfather. This clever handling of the conspicuous garb simultaneously demonstrates Cedric's sex identity and his typical willingness to please. Rosemont also counteracts Little Lord Fauntleroy's notoriety as a sissy by showing his pluckiness as he learns to ride his new pony—a scene from Burnett's romance Selznick's film had omitted. Because the 1980 film typically presents Cedric as an insouciant American boy, viewers are likely to find Schroder's expected tears more palatable than Bartholomew's.

Sir Alec Guinness plays his role with greater restraint than his 1936 predecessor. And in its portrayal of the transformation of the cantankerous snob into a doting grandfather and responsible landlord, the 1980 film shows greater concern for psychological and social realism. The 1980 earl credibly resists change longer than the earl in Burnett's book or Selznick's film. For much of the film, Guinness keeps his face stonily immobile, as if disdaining to respond to the inferiors surrounding him, his grandson included.

Much of their developing friendship is portrayed nonverbally in a series of tableaux in which the camera tells the story and suggests that the earl's change occurs over a period of time. The earl and Cedric are shown looking at paintings of their ancestors, viewing a dungeon in the castle, overseeing preparations for a party, reading together by the fire, playing baseball and kickball outside. During this sequence Guinness as the earl becomes increasingly relaxed and mobile, which

prepares for his later tears and gestures of sorrow when he
learns he will probably lose Cedric as his heir. The earl's un-
bending attitude toward his social inferiors is similarly re-
versed grudgingly and gradually. In Burnett's book and
Selznick's film, the earl immediately blesses Cedric's desire to
aid one of the earl's indigent tenants; in the 1980 screenplay,
however, the earl forbids this charitable act and later simply
accedes to Cedric's public announcement that his grandfather
did intend to perform it. Cedric also has to shame the proud
earl into improving conditions for his tenants in Earl's Court;
in a scene not found in the book or previous film, Cedric and
the earl ride through the village's sewer-ditch streets, and the
embarrassed earl later orders rebuilding in order "to improve
the vaue of the property."

The film's emphasis on the social themes in Burnett's romance is seen especially in its treatment of Cedric's mother.
From the beginning Connie Booth plays her as a proud working woman who resents the earl's presumption that his wealth
and social prestige allow him to take her son from her. She
appears most often in practical clothes with her hair efficiently
tied up and slightly mussed; her angular features underscore
her quick retorts when she feels she is misunderstood or under-
rated. Compared to the curved, curled, elegant child-woman of
the 1936 film, in fact, this 1980 Dearest is almost severe. Mrs.
Errol and Cedric exchange fewer physical expressions of en-
dearment than in the earlier film, and her maternal love is
shown more by her defense of her claims on the boy during
conversations with the earl's lawyer and the earl himself. She
frequently stands up to these venerable gentlemen not only on
the subject of Cedric's welfare but also on the issues of national
and social pride. For example, in a scene totally invented by
the 1980 screenwriter, in an argument about whether Americans are more rude than the British, Mrs. Errol has the last
word: "I thank God each day for the revolution that freed us
from aristocratic arrogance and ill temper. We won that war
and I have no intention to fight it again." Mrs. Errol's animus
against the earl is caused by more than his snobbery. In scenes
from the book omitted from the 1936 film, she is shown minis-
tering to the earl's tenants, whose destitution is graphically

indicated. Through its portrayal of Mrs. Errol, the 1980 film thus links the rights of a widowed working mother with a broader concern for social justice.

While the scenes of misery in Earl's Court heighten the social melodrama suggested in Burnett's text, the 1980 film plays down the personal melodrama in Burnett's denouement. We are not shown the rival heir, and his mother appears only briefly, when her perjury is exposed. After the false claimants are dispatched, the film concludes in a celebration that weaves its earlier social themes into its portrayal of Cedric's peronal triumph. In Burnett's book and Selznick's film, the joyful occasion is Cedric's birthday, but in the 1980 film it is Christmas. This change was probably motivated by a hope that the film would become a Christmas television regular—while it premiered just before Thanksgiving in 1980, it was rerun the week before Christmas in 1981. But the Christmas celebration also affords opportunities for underscoring the story's emphasis on the innocent power of children: as "O Little Town of Bethlehem" plays in the background, children prepare a crèche in church, and Christmas trees appear in a renovated Earl's Court. The Dorincourt celebration is a magnificent feast for the servants, held not in their own quarters as had been customary, but in the great hall—at Cedric's request. The film's final shots, however, demonstrate that its emphasis on social themes does not cause it to neglect the romantic sentiment surrounding its hero. In a curious throwback to techniques used in the 1936 film, the camera moves in for a close-up of the earl's hand topping those of Cedric and his mother before it moves back for a panoramic shot of the decorated great hall crowded with celebrants.

A few decades from now Rosemont's 1980 television film of *Little Lord Fauntleroy* may seem as much the product of its time as Selznick's 1936 movie does now. However, because its threads of psychological and social realism intensify rather than subvert satisfaction in its fairy-tale plot, and because of the quality of the acting and production, the 1980 film will probably be able to engage an audience as long as Burnett's 1885 romance and Selznick's 1936 film have.

Kidnapped—Improved Hodgepodge?

W. M. von ZHAREN

"Take a message to my father, the King. Tell him the pretender to the English throne has been thrashed this day on Killoden moor. And that bonny Prince Charlie, as he calls himself, is in flight in the heather. Tell him that it only remains for the pacification of the Highlanders to begin, that this is underway. Take that message to King George and tell him further that we have taken note that the public orders of the rebels yesterday was to give us no quarter. And they, therefore, may expect none. We shall end this nonsense once and for all so that never again will the Jacobite rebellious spirit disturb the peace of our two countries. This generation must be wore out before Scotland is quiet again. Never again will the presumptuous Stuarts lay claim to the British throne. Their escapade is over. They have dared, and they have lost. Inform my father that upwards of three thousand prisoners are on the roads to Edinburgh to be cast into jails pending their transportation—or execution. There will be no more rising of the clans in Scotland."

As an authoritative British voice reads this passage amidst cannon explosions and the screams of women and children, a montage of widescreen long shots of battlegrounds shows us twisted and mangled bodies. Red-coat uniforms mingle with blood of the Highlanders. Low-angle medium shots show the oppressors, the British. A close-up reveals the anguish on the face of a mother holding the torn body of her son. Thus begins director Delbert Mann's 1971 film version of Robert Louis Stevenson's *Kidnapped*. Mann's fourth collaboration with producer Frederick Brugger, and the fourth cinematization of *Kidnapped*, this new production included its sequel *David Balfour*, originally published as *Catriona*.

An over-the-shoulder shot depicts recently orphaned David Balfour watching a train of ragged prisoners; the British have ruthlessly checked an uprising of the Highlanders in the eighteenth-century Jacobite Rebellion. Davie (as he is called in the film) walks behind the captives, ending his journey at the house of Ebenezer Balfour of Shaws, his parsimonious uncle. The theme of Stevenson's *Kidnapped*—Davie's attempt to gain his rightful inheritance—is interwoven with the historical thread of Highland resistance to Red Coat oppression.

A brief summary of the film is in order at this point: Ebenezer, fearful that Davie will discover he is the rightful inheritor of Shaws, first tries to arrange for his death in a fall from a tower and then has him kidnapped aboard a ship bound for the Carolinas, where he will be enslaved. The ill-fated ship, however, runs down a small boat in the fog and Alan Breck Stewart, a proscribed Jacobite outlaw on his way to France to procure funds to encourage the rebellion, is brought aboard. When Davie discovers that the captain plans to murder Breck for his gold, he immediately befriends him. A fight ensues and Breck emerges triumphantly. The brig runs aground during a violent storm, and Davie and Breck are washed ashore. They head for the home of Breck's cousin, James Stewart, who, weary of the bloodshed, has attempted reconciliation with the British. It is here that Davie meets Stewart's daughter, Catriona. The next morning Mungo Campbell, the British collaborator, arrives with troops, and during the ambush that follows, Campbell is shot, Stewart is wounded and captured by the Red Coats, and Davie and Breck barely escape with Stewart's daughter. That evening they rest in the cave of Cluny McPhearson, who wins all Breck's money at cards and gives it to Davie, who tries to restore it to Breck. The proud Scot refuses to take it and they argue, going so far as to draw swords against one another.

At this point Catriona learns that her father is alive and has been imprisoned in Edinburgh. They all head for that city, where they learn from Breck's lawyer-cousin, Charles Stewart, that James Stewart is to be hanged for the murder of Mungo Campbell. Charles reluctantly assists Breck in procuring passage on the next ship to France; he not only forces Ebenezer to pay for this passage but also gets him to admit that Davie is the rightful heir to Shaws. Davie endeavors to persuade the Lord Grant, Advocate for the English in Edinburgh, of Stewart's innocence in Campbell's death but is warned that if he testifies to this he will only endanger himself. Nonetheless, Davie places his name on the defense witness list. Catriona vainly begs Davie not to give evidence at the trial, to take his inheritance and settle on his estate with her, away from bloodshed. Distressed by the thought of losing both her father and Davie, Catriona next pleads with Breck, who has gone into hiding while he waits for a boat, to forget the rebellion and help her rescue her father. He initially thinks she has lost her mind, but he eventually acknowledges to himself that there is little popular support for the Highland resistance and that the rebellion is truly lost. Catriona and Davie wait for him on the shore as the French ship lands to take him to safety. But at that moment he has arrived at Edinburgh castle to give himself up to the English, to sacrifice his life and his beloved cause for James Stewart.

The mainspring of Stevenson's novel *Kidnapped* is the situation of an orphaned boy forced to seek financial refuge in the Highlands and later being reinstated as the rightful heir in his inheritance. There are, of course, other occurrences of great interest: the Jacobite romance and rebellion; the murder of Colin Campbell; the skillfully drawn and authentic picture of Crommond and Queensferry in the eighteenth century. However, these elements only oil the mainspring, keeping the basic plot moving. Another subservient component is a tour through Scotland, a type of topo-cosmography of the Highlands. Yet an essential unity is found in this summary:

In June of 1751, orphaned David Balfour, after seeking out his uncle, discovers that he has the legal rights to the estate on which his uncle resides. The villainous uncle, therefore, has him kidnapped by seamen led by the miscreant, Captain Hoseason; they plan to sell him into slavery. While on this voyage to the Carolinas, the brig (named the "Covenant") over-runs a small boat and from it is rescued Alan Breck Stewart, the Jacobite rebel. When the crew attempts to murder Breck in the ship's roundhouse, David assists him in defeating the crew.

The boat is then wrecked, David survives and reaches a small island, Erraid, off the coast of Scotland. After a few days fishermen point a way for him to cross to the mainland at low tide and he then begins his search for Breck in the Highlands, following the signs Breck has left for him. On this journey he meets various Highland characters from a catechist to a snuff-addict.

The remainder of the book begins as he witnesses the murder of Colin Campbell of Glenure. Near the scene of the ambush, he discovers Breck, and together they flee into the hills seeking refuge from the Red Coats. During their wandering—described in great detail—David learns of the plight of the Highlanders. Later in the journey Breck and David quarrel over Breck losing his money in a card game. The argument lasts several days until the anger "oozed all out" of David. Reconciled, they reach their destination, the Lowlands. David claims his inheritance with the aid of Breck and a lawyer. David decides to assist innocent James Stewart who has been accused of the Campbell murder. After a parting marked by deep sorrow, Breck escapes from Scotland. The book ends abruptly.

David Balfour begins where *Kidnapped* ends. David unsuccessfully attempts to give evidence at the trial of James Stewart. During these endeavors he meets pernicious, ebullient Barbara Grant, the Lord Advocate's daughter. He also encounters Catriona, the daughter of shiftless, odious James More Drummond and immediately falls in love with her. Later, he is captured and taken to Bass Roc until the trial is over. After his escape, he and Catriona sail to Holland, where after a lengthy and heated emotional relationship, they marry. But this does not occur until Breck, still hiding from the British, has reentered the text for a brief visit and Catriona's thieving father dies.

In later years, one fuzzily recalls a childhood reading of *Kidnapped* and *David Balfour* as a series of stimulating moments: the sword fight of the round house, the destruction of the "Covenant," the survival on Erraid, the fear of the Lord Advocate. In rereading these novels as an adult with no aspirations toward learning topography, it is just as easy to succumb to prolonged feelings of tedium. Although the two novels contain vignettes which are perhaps masterpieces in themselves, they are nonetheless masterpieces ill-placed. The two narratives contain interregnums that are often exasperating: the plot is more than loosely constructed and capitulation to childhood memories forces the reader into episodes or descriptions unrelated to the rest of the narrative. Such selections as "his Journey in the Wild Highland" and "Journey into Holland and France" seem to be endurance tests for the reader rather than narration. Complications frequently stem from chance. Stevenson appears to have written with threads of a patchwork quilt rather than an adventure story. Particularly in *David Balfour*, excitement is secondary, only an occasional byproduct of the travel-illustrated tour of Holland and France and "true confessions" of the banal love declaration which dominates— no, suffocates—the novel. The courtship restrictions would not be accepted by youths of today. Stevenson wrote *David Balfour* at a time in his life when dollars and pounds may have meant more in his vision than good narrative.

Stevenson seems to have muddled through brief unity of exposition only to arrive at the new germinations for another excursus, approaching the two novels as if from different views. In such episodes as the piping contest between Breck and Robin Oig or the Tale of Tod Lapraik, events are incidental with David as a driftage, bobbing in and out until the final pages of *David Balfour*, wherein a sudden revelation of narration and a happy ending is quickly produced.

Sometimes Stevenson's interest seemed to flag as did his topic, resulting in slow, catenulate episodes. For example, in *Kidnapped* the chapter entitled "House of Fear" and the final section of the book seem to have been included only to unite *Kidnapped* with the beginning of its sequel—or perhaps to allow Stevenson to address the Highlands' frustration of that time.

There was one basic and acute difficulty in characterization: although Stevenson was well-versed in Scottish topography and history (even aspiring to hold a chair in history), he admittedly had sparse knowledge of the Gaelic mentality. He attempted to cover this inadequacy by depicting the Highlands through the responses of a Lowlander, entangling him in the aftermath of the rebellion. Sometimes it worked, sometimes it did not.

David is by his very background of homespun decency a rather uninteresting, priggish character. He is devoutly Protestant, Whig, and punctilious—and his mind usually responds to experience blandly. In fact his dour rationality is only affected by Catriona. However, in matters of courage and duty he is beyond reproach.

In *David Balfour* another dimension, though limited, is added to David's character. He develops a rather "confessional" stance, a psychological aura never seen in *Kidnapped*. He pretends to assume the role of a weakling, experiencing recurrent feelings of highly emotional self-pity.

Stevenson created a more memorable character in Breck, whose swashbuckling verve is derived more from what Stevenson perceived "ought" to be characteristics of a Gaelic rebel than was his clear comprehension of the Highland predicament. He is a bonny fighter, but his gallantry is static, his humor lifeless in many of the pages.

Minor characters with comparatively strong and memorable qualities do surface—in particular Barbara Grant, a fiesty, tenacious young woman who would have been a suitable match for Breck—but the two major characters, David and Breck, present an unmet challenge for development. Because Stevenson simply could not comprehend the Celtic mind, Breck seems artificial. Furthermore, at the abrupt ending of *Kidnapped*, the reader is dismayed to discover that no hero has been established. *David Balfour* is equally unimpressive as the reader anticipates this distinction but is instead given only the introduction of Catriona's further coquetishness.

What, then, is the point of Breck other than an artificial antithesis for David Balfour? The novels never quite answer this; fortunately, the film is ameliatory.

The narrative failings of *Kidnapped* and *David Balfour* are not transferred to the screen. The strengths are. By stripping various characters from the script (including, unfortunately, Barbara Grant, who would have added an additional quarter reel to the finished product), and encapsulating only major ideas (surely necessary when two lengthy narratives are committed to celluloid), succinctness is gained. The novels are easily accessible to episodic narrative and Mann takes advantage of this, but in the film each element is related to the whole of the work. Distilling and compacting two novels, Mann kept the film's *content* somewhat similar to the originals. It is in the *form* of the two media that dramatic change occurs, for he seized the opportunity to manipulate images of travel and adventure so splendidly that the travel-log of Stevenson's works seem almost superfluous.

The director elevates the historical component of *Kidnapped* to current crisis relevancy by accentuating from the opening moments the oppression of the oppressed. The film is far more rebellious and political than the two novels. With period color, this continues as an essential unity through the last scene in which Breck enters the castle gates of Edinburgh to surrender amidst a cacophony of chain clanking and vociferous admiration of him by bound Highland prisoners. This harmony is certainly as poignant in scope as the search by Davie for his rightful inheritance, a theme treated by Mann in a much more straightforward way.

The focal characters, Davie (Lawrence Douglas) and Breck (Michael Caine), also are given more credibility. This is managed in several ways: Davie is not subjected to the tedious and unbelievable confessional encounter with Catriona in Holland. The intolerable wooing episodes of the novel have been brilliantly pruned to only a handful of scenes: the cave of McPherson where the two lie parallel but not touching, listening to the sounds of the card game between Breck and McPherson, the intensity and gentleness carefully balanced through well-designed lighting and the audio-super-imposition of a moving "Scottish" ballad (written by Roy Budd and Jack Fishman, sung by Mary Hopkin); a parting and reuniting scene of Catriona and Davie after the cave incident, punctuated by long shots of spectacular scenery shot in the Highlands of Western Scotland; a romantic yet suspenseful flight through the heather; the acquisition of the House of Shaws and Catriona's advice to Davie to get out of danger by settling with her there; and Catriona's realization and expression to Davie that she could not bear to lose both her father and him.

Through skimming off layers of tedium in the novel's

Davie, the film allows him to emerge with values of innocence, yet courage and perception, as seen in this exchange between him and the Lord Advocate (Trevor Howard):

> LORD ADVOCATE: Well, then, you came here to testify; let's have it. But before you begin, let me warn you to volunteer nothing beyond the questions I shall ask. Nothing.
>
> DAVIE: I understand. But I couldn't be party to concealing information for want of the right question.
>
> LORD ADVOCATE: Mr. Balfour, a great issue hangs on this.
>
> DAVIE: An innocent man's life.
>
> LORD ADVOCATE: Thousands of innocent lives. Lives that are mine to protect.
>
> DAVIE: I understand that.
>
> LORD ADVOCATE: But you do not understand my position. The Highlands can be ruled only through the Campbells and one has been foully murdered, on Stewart ground at that. Have they no right to justice?
>
> DAVIE: Yes, my Lord, but not to vengeance.
>
> LORD ADVOCATE: In the Highlands, the difference is small. Mr. Balfour, I nurse in these two hands the interest of this country. Will you bring your country down to protect the life of one man?
>
> DAVIE: That man is innocent! And if to prove it the country has to fall, then it has to fall. There's no other way.

Mann's Davie is innocent, not shallow, nor does he have the Whiggish Protestant air that Stevenson wished to project.

The film also manages to accentuate the contrast between Davie and Breck through the casting of Michael Caine as Breck. The debonaire Caine replaces the novels' childishness with humor, bravura, romance, and rebellious agony (although one reviewer noted that he sometimes looks like a double agent disguised for a fancy dress ball). The syntonic humor and energy conveyed by Caine's performance changes the possible pseudo-hero of the novels into a more spirited rebel. Caine seems to enjoy his role as the dashing Breck, adding to many lines a mixture of engaging swagger, intelligence and risibility. For example, as the anxiety level of the audience rises during the beginning of the roundhouse battle scene, Breck, responding to the smallness of the roundhouse, quips: "More's the pity. My genius is with the cut, slash, and upper guard." Though these lines are similar to the lines of the original, it is Caine's impudent wit in delivery that makes them memorable.

In addition the film has added effective sketches of several other characters. Vivien Heilbron gives the role of Catriona a proud, sturdy, uncomplicated interpretation, creating a character possessing a strong feeling for the grandeur of her homeland. Ebenezer, played by Donald Pleasance, grows from a curmudgeon, etiolated under the weight of his own selfishness, to a character the viewer can trust as being at least true to his ideals even in his final moments. He becomes almost likable simply for that reason, as shown in a well-executed scene. As Ebenezer is dying, Davie is called to his uncle's side by the physician; the dramatic lighting and music suggest that the uncle is about to make amends:

UNCLE: Davie, Davie.

PHYSICIAN: I think he means for you to go nearer. He wants to tell you something. [*Excellent Gaelic accent*]

UNCLE: Davie, send the doctor outside.

DAVIE: Would you mind, Doctor?

PHYSICIAN: Oh, of course.

DAVIE: What is it, Uncle? [*Pause as Davie draws his ear near the lips of his Uncle*]

UNCLE: Ah, I just want to tell ya; [*Pause*] Donna let him charge ye too much. [*The Uncle dies.*]

In construction the film is loosely divided into two reels and two concepts of action. The first half relates physical action, getting underway with an energetic promenade of adventures: the Red-Coat mass murder, the kidnapping, the roundhouse battle, the shipwreck and survival. Psychological action dominates the second half: the meeting of Davie and Catriona, the verbal and mental challenge of the Lord Advocate, the quarrel between Davie and Breck, the death of the Uncle, and the surrender of Breck to the British.

Perhaps because of this "denouement reversal" of physical action, and because of the need for the audience to comprehend far greater psychological drama following intense physical drama, the film may seem to lose pace during the second half. But it is only the loss of physical action. Though Stevenson's *David Balfour* has little plot and few causalities, Jack Pullman has remedied this by presenting a trim, well-developed screenplay in which eloquent interludes are intermingled with dramatic events.

The film also achieves something neither of the two novels achieved—a conclusive ending. The suspense lingers until the final shots, however, as Catriona first begs Breck to forget the endless, useless fighting and to assist her in saving her father, James Stewart:

> BRECK: Would you have me desert them? I'll not do it. Not for James. Aye, I'll die for Scotland but not for HIM!
>
> CATRIONA: Aye, you'll die for Scotland but who wants you to? WHO WANTS YOU TO? It's all over, Alan, cannya no see? It's finished. FINISHED! There's no more fighting in us!
>
> BRECK: It's not over. Not yet. We'll come again. They're waiting for us to return. They're just waiting for us to come back.

The flashback scene in which Breck remembers the suffering caused by the fighting is one of the most poignant pieces of cinematography in the film. There is a dissolve to a montage: heather, the mountains, battle scenes dominated by red blood and Red Coats, faces of those who died, the ambush of Mungo Campbell, the pleading of Catriona—all intermixed while Cluny McPherson and James Stewart's admonitions as well as the lilting theme song echo in and out of the shots.

Davie and Catriona are waiting for Breck to arrive at the ship that is to transport him to safety. But the final shots show Breck walking through the gates of Edinburgh castle to surrender. He stops at the entrance and a medium shot reveals a touching view of him taking a final look at his beloved Highlands and freedom. The camera lens takes the audience through the exhilaration stemming from the Highland grandeur and the sobriety of political reality.

What, then, are the reasons for this successful film adaptation? The film only marginally duplicates the weaknesses of the novels and accentuates the strengths. Mann has been convincingly able to set his *Kidnapped* into a historical-political context with appropriate psychological perspective on the characters. By interpreting the novels as a demonstration of the struggle against oppression, and the emotional pain of a bloodied country, Mann gave them contemporary relevancy. Through trimmed scriptwriting, Pullman has given immediate credibility to both major and minor characters, and eliminated the frequent and irrelevant *longeurs* introduced by Stevenson. Through the brilliant camerawork of Paul Beeson, the natural and period setting of Highland beauty become Stevenson's "scenery of dreams." He has a feel for widescreen composition—his long shots seem nineteenth-century Romantic canvases—and he exploits the cinema's potential for both panoramic views and detailed close-ups.

If successful film adaptation means tight construction that omits little from the original text, then *Kidnapped* is an utter failure. However, if success depends on selecting ideas and essence from a novel with the intent of capturing its spirit and intended direction, then *Kidnapped* has met its goal.

Mann has taken two mediocre novels and produced a much better than average film, a more densely unified artistic achievement.

"I've seen the movie":
Oz Revisited

CAROL BILLMAN

Critical books and articles about L. Frank Baum, his Oz novels, their dramatic and cinematic adaptations, and about Oz as a distinctly American cultural phenomenon have recently been published at a pace more accelerated than that of the two score Oz novels succeeding *The Wonderful Wizard of Oz*. Nevertheless, the following comparative analysis of Baum's prose fantasy written in 1900 and the 1939 film adaptation, *The Wizard of Oz,* may be useful because most contemporary readers inevitably come to the prose after the film version has been firmly impressed upon them—and they continue to read and analyze *The Wonderful Wizard of Oz* in terms of the visualization. In addition, the extraordinary number of plays and films based on the Oz fiction raises interesting questions about the attractions of this material, and about the possibilities inherent in actually creating in visual form the world Baum imagined. The 1939 Victor Fleming film reworks both the strengths and weaknesses in Baum's first Oz novel and in so doing earns the position it occupies in readers' minds as the authoritative work to which all other tellings of the story, even the original one, must answer.[1]

Editor's note: This is a revised version of the article which originally appeared in *Literature/Film Quarterly*, Vol. 9, No. 4, 1981, pp. 241–250. Reprinted by permission.

[1]Four directors actually worked on the MGM Oz film, though Fleming is credited with the work: Fleming, George Cukor, Richard Thorpe, and King Vidor. It was Vidor, in fact, who actually directed the film's black-and-white Kansas sequences.

One thing the novel and film share is their sanguine depiction of a fantastic land in which success comes to those who believe in themselves and where human ingenuity underlies the ruler's wizardry. Optimism is more prevalent in the film, where even life in Kansas isn't so dreary. Baum begins his novel by describing the dulled and isolated land, dwelling and people:

> When Dorothy stood in the doorway and looked around, she could see nothing but the great gray prairie on every side. Not a tree not a house broke the broad sweep of flat country that reached the edge of the sky in all directions. The sun had baked the plowed land into a gray mass, with little cracks running through it. Even the grass was not green, for the sun had burned the tops of the long blades until they were the same color to be seen elsewhere. Once the house had been painted, but the sun blistered the paint and the rains washed it away, and now the house was as dull and gray as everything else.
> When Aunt Em came there to live she was a young, pretty wife. The sun and wind had changed her, too. They had taken the sparkle from her eyes and left them a sober gray. . . .[2]

Fleming's Kansas, on the other hand, despite its nasty neighbors and weather, is fairly cozy: the farms are comfortably enclosed by fences, and life on these farms is not such a singular endeavor. Dorothy's aunt and uncle have three jovial hands to help them. And the Harold Arlen/E. Y. Harburg music in the film underscores the upbeat treatment of both Kansas and Oz. To those stuck in the former, for example, there is still the possibility of an Oz "Somewhere over the Rainbow," and in the latter, contemplation of evil is denied by the celebratory "Ding Dong The Witch Is Dead."

Another common denominator for the novel and the film is pervasive moralizing. Despite Baum's disavowal of the preceding American tradition of moralistic children's literature, his tale is, quite obviously, a lesson in belief, or the power of positive thinking. The injunction to look within for the wherewithal

[2]The Ballantine Books edition (New York, 1956) is quoted. Subsequent quotations will be documented in the essay.

to succeed is belabored by the Wizard as he gives the Scarecrow, the Tin Woodman and the Cowardly Lion outward signs of brains, a heart and courage, respectively. And the final words of the novel, Dorothy's remark "and oh, Aunt Em! I'm so glad to be at home again!" are but thinly disguised didacticism: there is no place like home, even though the grass always seems greener on the other side of the fence. In the film the same points are made, perhaps even more decisively in the case of homely satisaction; Dorothy reassures Aunt Em she will never run away again.

The cheery tone and overt moralizing in the film and novel no doubt explain in part the popularity of both. The film uplifted spirits at the end of the Depression decade, and the novel had come along at another time when Americans needed their faith in themselves bolstered. In the last decade of the nineteenth century, social classes had separated, not merged, and the once-held belief that a piece of land or a respected place in the work force was the American birthright began to falter as the frontier disappeared and industrialization made the rich richer. Asked to explain the early twentieth-century popularity of *The Wonderful Wizard of Oz* and the subsequent Oz books, Baum's son said: "A disquieting gulf was growing between the new rich and the new poor; the cities knew the problem of the slums; and the farmers felt an unaccustomed financial stress."[3] But when readers today encounter the novel without the same external, or social, context brought to it by Baum's first audience, what stands out is the inherent confusion within the work iself.

This confusion is the result of the clutter that is manifested everywhere in the book. The land of Oz is not one but four lands—the countries of the Munchkins, the Winkies, the Quadlings, and the Gillikins—as well as the central district of the Emerald City. There are, moreover, four witches, along with the Wizard, who exercise authority over the people of Oz. And the variety of this patchwork fantastic world is fully explored. Dorothy and her companions travel west through Munchkin

[3]Quoted by Selma G. Lanes in *Down the Rabbit Hole: Adventures and Misadventures in the Realm of Children's Literature* (New York: Atheneum, 1971), p. 100.

country to the Emerald City, then farther west to confront the Wicked Witch of the West at her castle, back to the Wizard, and off again south into the Quadling country. The narrative moves forward in episodic spurts as the travelers set off time and again on another quest (to reach the Wizard, kill the Wicked Witch of the West, find the castle of Glinda the Good). On each segment of their trip moreover, the party encounters a host of wondrous obstacles—on the first leg of the journey, for example, they are impeded by a great ditch, a forest populated with Kalidahs, and the deadly poppy field—not to mention the delays suffered once the group arrives at the Wizard's palace. During their travels south they come upon the china country, the description of which occupies Baum's entire twentieth chapter, even though this set piece has nothing to do with the character's immediate goal to meet Glinda. Here and elsewhere it appears that Baum's inventiveness led to the inclusion of charming vignettes that exist for their own sakes, having little bearing on the larger narrative but diffusing its pattern and pace.

Readers are often puzzled, too, by Baum's expansiveness in the matter of characterization. Beyond the duplication of good and evil witches, there are Dorothy's multiple traveling companions. And why the odd assortment of a man of straw, another of tin, and a lion? The first, of course, is a carryover from the Kansas countryside, but the other two seem to be the whimsical inventions of an author not averse to mixing his separate "brainstorms." Multiple protagonists are not uncommon in children's literature—the four children in C. S. Lewis's Narnia Chronicles, for instance—but here their separate origins and individual goals contribute to the lack of narrative focus and divert the readers' attention from the author's main character, Dorothy. Readers invariably ask: whose story is this?

Because of the jumble of narrative episodes and of the characters involved, Baum's fantasy leaves many readers with the sense of a story that spills over and meanders, and, with the sense of a fantastic land that, while ruled over by four witches and a Wizard, is fundamentally unruly. Nor does the creator of this world, Baum himself, manifest control of his

Humpty Dumpty creation through either his structuring of the Kansas "frame" for the fantastic adventures or his mode of narration.

While the theme of belief in one's own abilities emerges plainly from what goes on in Oz, what Baum is trying to say about Dorothy's awareness of the value of home is not evident anywhere in *The Wonderful Wizard of Oz*. His intentions in developing the realistic frame for the Oz adventure are particularly unclear. At the outset, as shown above, he dwells on the grayness of Dorothy's surroundings and on her loneliness. Yet no sooner has she been transported to Oz than she tells the Munchkins that she wants to go home. But in response to the Scarecrow's query about the nature of Kansas, Dorothy tells him "how gray everything was there" (p. 33). The Scarecrow then says "I cannot understand why you should wish to leave this beautiful country and go back to the dry, gray place you call Kansas," to which Dorothy replies:

> That is because you have no brains. . . . No matter how dreary and gray our homes are, we people of flesh and blood would rather live there than in any other country, be it ever so beautiful. There is no place like home.

For the reader, the Scarecrow's questions remain. Was Dorothy initially eager to get away from the oppressive sameness of Kansas? If so, it is hard to understand her wish to go home so soon. If not, why did the author go to such lengths to suggest an oppressive environment? At the end of the novel Dorothy returns to a Kansas no longer described as dulled or lifeless. Is Baum trying to say something about the regenerative function of the Oz trip—that is that it supplies the imaginative sustenance necessary to make life in Kansas tolerable for the girl? If so, he has only intimated this function in the vaguest of ways, by offering the possibility that the two depictions of Kansas in the frame are reflections of Dorothy's perception.

The question of narrative point of view leads to a final manner in which Baum disorients readers or, at least, provides no sense that he is in control of the way his story unwinds. In the frame there is only the remote possibility that readers perceive Kansas through Dorothy's eyes; in Oz no perspective is clear. No identification with any character is encouraged, nor does Baum create a narrator to tell his story, as is often the case in fantasy, especially fantasy for children, in which an omniscient persona is frequently in control of revealing the fantastic world to the reader. The story of Oz unfolds as a drama, through paraphrased action and the dialogue of the characters; Baum presents his story as unobtrusively as did the tellers of the fairy tales. Accordingly, the few instances (of a narrator) in the book are jarring.

This lack of perspective coupled with Baum's tendency to include all that came to mind beg reader interpretation. There is an inclination to explain the frame as indicative of Dorothy's changing point of view. And one reader labored to explain the needs of Dorothy's three traveling companions as precisely those qualities Dorothy herself lacks. In other words, Baum's additive approach to subject matter and his inconspicuous manner of storytelling beg the reader to be as imaginative as he was in creating the story and as inventive as the Wizard in turning out something to be believed in. The MGM film then, can be seen as one interpretive "reading" of Baum's amorphous narrative.

Similarities in terms of upbeat moralizing notwithstanding, the film is undeniably a cinematic adaptation of the original novel. One aspect of the adaptation is deletion. The episodic meanderings of the Baum narrative, for example, have been radically edited—no mention, for instance, of the anticlimactic venture into the land of the Quadlings. Moreover, the various obstacles the screen characters do encounter are integrated; for example, the apple-pelting trees and the deadly poppy field are presented as the machinations of the Wicked Witch of the West. And the existence of multiple protagonists is not problematic in the film, perhaps because we *see* that Dorothy, as opposed to her carefully costumed partners, is flesh and blood, a point more easily made in the cinematic medium.

The best illustration of the fact that Victor Fleming and those he worked with interpreted the story, concerns the straightening out of the imperfect cues Baum gave readers in his frame. In the film, Dorothy's inclination to escape is evident—before the cyclone she actually runs away from home. And it is equally plain that she has learned the lesson, "no place like home," *before* entering Oz, since she rushes home after Professor Marvel tells her how much her aunt misses her. The adventure in Oz becomes a dream, the likely result of her guilt at running away from home. It has indeed a nightmarish aspect in that it separates Dorothy from family. (Significantly, Aunt Em and Uncle Henry do not appear in her dream while others who surround her in Kansas do.) Given the film's extended preliminary treatment of life in Kansas, it is both understandable and predictable that Dorothy should want to go home as soon as she touches down in Oz. And the strange adventure, wonderful as it is, merely reminds her of the comforts of home, a place that is, as noted, far less stultifying than the Kansas farm depicted in the novel.

But *The Wizard of Oz* surpasses the novel not merely because its creators untangled the twisted storyline or the muddled themes of Baum's work. Other factors contributing to the film's success concern the story's immanent potential as film. Baum's narrative style made the work readily adaptable; the dramatic presentation of the written story must account in part for the long tradition of adaptations on film and stage. Specifically, the absence of a narrative persona is conventional rather than unconventional in film. The real invitation of the novel to be turned into a visual story, however, is the vision that underlies Baum's often disorderly selection and arrangement of the pieces comprising his make-believe world. One thing that undeniably makes Baum's work popular and memorable is the concept of Oz—the color-coded quadrants, the Yellow Brick Road, and the Emerald City. This fantastic world appeals undeniably to readers' visual senses. Here, for example, is the first look Baum provides readers of the Emerald City:

> Even with her eyes protected by the green spectacles, Dorothy and her friends were at first dazzled by the brilliancy of the wonderful City. The streets were lined with beautiful houses, all built of green marble and studded everywhere with sparkling emeralds. They walked over a pavement of the same green

marble, and where the blocks were joined together were rows of emeralds, set closely, and glittering in the brightness of the sun. The windowpanes were of green glass; even the sky above the City had a green tint, and the rays of the sun were green. (p. 100)

Seeing is believing in Oz. In the film, a series of spectacular vistas appear before the travelers. The expanse of the dreaded poppy field is captured, as is the overwhelming aspect of the castle of the Wicked Witch of the West, teeming with guards and imposing in size. And the Emerald City is properly bedazzling at first view. Finally, the cumulative effect of these vistas is that viewers of the film do—as readers of the novel do not—have a point of view. We see things along with the four travelers, and we share in particular Dorothy's awe at the foreign and marvelous things she sees.

Special visual effects, moreover, are put to intelligent use in the film; they enhance the visual dimension of the story. Arnold Gillespie, director of special effects, and his staff invented a thirty-five-foot muslin cone suspended by an overhead crane to re-create the cyclone that transports Dorothy to Oz. They also made visually credible and frightening the scenes involving the winged monkeys. And a scene with special visual potential was inserted—the sky-written message from the Wicked Witch of the West, "Surrender Dorothy."

The deliberate and masterful use of color and of artificiality in set design best explains the visual success of *The Wizard of Oz*. Experimentation in mixing techicolor scenes with those shot in black and white (sepia in the original prints) works to support the narrative in this film. The black-and-white sequences in Kansas prepare for the colorful splendor of the fantastic world. In addition, Dorothy's dreaming in color makes sense. Further, the stylized, handpainted backdrops, combined with fullsize actors and obviously artificial scenery (as the flowers in Munchkinland) by means of matte photography, underscore the fantastic, brittle quality of Oz. Artificiality is as effectively obtrusive in the Fleming motion picture as it is not in his other 1939 work, *Gone With The Wind*.

The urge to visualize children's fantasies in live action film has long been in evidence, from the adaptation of Frances Hodgson Burnett's *The Secret Garden*, 1949 (which also blends color with black and white footage) to more recent attempts like *Chitty Chitty Bang Bang* (1968) and *Willy Wonka and the Chocolate Factory* (1971). But none of these efforts is as technically creative or as popular as *The Wizard of Oz*. Cinematic adaptation of children's fantasy is not easy to do, as the furor over Disney's animated interpretations demonstrates. But *The Wizard of Oz* transcends its original in American popular culture, and by acts of both omission and commission the makers of the film produced a vision that deservedly overlays and conditions readers' responses to L. Frank Baum's *The Wonderful Wizard of Oz*. The film's inventive approach to make-believe is after all, what the wizardry of Oz is all about.

All About a Boy: Kipling's Novel, M.G.M.'s Film

WILLIAM BLACKBURN

An American filmmaker I know once attempted to elucidate for me the sins of film critics. He gave me to understand that sins are stale, flat and unprofitable—with the most unprofitable of all being the critic's insistence on approaching the film as if it were something other than a film and on judging it as if it were, for example, a novel. Such a critic is, in short, someone who makes a living out of going to restaurants, eating the menu instead of the dinner—and then howling for the blood of the chef.

Film and prose fiction do of course have elements in common; neither can ignore with impunity such fundamentals as plot, characterization, setting, and imagery. Occasionally, a film can profit from a novelist's mastery of visual elements; an obvious example is Ken Russell's *Women in Love* (1969), a film which owes a good deal of its power to the visual and iconographic quality of Lawrence's imagination. Still, despite their common elements the film and the novel are significantly different artistic media. Pauline Kael is surely right when she informs us that "It's a gross deception to pretend that you can get the same things out of a movie that you can get out of a great novel." But it is an equally gross deception to pretend that a mediocre film is somehow less vulnerable to criticism than a mediocre novel. The criteria of criticism may differ, but the critical principle remains the same: every work of art should pursue the kind of excellence proper to itself. The filmmaker's fidelity to a prior text is not the point at issue. Whether a film is good or bad does not depend on its "literary"

101

qualities but on whether or not it is a coherent and autonomous creation. We do not want to eat the menu instead of the dinner—but we do want a work of art to provide us with some sort of genuine nourishment.

The critic of children's literature should be particularly sensitive to the need to distinguish kinds of excellence—for children's literature has long endured the sneers of those who deny that literature any capacity for excellence whatsoever. Even those who ought to know better can slip easily into condescension when confronted with a chldren's book written by a "serious" author. For example, in his discussion of Rudyard Kipling's *Kim* in the *Oxford History of English Literature,* (1963) J.I.M. Stewart begins by warning his reader that "whether or not there be irony in the fact, Kipling came nearest to a successful novel in a book for young people—for we lose contact with *Kim* (1901) when we regard this story of an orphan white boy gone native, and using his native cloak of invisibility to become a peerless Secret Service agent, as other than essentially that." F.J.H. Darton falls into the same error when, in *Children's Literature in England* (1966), he tries to defend *Kim* by insisting "it is all about a boy." Both critics by failing to give adequate consideration to the kind of excellence Kipling's novel is seeking. Neither questions the fact that *Kim* is a splendid yarn, but each assumes that, because *Kim* is a splendid yarn for children, there is little reason to give it the same sort of attention we give to a serious novel (i.e., a novel written for adults).

This assumption is, of course, nonsense precisely because a good book for children is simply a good book. Such a book does not lose its appeal when the reader finally stumbles over the leaden threshold of maturity. No good children's book speaks only to children: it speaks to all readers endowed with the wit to appreciate its proper excellence. The task of the critic of children's literature, like that of the critic of film, is to discern the excellence proper to his subject. The necessity of doing so becomes apparent when a work of "children's literature" is adapted for the screen. How are we to judge the merits of such a film? A comparison of Kipling's novel with MGM's version of *Kim* (1951) suggests one answer to this question.

Since Kipling's novel is so rich in exotic locale and high adventure, and since it offers a variety of characters ranging from the sternly ascetic Teshoo Lama to the richly profane Mahbub Ali, one may well be surprised that it took *Kim* fifty years to make the transition to the screen despite the fact that filmmakers began showing an interest in Kipling's work as early as the 1920s. Plans for a film version of *Kim* (Metro) to star Freddie Bartholomew and Robert Taylor were announced in 1938. The advent of World War II slowed Hollywood's production; the project was taken up again in 1942, only to be dropped after a protest from the War Information Office. Not until Victor Saville's *Kim* (1951), a full half century after the novel's publication, was Hollywood able to mine the riches of Kipling's work.

With so much time to prepare, Hollywood really ought to have done better. Since the film had a lavish production budget, it can scarcely help doing some things well. For example, the opportunities for vigorous action and visual humor are generally well utilized; there is an inevitable gymnastic quality to all Errol Flynn's films. Lovers of Kipling's superb dialogue will be surprised and pleased to recognize portions of that dialogue in the film; the screenplay (by Leon Gordon, Helen Deutsch, and Richard Schayer) likewise shows a noticeable fidelity to the plot of Kipling's novel. Choosing Dean Stockwell to play the part of Kim was an inspired stroke of casting and Flynn is, in himself, at least inoffensive as Kim's Pathan mentor, Mahbub Ali.

If money and diligence and an established star should have guaranteed the success of Saville's *Kim,* but with all the advantages of a big budget, exotic locale, and an action-crammed plot, the film somehow goes wrong. It does not go wrong simply because it fails to mimic Kipling's novel. One can condone the changes of plot necessary to give Flynn prominence on the screen, or to develop Kim's character (as when Saville has Kim steal a new pair of glasses for the Lama). One can likewise overlook the long and familiar arm of gratuitous coincidence. But as the film grinds on one cannot overlook the growing conviction that it takes more than Errol Flynn and elephants to make a good movie. A sympathetic reviewer summed up

Saville's *Kim* as "ornate, lavish, but curiously lacking in genuine atmosphere, vitality, or period sense"; she might have gone on to say that the film also lacks any genuine sense of its own purpose.

Even as an action film, *Kim* falls short. For all his swashbuckling, and top billing Flynn really has little to do, and is often the victim of poor choreography; he spends an inordinate amount of time standing around looking like a particularly amiable and earnest circus bear. In addition, for all its lavish budget, the film is sloppy about background—as Kipling manifestly is not. (Only Flynn and Paul Lukas went on location to India: the rest of the film was shot in Lone Pine, California. This can be excused as standard operating procedure. But why then did the filmmakers go to so much trouble and expense to make a troop of *saddhus* resemble a troop of dancing elephants?)

It is in the area of characterization that the film seems most determined to throw away the advantages offered by the novel. Flynn does not mean, but be; Paul Lukas, as the Teshoo Lama, a cranberry-swathed kindly old soul compelled to depict spirituality as platitudinous absent-mindedness, is a Polonius of the Punjab. Most telling of all is the film's failure to achieve real depth or coherence in the character of Kim.

Talented though he is, there are certain things young Stockwell cannot quite bring off. His maledictions, for instance, are stilted and wooden; Kipling's hero is made of sterner stuff. The real problem, though, is that Saville seems bent on interpreting Kim as if he were Tom Sawyer in pajamas. (For example, the novel stresses the self-discipline which Kim's desire for education requires him to impose on himself; the film shrinks this to a series of confrontations between Kim and various sanctimonious louts who all scream at him: "That's not the way we do things at St. Xavier's.") Reducing Kim to a pretty prankster, the film consistently denies him the responsibilities and decisions with which he is confronted in the novel. Kipling has Kim save the Teshoo Lama from the Russian agents, but Saville gives this role predictably enough, to Mahbub Ali—and Flynn is far more genteel than Kipling's hero.

Saville's film is weak not because it is insufficiently faithful to Kipling's novel, but because it fails to make determined use of the resources available to it. Our advantages betray us. Perhaps the very richness of Kipling's novel discouraged invention on the director's part; perhaps the belief that Kim is only "all about a boy" tempted him away from seeking the kind of excellence appropriate to an adventure film. That such excellence is not forbidden by the novel, but rather encouraged by it, is shown by the book's wonderful integration of character and action. Supremely entertaining in their own right, the adventures Kipling gives Kim are all milestones in his development. That is, plot and character rest on a firm thematic foundation; at all levels, the novel addresses itself to the problems of maturation—without once ceasing to be superb entertainment. Saville could have learned much by studying the careful design of Kipling's novel.

In the novel, the comradeship of the boy and the Teshoo Lama is of central importance, and their quest for the River of the Arrow is certainly much more than the pretext for colorful adventure which the film makes of it. The Lama is a venerable holy man, seeking a river "whose nature . . . is [such] that whoso bathes in it washes away all taint and speck of sin." By contrast, the thirteen-year-old Kim, who "did nothing with an immense success," is a gloriously natural boy who loves intrigue and "the game for its own sake."

Kim has a quest of his own—the search for his father's regiment and his own identity—but is barely conscious of it as a sort of family legend. He has no real sense of vocation or direction and the need for purpose and discipline is one of the most obvious lessons the boy has to learn from the old man. Of all the adults Kim meets, the Lama is one of the most effective in convincing him of the value of discipline; the regimen which the Lama imposes on himself is a clear parallel to the discipline which Kim will have to practise in the Great Game of espionage. There is therefore less incompatibility than one might expect between Kim's role as the old man's disciple and his role as a government agent. All Kim's mentors teach him the value of discipline, and this discipline is one of the great bridges joining East and West in the novel. In Saville's film,

Kim merely learns to shoot straight and save the wagon train.

In their different and imperfectly understood quests, both Kim and the Lama have major limitations. Kim's are the natural limitations of boyhood; he is undisciplined, and, for much of the novel, takes not the slightest interest in the question "what is Kim?" The Lama likewise fails to know himself. He can tell Kim sternly that "affection is no part of the Way." Confronted with the rich spectacle of life on the Great Trunk Road, "the lama never raised his eyes. . . . He looked steadily at the ground . . . his soul busied elsewhere. But Kim was in the seventh heaven of joy." It is perfectly clear to the reader, however, that the Lama is not indifferent to worldly attachments. His head and his heart are at odds. It is obvious that he loves Kim, and that, as one character says, a good householder was lost when the Lama chose to become a monk. A Buddhist might argue that true enlightenment is characterized by the balance of *prajna* (insight) and *karuna* (compassion). Deliverance is not to be found by fleeing the world—on this point both Mahayana doctrine and Kipling's novel stand firm. Kipling shows us that, unti the Lama comes to terms with his own compassion, until he finds a place for human love in his vision of freedom, he will not find the deliverance he seeks.

So the Lama, though he is obviously one of Kim's most influential teachers, also has something to learn. While Kipling continually encourages us to admire the Lama's kindness and wisdom and tenacity, he also suggests the limitations of his vision. "What profit to kill men?" asks the Lama of an old soldier, a veteran of the Great Mutiny. The soldier replies: "Very little—as I know; but if evil men were not now and then slain, it would not be a good world for weaponless dreamers. I do not speak without knowledge. I have seen the land from Delhi south awash with blood." It is in this context that the novel requires Kim to resolve the claims of contemplation and action. When the Lama tells Kim that "to abstain from action is well—except to acquire merit," the boy replies: "At the Gates of Learning, we were taught that to abstain from action was unbefitting a Sahib. And I am a Sahib." Though Kim accepts the discipline of service, he cannot renounce the world of action. No less than the Lama, Kim has, as one of the key phrases of the novel puts it, two separate sides to his head. Like the Lama, he too must apparently choose between worldly affections and dedication to a goal.

There are, of course, characters in the novel who do not show this sort of inner split, or who have resolved it successfully—Lurgan, Mahbub Ali, and Hurree Babu, for example. Their presence suggests that one of the fundamental patterns in the novel is the change from a state of inner division to a state of integration. We see this pattern at work as the quests of Kim and the Lama come increasingly to parallel each other. Kipling would have us believe that the virtues of one vocation are in fact those of the other. Like the Lama, Kim aspires to "seeing the world in real truth." Colonel Creighton's stern warning that "there is no sin so great as ignorance" might well have come from the Lama's own lips. The test of the jar, when Lurgan attempts to hypnotize Kim, recalls the Lama's struggle against error and delusion. We recognize Kipling's pun when he tells us "how religiously Kim kept to the contract with Creighton." It is no accident that, early in the novel, a farmer describes a canal built by British engineers as running "straight as an arrow" across his fields. When Kim asks himself "'how can a man follow the Way or the Great Game when he is eternally pestered by women?'" we note that his new awareness of himself as a man is bound up with his awareness of the Lama's Way and the Great Game of the secret service as parallel vocations.

The possibility of a secular career parallel to that of the Lama, a career combining his sanctity with a life of duty and action in the world, is what Kipling is suggesting through this series of elaborate correspondences. It is in Kipling's deft use of these correspondences at the close of the book that the true art of what he called this "nakedly picaresque and plotless novel" betrays itself.

Kim's trial is complex. He is tempted to abandon his new vocation, to cling either to the Lama or to the woman of Shamlegh. Though he resists these temptations, his situation becomes precarious indeed after the Lama is wounded by an enemy agent at a remote spot in the mountains. The boy is thrown entirely on his own resources. The village where they find shelter is, in a very real sense, "the world's end" for Kim. The window of their hut overhangs an abyss, and Kim throws "all he meant to lose"—notably the books and surveying instruments of the Russian agents—into this abyss. He seems on the brink of a desperate decision to renounce both his education and His Majesty's Service. The Lama's stern example steadies the boy. He remains true to the Service and the Lama both, bringing the old man to safety and reporting to his superiors before succumbing to fatigue and nervous strain. After a massage "which took him to pieces all one long afternoon," Kim sleeps for thirty-six hours, then rises from the dust feeling he "must get into the world again." When the question "What is Kim?" recurs, he bursts into tears, and then "with an almost audible click he felt the wheels of his being lock up anew on the world without. Things that rode meaningless on the eyeball an instant before slide into proper proportion. . . . They were all real and true . . . clay of his clay, neither more nor less." We understand the symbolism of Kim's rebirth. His affirmation of life in the world, his acceptance of India and her peoples, is also an implicit acceptance of his career of service to the "clay of his clay." He has made the choice—which will determine the rest of his life.

His choice is further illuminated by the Lama's experiences. After the attack on the hillside, the Lama's relations with the world also reach a critical point. Like Kim, he undergoes a profound struggle, then renounces selfish revenge. Like Kim, he too comes to the moment of proof and the end of his quest. He seeks the peace of meditation, and, for the first time, "the wise Soul loosed itself from the silly Body and went free . . . . I knew the Soul had passed beyond the illusion of Time and Space and of Things . . . . I knew that I was free . . . . Then my Soul was all alone and I saw nothing . . . having reached the Great Soul." Just when freedom is within his grasp, when the fulfillment of his lifelong quest is upon him, the Lama must make what is apparently a final choice between the eternal and the temporal, the spiritual and the profane. Out of love for Kim, the Lama, not without "strivings and yearnings and retchings and agonies," tears himself from the Great Soul and returns "to my *chela,* lest he miss the Way." Now the Lama has finally balanced compassion and wisdom, and so wins the kind of salvation the novel makes comprehensible to us. Since the Lama has finally resolved the claims of love and the claims of law, his quest is over at last; emerging from his meditation, he "saw plainly the River of the Arrow at . . . [his] feet."

So Kipling tells us that the spiritual and the profane are not incompatible; the twain do meet after all, as they have a habit of doing in his work. But what are we to make of the Lama's certainty that he "has won Salvation for himself and his beloved," that Kim "will be free as I am from all taint of sin— assured as I am when he quits this body of Freedom from the Wheel of Things"? Whatever its theological foundation, the statement is true because Kim has found the kind of secular vocation that will permit him to live in the world without forsaking the Way. So, in this sense, the Lama's early intuition that Kim "is not . . . of this world" is borne out. Nor is the Lama far wrong when he insists that Kim will "go forth as a teacher"; the Lama is himself "a Teacher of the Law," but so also are Lurgan and Colonel Creighton and Mahbub Ali, whose ironic gratitude that "the boy, sure of Paradise, can yet enter government service" we are obviously expected to share.

One of the Lama's major functions in the novel, then, is his eventual and largely unconscious blessing of Kim's work for the British goverment. This is why it is so important that he attains his goal by learning to balance the claims of law and the claims of love. Furthermore, the Lama recognizes only a man's merit, not a man's color: "To those who follow the Way, there is neither black nor white, Hind nor Bhotiyal"; to those who live by the Law, matters of caste and creed and color are "nothing." The implication is that Kim can achieve the same sort of balance in his career of Imperial service.

In this manner, in what many have dismissed as a story for children, Kipling embodies his vision of what the British Empire might be. Few readers, it might be objected, would seek to wring such meaning from the book; in fact, such close reading is not at all necessary to the enjoyment of Kipling's novel. (In his Preface to *Life's Handicap* [1899], Kipling observed happily that "grown men are but as little children in the matter of tales.") And what has all this to do with Saville's *Kim*?

What is important is grasping how deftly Kipling realizes

the particular excellence of which an adventure story for children is capable. (Kipling would have understood C. S. Lewis's remark that you decide to write a children's story "because a children's story is the best art-form for something you have to say.") This story of a boy's growth to maturity reveals a vision of empire worthy of adult attention, and every one of Kim's escapades serves to illuminate this vision. High adventure rests on a firm thematic base. Plot and characterization are given focus because Kipling knows precisely what he is about in depicting Kim's development, and his tale of splendid adventure is also a splendid marriage of character and action.

Saville's *Kim*, with its determination to lumber Mahbub Flynn into center stage whenever possible, minimizes the development of Kim's personality and denies itself the unifying power of the boy's struggle to maturity. Of course Saville and Co. need not have aped Kipling—but they should have found some basis of their own integrating character and action. (Kurosawa, for example, is a master of such integration; without it, his masterpiece, *The Seven Samurai* (1954), would be merely another dreary *chambara* bloodfest—maniacs in period costume butchering one another with swords.) But Kim's development is neglected—and a vacuum results. Saville's film falls short, not because it strays from the "literary" values of Kipling's novel, but because it finds nothing at all to put in their place. The film leans on the novel, instead of using the resources of the cinema to support itself. Since the filmmaker fails to seek an excellence proper to his medium, the film cannot pretend to offer more than creaking and labored entertainment.

There is a saying among the swordsmen of Japan: "When the heart is true, the sword is true." Saville's *Kim* has no heart and therefore it has no truth. And all the swords and elephants of India, all the acrobatics of the dashing Mr. Flynn are helpless to confer upon it even the slightest touch of the life which draws readers year after year to the pages of Kipling's novel.

Children, Daffodils, and Railways

KEITH C. ODOM

"They were not railway children to begin with,"[1] the story commences, but that is practically all they were known as by the end. *The Railway Children* has been considered a classic of children's fiction since Edith Nesbit first published it in 1906, and Lionel Jeffries wrote and directed the EMI film in 1970 secure in the knowledge that many would still know the book. Though its characters are not Bastables or Wouldbegoods, names which E. Nesbit gave her most famous characters, the inhabitants of *The Railway Children* novel are sympathetic, winning, and natural. E. Nesbit wrote an entirely different novel with new characters whom she never used again, though she could have with good effect. They and their episodic adventures could lend themselves to a series, as was demonstrated by the BBC Television series that preceded the film.

Three children—Roberta, Peter, and Phyllis—originally lived with their parents in an upper-middle-class suburban London villa, semi-detached to be exact. Father (Ian Cuthbertson in the film) is in the Foreign Office and provides for his family modern conveniences, servants, and trips to the theater. Suddenly and inexplicably Father leaves home, and the children and their mother are so poor that they must move to a rural cottage near a railway line. The cottage, Three Chimneys (probably named for E. Nesbit's sister and brother-in-law's cottage in the Peak District of Derbyshire), becomes the setting for many adventures in which the children come off

[1]E. Nesbit, *The Railway Children* (Harmondsworth, England: Puffin Books, 1960), p. 9. Subsequent references will be cited in the text.

as railway heroes: they make friends with Perks the Porter (Bernard Cribbins), the Station Master, and a rich old commuter (William Mervyn); they aid a destitute Russian refugee (Gordon Whiting); they save a train from a landslide; they give the Porter a wonderful birthday party; and they rescue the old gentleman's grandson when he is injured in the railway tunnel. Small wonder that they also manage to obtain their father's return from an undeserved prison sentence by enlisting the old gentleman's aid.

At one adventure per week there are enough in the novel for a mini-series at least. The adventures, while rather too coincidentally frequent for most children to encounter, are realistic and exciting enough to keep a novel or film going. The child characters themselves are upstanding enough to convey the requisite themes of fair play and generosity, and natural enough to quarrel and make mischief like real children. The mother (Dinah Sheridan) is controlled and responsible—more playful in the book where she writes poems for the children but in the film more a person of business and of enforced creativity. The origin of these characters and events is sufficiently autobiographical to be remarked upon. These children reflect both E. Nesbit's own offspring as well as herself and her brothers a generation earlier. Perhaps the Bastables did too, but they were more pert while these were more naive.

E. Nesbit and her lovable but philandering husband Hubert Bland supported themselves by writing as the mother does in *The Railway Children*. Mr. Bland's actions, especially with other women, were erratic enough to cause his wife to imagine life without him, though perhaps her father's death when she was four may have attracted her to the subject of orphans. At any rate her novels often portrayed orphaned children, though, as with the Bastables, it was not always the father who was missing. The Railway Children's mother speaks of how loving *her* mother was, however. In her *E. Nesbit: A Biography* (1966), Doris Langley Moore relates how E. Nesbit and her brothers played along the railway near Knockholt, and perhaps her own children did too, because she dedicated the book to her son Paul "behind whose knowledge of railways my ignorance confidently shelters" (p. 8).

Whatever particular English locale E. Nesbit may have

had in mind, perhaps in Derbyshire or further south, the Keighley and Worth Valley Railway in West Yorkshire was ideal for the filming, having tunnels, cuts, curves, and hills appropriate as settings for the incidents in the novel. Because the film was set in a well-known tourist area along a line preserved by railway history buffs, the local names were retained in the film, though the novel rarely used place names except for the houses: Edgecombe Villa and Three Chimneys. In particular, the Victorian railway station at Oakworth, which is still handsomely preserved, retains its real name. Mother tells the children that they are moving to Yorkshire to a house called Three Chimneys. The house used in the film still stands a few miles up the line at Oxenhope. In between are the picturesque streets and churchyard of Haworth, which serve as the film village of the Railway Children, and the doctor's house, which is actually the Brontë Parsonage Museum.

Edith Nesbit was also very athletic—a tomboy when young and physically active with her children, beating them at footraces and the like. The mother in her novel was more ladylike and, perhaps, less of a cook and housekeeper; she wrote clever lines for special occasions and did not race and play with her children. E. Nesbit depended upon her own mother and kept loving contact with her until the old lady died at eighty-four.

Some biographers believe the autobiographical impulse for *The Railway Children* weaker than that in her earlier books. *The Treasure Seekers* (1899), for example, relates to the early years of her marriage when, with two babies and a living to make, she had over an extended period to nurse her husband back from a serious case of smallpox. This setting would explain why, with all her other troubles and responsibilities, the mother of the Railway Children nursed first a sick Russian refugee and then an injured boy. Undoubtedly E. Nesbit drew on that and other personal experiences: romping with her brothers when she was young, writing for a living, raising several children, nursing a sick husband, and entertaining a large circle of great and not-so-important friends. All through the long years of marriage the Blands regularly entertained many acquaintances, including members of the Socialist Fabian Society which they helped to found.

In all her children's books, she never felt that she should

talk down to her young audience in her orally readable style, and she allowed her own children more freedom than most enjoyed in that era. Though today the personal tone of the narration might seem a bit precious, didactic, or sentimental, it hit just the right note for that time and even slightly later when, as Moore tells us, it was the favorite childhood reading of Noel Coward.

To present-day ears the narration sometimes does have an unexpectedly childish tone; for instance, the watches rewarding the children's heroism, "each . . . had a blue leather case to live in when it was at home." The narrator is carefully didactic, frequently employing the phrase, "You see," and then the explanation. No one could hear Phyllis call the train a dragon: "You see the train was shouting, too, and its voice was bigger than hers" (p. 190). The injured boy, Jim (Christopher Witty) utters lines in the book as well as the film which strike one as excessively whiney: "You won't think I'm a coward if I faint again, will you? I really and truly don't do it on purpose. And I do hate to give you all this trouble" (P. 209).

The novel's structure as well as the narrator's usually objective style lent itself to translation into film. The episodes are solidly rendered—separable though linkable—and can be conveyed with visual interest. From the opening words,"They were not railway children to begin with," to the closing "we may just take one last look, over our shoulders, at the white house where neither we nor anyone else is wanted now" (p. 240), the narration rarely fails to interest the reader and to provide continuity; for example, in the children's mysterious change of fortune and residence from suburbia to a tiny village and its nearby railway line.

Luck and coincidence also add tightness and symmetry to the episodic story line; for example, when the rich old gentleman turns out to be the injured Jim's grandfather and pays for his recuperation under Mother's care. Continuity is also achieved by pairing: Father was a prisoner and captive and so was the Russian author; the Russian was an invalid and so was Jim; Roberta had a birthday party and so did Perks; the railway almost had a disaster (landslide) and so did the canal barge (fire); Peter was a coal-burglar and Roberta was an engine-burglar; and, speaking of illnesses, Mother was ill twice, once after the trial and once after the family moved. Instead of being mere repetition, the continuity provided a sense of progression and motivation as well as order and symmetry. It was almost as if one version of an episode gave rise to another version of the same episode. The novel would have been repetitious if the second of each pair had not provided some important differences and some impetus toward the ending. The sick Russian, for instance, is different from the injured schoolboy. Strangely, though the Russian's problem is solved, the boy's problem is left in limbo at the novel's end. The film writer, Lionel Jeffries, remembers to send the boy home. As the train pulls out, Roberta grasps his hand and runs along the line. In a remark coined for the film, Peter whispers, "They'll have to get married now!"

Whom Roberta, or Bobbie, married is never revealed in the film, but the subject comes by implication in the film's openng when a grown-up Roberta enters a room of toys and momentos, and turns on the little music box with the flying dove. Those musical and visual themes lead the viewer into the film credits and then to the beginning of the story. Nostalgic memory is a theme in the film, though not in the novel. The nostalgia is expressed first by having the children pose for a photograph and then is reinforced by several idyllic walks through fields of buttercups. As Jay Cocks says in the *Time* review (November 15, 1971), the film is a kind of "elegy for an era."

Roberta is given a firmer central role in the film than in the novel. Whether she represents Edith Nesbit or one of her daughters is not clear—nor is it important, though the book has a more realistic tone than the film which several times uses cinematic techniques for memory and dream. When father appears at the beginning and end of the film, a still shot draws special attention to him, and when Roberta enters the dining room for her birthday party, she virtually floats into a haze of greenery and candlelight.

For other occasions, scenes in the film reproduce C. E. Brock's original illustrations in the novel, especially the train being flagged so it wouldn't hit the landslide, afternoon tea for the old gentlemen being provided by Phyllis (she, by the way, is pictured wearing a large tam in the first illustration and so she wears one all through the film—even to bed), Perks talking to his wife about the birthday party, the boy lying injured in the railway tunnel, and the children being visited by their Old Gentleman.

Rich in detail and event, the novel had to be tightened for the film. In some cases whole adventures are omitted, such as the time when the children rescue the bargee's baby from the burning canal boat. (Who needs a canal with all that railway?) In the novel but not in the film Roberta steals a ride on the railway engine to find a repairman for Peter's toy engine, and Peter discovers the railway signal man asleep at his switches. Some characters are merged or eliminated. It's Perks who repairs Peter's broken toy engine—not the fireman's second cousin's wife's brother—and there is a very active station master in the novel who is home with a broken leg in the film leaving only Perks to do everything at the station. Mrs. Viney is never replaced at the end by the overly efficient cook and maid.

Sometimes events are compressed: the visit of Aunt Emma at Edgecombe Villa, the discovery and rescue of the injured boy in the tunnel, and the tying of Peter with ropes when the girls tired of his obnoxious behavior. Since there was no station master to catch Peter when he stole the coal, it was up to Roberta and Phyllis to show him the error of his wicked ways. Peter's injury by the rake is omitted, so Perks's gift of magazines wrapped with the telltale newspaper about Father was done in return for his birthday party, not for Peter's convalescence. Only a few times did interest dictate that more be told in the film, such as during Jim's convalescence when the children entertained him with a Pollack's Toy Theatre.

Everything necessary to know is brought into the film in some logical way. While exercising economy of characters and events, director-writer Lionel Jeffries had to compensate for E. Nesbit's curious and protective reticence about naming people and places. The novel's Old Gentleman is disconcertingly anonymous, but toward the end of the film he becomes Mr. Fitzgibbon. The novel's children have no last name, but someone on the film must have noticed that Peter has a Waterbury watch in the novel—that name became the family name in the film. The reason for the novelist's reticence is unclear because most other characters were named, including Perks the Porter and Dr. Forrest (Peter Bromilow). The attention to details from the novel is revealed in the film when even the brass plate on Dr. Forrest's gate (actually, the Brontë Parsonage gate) is shown as E. Nesbit described it. Cinematic methods also provide other details of description and narration. Dr. Forrest, the omniscient narrator tells the reader, is somewhat poor himself. When the doctor first appears in the film, he is stretched out on the lawn before his house (he doesn't have much to do), and from the viewer's angle of vision one can see that there are large holes in the soles of his shoes.

The simple life of an even poorer Albert Perks is shown when the children approach his house with the birthday gifts. In the novel the Perks boy calls to them from the wash house that his mother is "a-changing of herself." In the film he is sitting on an outdoor privy behind a scarcely adequate door. Here too is the opportunity for the children to avoid too much saccharine sentimentality. Their careful birthday plans backfire when Robert forgets to tag the gifts, and Perks angrily refuses what he thinks is charity. The occasion is barely saved in both the novel and the film as the remorseful children read him the good wishes of his neighbors.

An excellent comedy turn in the film was the addition of a local brass band at the awards ceremony after the children saved the train from the landslide. The band members keep getting their music mixed up, and the result is a terrible cacophony that sends the director (David Lodge) into a frenzy. When he finally gets them straightened out and turns to the audience, the audience has gone. The director's throwing his fancy cap onto the station platform and stalking away was a visual delight. The scene was compatible with the rest of the tale but was provided by Lionel Jeffries and not by Edith Nesbit.

Background music for the film, as opposed to the comic band scene, ranges from serious, when the Scotland Yard men come for Father; to threatening, after Peter catches the housemaid Ruth (Ann Lancaster) in a booby trap; to pleasant, when the children skip through the buttercups. Aunt Emma, on her way to India as a governess, appears at Edgecombe Villa accompanied by sitar music, and the Scots Flyer hurtles through Oakworth Station amid the sound of bagpipes.

Camera and audio techniques are more effective, however, though not greatly innovative. The terrain is a natural advantage, since the photogenic hills, valleys, and moors of the Worth Valley around Haworth closely resemble E. Nesbit's key descriptions. The train does rush into and out of tunnels with a roar, and one can see it through the buttercups from Three Chimneys (though this is not possible in the actual location).

Some impressive camerawork occurs when Ruth, dripping from the booby-trap water bucket, walks straight into the camera turning her head first to one side and then to the other while Peter and the girls cringe in a corner of the bathroom. When Ruth slaps Peter and tells him that he'll end up the same as his father, Mother discharges her. Though sorely provoked, Ruth has been characterized all along as potentially nasty; the family's fall from respectability somehow offended her.

Fortunately, very few uses were made of camera tricks such as freezes (Father in both cases) and slow motion (Ruth's angry movement toward Peter resembled slow motion somewhat but may not have been). Director Arthur Ibbetson uses three basic cinematic techniques to tell the story: 1) cutting back and forth—for example, from Mrs. Viney and Mother to Peter and Dr. Forrest and from the engine to the children and back to the engine; 2) transitions by using voice-over to lead into the next scene; and 3) tracking shots up hills and down, up through fields of buttercups to Three Chimneys and down from Three Chimneys into the valley where the railway runs. Twice a dreamlike effect was achieved, first in the haze of greenery and lighted candles of Roberta's birthday party and then near the end when Father appeared out of the steam from the train. A strong and sudden transition with a sort of liquid significance cut from Mother's quiet tears after Roberta's party to the violent rainstorm on the railway platform just before the Russian refugee collapses.

Though well received, the film struck many reviewers as sentimental and juvenile in places. John Russell Taylor, however, says in his *Times* (London) film review (December 18, 1970) that after the children get to Yorkshire "the comedy and the sentiment are kept perfectly in balance, and the period background is realized with an unobtrusive accuracy which keeps even E. Nesbit's rosier imaginings firmly anchored in reality." It is juvenile in most cases, except when attempts are made at adult comedy as in the aftermath of Perks's birthday when he and "the missus" (played by Deddie Davis) enjoy a bit of bedroom humor. After the Perkses close the curtains around their bed there is a pause and then Mrs. Perks says, "All right, Bert, as it's your birthday." What Perks does is reach outside the bed curtains and uncork the wine bottle.

The sentimental elements are too short-lived to damage the entire film, though two problems remain. One is that in casting the film the two younger children appear to be switched in ages with Peter smaller and thus younger than Phyllis who is larger and thus older, instead of the reverse as E. Nesbit had them in the book. The film writers, however, still characterized Phyllis as younger than Peter, causing her to appear rather simpleminded. Peter's shoelaces never came undone as hers did continually, for instance, and Peter could say "extraordinary," whereas poor hulking Phyllis could only say "stronery" as she had in the novel (p. 235). Perhaps casting choices depended upon what moppets were available, and the young people chosen (Jenny Agutter as Roberta, Sally Thomsett as Phyllis, and Gary Warren as Peter) were otherwise quite capable in their roles.

The other remaining problem was pointed out by original reviewers of the book as well as recent reviewers of the film. Father's sudden disappearance is kept from the children for no apparent reason and merely serves as a flimsy plot gimmick that permits the children to have all of their interesting adventures. Since reviewer complaints date back to 1906 (*Outlook*, October 27, p. 533), the reason is not that upper-middle-class children were more sheltered in those days. As a matter of fact, in the novel the Old Gentleman says, with the author's apparent approval, "I see, you trust your children and confide in them" (p. 224). This is also said in the film, but it is not true. Mother has kept from them the most important secret of all.

The audience feels some suspense, but it wears thin after a while.

Howard Thompson, in his *New York Times* review of the film (October 29, 1971), thought of a possible third problem. "Don't the endearing kids ever go to school"? he asked. The answer, provided by E. Nesbit's biographer, Doris Langley Moore, is that "E. Nesbit had little interest in school life and her *dramatis personae* seldom appear in situations where conformity and disciplines are admired." Both the novel and the film imply that Mother taught the children when she had time—something obviously easier to do in Edwardian days.

Psychology and Magic: Evocative
Blend or a Melodramatic Patchwork

VIRGINIA L. WOLF

The third of Frances Hodgson Burnett's children's novels (*Little Lord Fauntleroy*, 1886, and *A Little Princess*, 1905), *The Secret Garden* (1911) is her masterpiece and sustains its appeal in our own time, frequently appearing on the *New York Times* list of the ten books most often read by children. It has often provoked serious and stimulating criticism, most notably Phyllis Bixler's prize-winning essay in *Children's Literature* (1978), "Tradition and the Individual Talent of Frances Hodgson Burnett: A Generic Analysis of *Little Lord Fauntleroy, A Little Princess,* and *The Secret Garden.*" However, perhaps, as some film theorists believe, a literary masterpiece seldom generates a brilliant film adaptation, form and content having already been nearly perfectly matched in the classic. Perhaps film simply cannot achieve Burnett's evocative blend of magic and psychology. In any case, MGM's 1949 rendition sacrifices the novel's powerful appeal, its symbolic resonance, and its thematic complexity.

In form *The Secret Garden* is what Northrop Frye in *The Secular Scripture* (1976) identifies as romance. Often employing the techniques of realism, the romance differs from realistic fiction in its overt patterning of polar opposite and highly unusual characters, settings, and events. The elements of romance are larger than life and function to engender wonder or horror in the reader. As Richard Chase points out in *The American Novel and Its Tradition* (1957), romance tends to oscillate between melodrama and pastoral (again see Bixler's article about Burnett's use of pastoral). Heightening the imag-

121

inative and sensuous appeal of characters, settings, and events, the prose of the romance functions like poetry to create richly symbolic images and to evoke intense emotions. Unlike realistic fiction, which earns our belief and respect by speaking to our heads and to our experience of what is, the romance reaches out to our hearts and to our dreams and nightmares about what might be.

The Secret Garden sings of life's triumph over death. The desolation with which the story begins slowly gives way to beauty and joy as the children—Mary Lennox and Colin Craven—the secret garden, Misselthwaite Manor, and its master, Archibald Craven, come alive. The huge, dark, closed-up manor and the barren wintery moor—like the hot, humid house in India, where all but Mary have died of cholera—are moving symbols of death as are the sickly, willful, and unloved children and the weedy locked garden. Details accumulate to equate the children with the garden, suggesting their affinity with nature and its power to teach them about life. Their effort to save the garden, furthermore, persuasively symbolizes the value of transcending self—of concern, involvement, work, and cooperation. As the children make the garden grow, they build their own appetites, strength, health, community, and joy. As their friendship with the robin nesting in the garden symbolizes, the children, hoeing, weeding, pruning, and planting the garden, fashion their own home or nest.

With the coming of spring, the garden blossoms, and the children run, shout, and laugh in delight. Even the house comes alive, its windows flung open to fresh air, its halls ringing with the sounds of children. When Colin Craven stands in the garden and shouts, "I shall live forever and ever," his father, far away on his travels, feels relieved of his misery for the first time in ten years. Some months later he dreams of his dead wife "in the garden," where ten years before she was fatally injured shortly before their son's birth. Miraculously healed in his grief, he awakens with thoughts of leaving for home. Though his return, like other incidents in the novel, is overly coincidental, it is emotionally appropriate, sustaining and then peaking the movement away from death and toward life. As the family walks back to the house together and the novel concludes, Burnett assures us that Misselthwaite Manor has come fully alive. Thus, symbols of life oppose symbols of death in a complex pattern reverberating with meaning and emotion.

Especially important to this pattern is the children's preoccupation with "Magic." They believe that Colin's mother's spirit is in the garden—as his father's dream of her there seems to confirm. She, so they deduce, sent the robin to show Mary the key, and assists the "Magic" in strengthening Colin's body. The garden the children see is the site of magic as evidenced in its own and their growth.

Their conviction that magic is at work in their lives begins, however, with Dickon, who, charming animals and supervising the rites of passage in the garden, is certainly larger than life—the figure of the god Pan even in his appearance. His mother, Susan Sowerby, furthermore, is another idealized character—a kind of Earth Mother, who, having twelve children of her own, seems to understand the children's every need. From afar, she provides this motherless twosome with the food, protection, and love they need to grow. The one time she enters the garden—after they have just sung the "Doxology" as a part of their celebration of the "Magic"—she reinforces their belief: "Th' Magic listened when tha' sung th' Doxology. It would have listened to anything tha'd sung. It was th' joy that mattered. Eh! lad, lad—what's names to th' Joy Maker." She also calls the "Magic" "the Big Good Thing" that "goes on makin' worlds by th' million."

Burnett herself supports the children's belief in less religious terms. In the last chapter she cites psychology as explaining the powers of thoughts and then proceeds to explain how good thoughts replaced the children's disagreeable ones to make them well. Whatever explanation we accept—a Christian god, pagan ones, "Magic," or psychology—the children's rites of celebration and their wonderstruck points of view stir us deeply.

The key to Burnett's mixture of realism and fantasy is Mary's (and later Colin's) point of view. It largely controls our experience of the novel's events. England, winter, moors, robins, spring, and people like Dickon, his sister Martha (Mary's maid), and his mother are new to Mary. She only partially understands them. Butnett gives us realistic explanations as storyteller, but Mary (and later Colin) always explains the source of joy as the "Magic." It is she who identifies Dickon as an animal charmer, his mother as "the mother," and Colin's recovery as the work of magic. Joy is so new to her that even the smallest pleasure is wonderful, and sharing her perspective, we intensely experience the miraculous nature of life itself.

Though bordering on fantasy, *The Secret Garden* violates the standards of realism at only a few points. There are three or four rather too fortunate incidences, and at one point Burnett adopts the robin's point of view, but otherwise if events seem wonder-filled, it is because we share the children's points of view and because Burnett has constructed such a moving fable. Indeed, her characterization of Mary, her uncle, and her cousin Colin is masterful, original, and complex. Minor characters, such as Martha, Mrs. Medlock (the housekeeper), and Colin's nurse, are also realistically drawn. Only Dickon and his mother seem too good to be true, and—for reasons already indicated—even they do not contradict our sense of the possible once we are captured by *The Secret Garden*'s pattern of mythic images.

Because many critics have explored the complexity of Burnett's characterization of Mary and Colin (see, for example, Marghanita Laski's *Mrs. Ewing, Mrs. Moleworth, and Mrs. Hodgson Burnett,* 1951; John Rowe Townsend's *Written for Children,* 1974; and Roger Lancelyn Green's "The Golden Age of Children's Books" in *Only Connect,* ed. by Sheila Egoff et al, 1969), there is little point in elaborating on it here. It is important, I think, to recognize her achievement and her contribution to literary tradition as one of the first writers for children to use thoroughly unpleasant children as protagonists and to portray convincingly the process whereby they change. Unattractive, totally self-centered, and sickly, Mary and Colin are nevertheless sympathetic characters. Burnett believably conveys their points of view and shows why they are as they are—their parents' having given them everything they wanted but attention. Though we come to understand how the parents may be responsible for their children's flaws, they too are portrayed with sensitivity and not as monsters. Misguided—and, in the case of Archibald Craven, overburdened with misery—they are victims who create other victims. Besides allowing us empathy, Burnett's characterization demonstrates that change is gradual, that psychological health rests upon physical well-being, that genuine concern for other people and things results in self-esteem, and that freely chosen and pursued work produces growth, which, in turn, evokes joy.

All of Burnett's techniques work to build and sustain mood, but none so more than her language. Both lyrical and incantational, as Phyllis Bixler points out, it sings repeatedly of "green," "Spring," "Magic," "awakening," "growing," and "alive." The Yorkshire dialect spoken by Dickon and his family, and increasingly by Mary and Colin, becomes the language of caring in *The Secret Garden*. Characterized by soft sounds and full vowels, using the formal but shortened "thee," "thy," and "thou" (most often tha' or th'), often clearly working-class in grammar, its vocabulary rooted in the earth, this dialect serves admirably to celebrate the natural wonders the children experience.

In writing the screenplay for the 1949 MGM movie, directed by Fred Wilcox, Robert Ardrey confronted several obstacles. First of all, the 300-page novel covering the events of a year had to be contained within a relatively short film length—somewhere around an hour and a half. Secondly, like drama, most films center around a conflict, build suspense to a climax at which the conflict is resolved, and then quickly end. Burnett's book, on the other hand, details a gradual change, essentially poetic rather than dramatic in form. Finally, because of it's heavily visual nature film must distort physical reality or create abstract images in order to communicate subjective states of mind, thereby also conveying a sense of unreality or fantasy that is perhaps confusing to the child viewer. Burnett, on the contrary, uses subtle narrative technique to blend psychological and physical realities without violating our sense of what is real.

Operating within the constraints imposed by a children's film, Ardrey offered roughly the same story, but he chose to compress the novel, to create suspense wherever possible, to add comic relief, to stress psychological explanations for the children's behavior, and, for the most part, to avoid distortion, coincidence, and fantasy. In other words, he chose to use the novel's realism, very nearly removing its magic.

Some romance elements remain. To a great extent, the film uses setting as the novel does, creating elaborate, unusual places to convey mood. The empty, ornate house in India, vultures circling above it, sets the scene. Huge Misselthwaite Manor with its dark maze of halls, locked rooms, and shrouded furniture, its formal and walled gardens, its secret garden, similarly speaks of richness in desolation. In the film, a raven, not a robin (obviously because only a trained raven could be found), befriends Mary (Margaret O'Brien) and shows her the key to the garden. However, it plays a less central role than the novel's robin. A raven adds an element of suspense to the film, but a robin *belongs* in the blossoming garden. Other features of the novel that support the children's belief in magic are similarly distorted or undercut. Though Dickon (Brian Roper) retains his pet fox cub, Captain, and the baby lamb, he loses Soot, his crow, and Nut and Shell, his squirrels. He, of course, does not play on a pipe to attract animals, but he takes on much of his mother's and sister's roles in the novel. His mother is essentially absent, except for one very brief scene. Seldom referred to, even by Martha (Elsa Lancester), she also has two fewer children.

Most important, however, is that the film's secret garden is never as believably special, let alone as magical, as it is in the novel. The introduction of technicolor into an otherwise black and white film, lending the garden scenes a rose-colored glow, fails in and of itself to impress the viewer. Yet this device very nearly carries the entire burden of conveying the garden's importance. The children act as if it is extraordinary, but they do so in terms of its being a private retreat. Not much is made of their working in the garden or of its gradual flowering. When Colin (Dean Stockwell) enters the garden, it is in full bloom (technicolor). He is not able to stand as he does during his first visit in the novel although he still manages to say, in one of the most miserably delivered lines of the movie, "I shall live

forever; I shall live forever." Because the children in the film
never speak of magic and this line lacks the context it has in
the garden, it seems melodramatic, if not downright ludicrous.

Indeed, the romance elements that survive in the film tend
to generate melodrama or sentimentality. Stripped of the
characters' subjective interpretation and of symbolism, these
elements are often incongruous in the film—there to manipulate the emotions but tacked on rather than integral to thematic development. The complexity of theme offered by the novel
is absent from the film. Rather than embody the meaning and
emotions held by the garden in the novel, the Hollywood garden is merely a place for children to get away from adults, to be
out-of-doors in the fresh air and happy together. Why the garden should prevent the children from being mean or from quar-
reling is not explained. Moreover, because few of the novel's
powerful associations with the garden are made, we have less
reason to believe in it as a source of happiness and health. In
any case, a scene near the end of the film, when the children
fear the sale of the house and the loss of the garden, effectively
betrays the thematic structure of the novel. If at this point
Mary Lennox can say, "I don't want to grow up" and Colin can
reassure her by saying, "It's a long time till we're grown up.
We're going to be happy in our garden," then the garden,
rather than a symbol of growth and life, becomes merely a place
to retreat and hide from life.

Ironically, it is partially Ardrey's rewriting for realism
that results in the film's unconvincing final scenes and in its
thematic incoherence. He picked up on and expanded the following passage in the chapter titled "A Young Rajah": "Once
they made him wear a brace but he fretted so he was downright
ill. Then a big doctor came to see him an' made them take it off.
He talked to th' other doctor quite rough—in a polite way. He
said there'd been too much medicine and too much lettin' him
have his own way." This short account by Martha inspired
Ardrey to create two scenes and to use psychology to structure
the movie's events. He introduces a London doctor with
psychological training. This doctor tells Colin (as well as Mary,
Dickon, and us) that nothing is really wrong with him, that his
father's fear that his son will be a hunchback has made him an

invalid, wearing unnecessary leg braces. Later in the movie the doctor visits Archibald Craven to follow up his report, reaffirming that Colin is potentially a healthy child.

The novel offers the same psychological understanding but more indirectly than does the movie. By creating the London doctor, Ardrey gets Colin out-of-doors, forces Archibald to return home to sell the house and take up his role as father, and accounts for his discovery that the children and the garden are flourishing. Psychology replaces magic to explain the film's events. The children treasure the garden as a release from unhealthy adults. They grow happier and healthier because of the fresh air and companionship. Archibald Craven becomes a responsible parent because the doctor forces him to see how he has harmed his son. But as psychology replaces magic, reason replaces wonder, and nothing in the movie convinces us that the secret garden is the marvelous place it is in the novel. Without a moving visual image or the children's perception of it as magic, the movie garden lacks symbolic resonance and emotional power.

Furthermore, Ardrey fails to realize the complexity potential in a psychological explanation of the events. Indeed, even as he eliminated magic in favor of psychology, he simultaneously simplified characterization and intensified events, diminishing realism. With the exception of Dickon, the characters' likable traits have been greatly reduced. Similarly, added details and music (by Bronislau Kaper) function to provoke a more pronounced, less complex response than the one called forth by the same scene in the novel. Melodrama and sentimentality result from these changes. For the sake of suspense, broad comedy, and a few tears, the move undermines its psychological emphasis. Considering the simplifications made, psychology serves only as one more means of manipulating the viewer's response—to evoke pity for the children and fear of the adults.

Mary and Colin are never convincingly more than rather nasty movie children. They never earn our admiration or love, but we do come to pity them. "I hate you" is the line that comes most frequently from both. O'Brien does show some sympathy for Stockwell and some affection for Roper, but Stockwell never convincingly reciprocates positive emotions. Neither, in any case, really change that much in physical appearance or behavior. Especially disappointing, if understandable, is that they both look incredibly healthy at the film's beginning. There is, of course, little time or reason for the rather major changes they undergo in the novel, so it is not surprising if they seem saccharine, rather than vital and involved, in the movie's final scenes. However, even much more gifted actors than O'Brien and Stockwell would have had difficulty earning our belief in characters whose supposed great change is never demonstrated or explained.

Even more striking are the simplifications of minor characters like Mrs. Medlock (Gladys Cooper), Martha (Elsa Lancester), the gardener Ben Weatherstaff (Reginald Owen), and Archibald Craven (Herbert Marshall). They represent the characteristics suggested by their names, none of the adults seeming fully human. The loquacious Mrs. Medlock becomes stern and forbidding. Loving Martha, spokeswoman for her wise mother, becomes chuckleheaded. Ben Weatherstaff, who in the novel participates in the children's celebration of magic in the garden, becomes a gruff intruder whose protection of their secret remains unknown until the end. And miserable, sensitive Archibald Craven becomes a glass-throwing, self-centered, passionate tyrant who, when he finally asks to see his orphaned niece Mary some time after her arrival from India, can only repeat, "I'd thought you might be beautiful."

These changes in characterization, supported by romantic music and other additions, provoke intense emotional responses, exaggerating the story's tendency toward melodrama. For one thing, such characters make Misselthwaite Manor more horrible, increasing our sense of apprehension during the first third of the movie. Especially suspenseful are scenes when Mary, hearing crying, searches through dark rooms with shrouded furniture looming like ghosts and mirrors reflecting her figure. The images frighten, the music is eerie, and, having met an array of adults who bully and frighten Mary, we expect the worst. Ardrey also increases suspense by having Mary, when she sees the branch crushing the chair in the garden, the axe still in the tree, suspect her uncle of murdering his wife.

For the same reason, he has Ben Weatherstaff lurk around the garden and intrude on the movie's one idyllic scene.

Besides suspense, the screenplay provides comic relief sure to induce giggles in children and to ease their tension. The tantrum scene quite effectively provokes laughter. More drawn out and played up than in the novel, it allows O'Brien and Stockwell to amaze and amuse us with ear-splitting screams and piles of broken crockery. Even more laughter is provoked in the scene in which the old doctor brings the London doctor to see Colin. Dickon and the animals are visiting, and the raven escapes with the old man's wig and the fox cub unties his shoes. Making the old doctor, who keeps Colin bedridden and in leg irons, look ridiculous and thus getting back at "bad" adults, this scene is very broad comedy. Much the same in their purpose to manipulate a response are the scenes provoking tears: the scene outside the garden when Colin tries to walk in by himself, the one when Dickon explains that Colin's father hates the garden because Colin's mother died of an injury suffered there, and the scene in which Archibald Craven storms into the garden, shoving Ben and then Mary down, to see Colin walk for the first time in his life.

The psychology, in other words, is superficial. Just as Ardrey nearly eliminated magic from the film but left unconvincing pieces behind, he—in the reverse—added a heavy dose of psychology for realism but reduced realistic characters to types, and realistic events to melodrama. Perhaps the sacrifice was to save time or quicken the pace. Perhaps the complexity of Burnett's characterization is too intimately bound up with the novel's "Magic" as conveyed by the children's points of view. Perhaps child actors and actresses cannot be expected to handle such complex parts. In any event, the cost was great.

At times suspenseful, funny, or sentimental, the film somewhat succeeds for children but fails rather thoroughly for adults. Less believable, complex, and moving than Burnett's evocative blend of magic and psychology, MGM's melodramatic patchwork quickly met with obscurity.

More Than a Magic Ring

GENE HARDY

When in 1937 American publishers proposed illustrations for *The Hobbit,* Tolkien wrote: ". . . let the Americans
do what seems good to them—as long as it was possible (I
should like to add) to veto anything from or influenced by the
Disney studios (for all whose works I have a heartfelt loath-
ing)."[1] Nine years later, even after the celebrated *Snow White*
and *Fantasia,* he complained that certain German illustrations
were "too 'Disneyfied' for my taste. . . [with] Gandalf as a figure of vulgar fun rather than the Odinic wanderer that I think
of" (*Letters,* p. 119). By 1961 he was still referring to the "vulgar elements in Disney" (*Letters,* p. 311). The direction of his
taste (as well as the fact that in his judgment Disney was
special rather than typical among American illustrators) is
indicated by the remark in yet another letter than an American filmmaker had "brought some really astonishingly good
pictures (Rackham rather than Disney)" (*Letters,* p. 261).

In his essay "On Fairy Stories" Tolkien wrote in 1938 that
illustrations served little purpose in fairy stories, even though
in themselves they might be valuable as pictorial art.

> The radical distinction between all art (including drama) that
> offers a visible presentation and true literature is that it im-
> poses one visible form. Literature works from mind to mind
> and is thus more progenitive. It is at once more universal and
> more poignantly particular. If it speaks of *bread* or *wine* or
> stone or tree, it appeals to the whole of these things, to their
> ideas; yet each hearer will give to them a peculiar personal
> embodiment in his imagination. . . .

[1] Humphrey Carpenter (ed.), *The Letters of J.R.R. Tolkien* (Boston:
Houghton Mifflin Co., 1981), p. 17. All future references to the letters of Tolkien will be identified in the text.

Tolkien was not wholly opposed to an attempt to transpose *The Hobbit* or *The Lord of the Rings* to film, however. His basically Aristotelian trust in the value of action, of plot, to the telling of any good story should have kept him open to the power of cinematic drama despite his distrust of illustrations. Objections he made to proposals by Morton Grady Zimmerman for an animated film verson of *The Lord of the Rings* were that the details were inaccurate in important respects and that tasteless exaggerations were being introduced into the story. He wrote to Forrest J. Ackerman, an agent for the film producers, that "The canons of narrative art in any medium cannot be wholly different; and the failure of poor films is often precisely in exaggeration, and in the intrustion of unwarranted matter owing to not perceiving where the core of the original lies (*Letters,* p. 270).

Ultimately the 1977 production by Arthur Rankin, Jr. and Jules Bass—or any other adaptation of *The Hobbit*—will be judged by a generation of observers who may or may not know what the original story held. Nevertheless those who choose not to invent their own stories but, for noble or ignoble reasons, depend on imitation of already successful works, are liable to the judgment of whether they simply reproduced the original (presumably for an audience which doesn't read), gave it a dimension which it lacked in the original form, or distorted it.

Before evaluating the animated film version, an examination is in order of Tolkien's *The Hobbit* both in itself and in the light of what the author thought about his own intention and success.

Like Aristotle, Tolkien asked himself what a successful work of art does, what effects it has on its audience that bring to them a sense of satisfaction peculiar to itself. In short, where does the "core of the original" lie which filmmakers may or may not perceive or preserve? He was also Aristotelian in his insistence on the primacy of narration, of plot. Some readers have mistaken him to say that action alone is all that counts, but to read him further reveals that though good plotting was a *sine qua non* of storytelling, it was not the whole. The necessity for competent plotting is not for itself or for one effect only (excitement or curiosity, for instance) but for a complex emotional response that at least on occasion involves being not merely amused but moved.

How, then, does a simple story like *The Hobbit* seem to take on allegorical proportions as it comes to life? The answer seems to lie in the mysterious ways in which the essential nature of the writer emerges in the story through the process of what Tolkien preferred to call sub-creation. The incalculable part of that process (except perhaps a bit in retrospect) is the role of the unconscious. Like writers as diverse as Madeleine L'Engle, Ursula LeGuin, and Walter Wangerin, Tolkien was entirely comfortable with (if sometimes bemused by) the operation of the unconscious.

Of the origin of *The Hobbit* Tolkien wrote to W. H. Auden that he remembered nothing about it except that he scribbled on the blank leaf of an examination paper the now famous opening line of the story. He added, "I did not and do not know why" (p. 215). More pertinent is his footnote in that letter suggesting that *The Marvelous Land of the Snergs* (1927) by E. A. Wyke-Smith was "probably an unconscious source-book for the Hobbits, not of anything else" (*Letters,* p. 215). Years earlier, at the time of the publication of *The Hobbit,* he had written to Stanley Unwin that "Mr. Baggins began as a comic tale among conventional and inconsistent Grimm's fairy-tale dwarves, and got drawn into the edge of it so that even Sauron the Terrible peeped over the edge" (*Letters,* p. 26). Some eighteen years later he reflected that he "had no conscious notion of what the Necromancer stood for (except ever-recurrent evil) in *The Hobbit,* nor of his connection with the Ring" (*Letters,* p. 216).

The unconscious process continued and became even more noticeable to himself in the composition of *The Lord of the Rings* as *The Hobbit* became "inevitably drawn in to the circumference of the great construction; and in the event modified it." Yet, he confessed, *The Hobbit* was written, "as far as I was conscious, as a 'children's story' " (p. 215). He recognized, however, the truth and applicability to himself of Gandalf's remark to Frodo that he was "meant" to do something. In this case it was to go on with the story of the Ring.

Ultimately Tolkien would say of his storytelling that "parts of it seem (to me) rather revealed through me than by me" (*Letters*, p. 189). And, with respect to his discovery of the Ents:

> I daresay something had been going on in the 'unconscious' for some time, and that accounts for my feeling throughout, especially when stuck, that I was not inventing but reporting (imperfectly) and had at times to wait till 'what really happened' came through (*Letters*, p. 212).

> I think a lot of this kind of work goes on at other . . . levels, when one is saying how-do-you-do, or even 'sleeping.' I have long ceased to *invent*. . . ; I wait till I seem to know what really happened. Or till it writes itself (*Letters*, p. 231).

So much for the role of unconscious thought processes in a writer. What happens in the mind of the reader? And ultimately does something of the same kind happen in the mind of a film viewer? And how much does that depend on an expectation that some role will be played by the unconscious in aesthetic matters and an allowance for it on the part of filmmakers?

Tolkien's reference to a story's "coming to life" is perhaps at least as much a description of an event in the mind of the reader as it is of what happens in the mind of the writer. While the reader's attention is seemingly taken up with the flow of the narrative, the more life a story has (or the more fidelity to the complexity of life) the more certain events, characters, images and even single words evoke an unconscious response in the reader. Part of it will be a universal response (related to the Jungian notion of archetypes) and part will be wholly personal. Fantasy has the special advantage that it almost always seems to be about something else, or something more. At the moment that Bilbo lay temporarily secure in the Eagles' eyrie, he dreamed all night long about "his own house and wandered in his sleep into all his different rooms looking for something that he could not find nor remember what it looked like."[2] And in doing so he causes in each reader/listener a welling up of memories and fears and hopes and even revelations of previously unconscious knowledge of one's self.

The fact that *The Hobbit* has teasing structural simi-

[2]J.R.R. Tolkien, *The Hobbit* (New York: Ballantine Books, 1965), p. 114.

larities to the grand epics of the past such as *The Iliad*, *The Odessey*, *The Aeneid*, and *Beowulf* has not gone unnoticed by readers who are familiar with the form. What is perhaps less obvious is that *The Hobbit* shares with them in its own peculiar way a function which is at most only partly conscious. While the mind of the reader/listener is consciously directed toward the surface events of the story (and in proportion as the narration is indeed genuinely engrossing) underlying values and meanings implicit in the interplay of character and action are communicated at a less than fully conscious level. Students of the epic have assumed for generations that the behavior of the epic hero not only reveals indirectly (and largely unconsciously) his own deepest nature but serves to implant in the audience a sense of what is indeed fitting in feeling as well as behavior. The society that preserves a particular epic and celebrates it need have no conscious awareness that more than an entertaining story is being preserved. But the very fact that one story persists in the minds of the people while others do not would point to a satisfaction of deeper needs and purposes than entertainment. Whatever the "official" standards of a society, its most deeply felt values are inculcated through emotional identification with the hero, who may indeed have a thousand faces, but seems ultimately to have one spirit.

If Bilbo Baggins seems far removed from the larger-than-life Odysseus, we need to remember Gandalf's own words about the futility of his search for "a mighty Warrior, even a Hero. I tried to find one; but warriors are busy fighting one another in distant lands, and in this neighborhood heroes are scarce, or simply not to be found" (*The Hobbit,* p. 33). So in an age without heroes (which is not necessarily the same as an unheroic age) timid Bilbo Baggins is required (by whom? by what?) to discover for himself and within himself the courage and wits to trigger if not control momentous events in the great world in which he is, after all, "only quite a little fellow."

And as he does so his story takes on characteristics of another, not unrelated genre, the fairy tale. Perhaps the fairy tale is, as has been suggested, derived from the epic. At any rate the two kinds of literature share a surface story of quest and adventure and risk of body, plus an inner story of the revelation both to the hero and to the audience of the conditions for success and for maturity of spirit, the chief of which is willingness to risk the death of self. Perhaps the connecting link between the epic and the fairy tale sources for *The Hobbit* is Bilbo Baggins himself, the typical young, untried, and unrespected figure of the fairy story who undergoes adventures that one would properly expect to belong to the grand epic, right down to the heroic battles at the end.

The inner story of the growth into mental and spiritual maturity by Bilbo Baggins flows just under the surface of his adventures with trolls and goblins, spiders, elves and men. It surfaces in quick revelation of the deeper significance of Bilbo's behavior at key points in the story. The reader or filmmaker who fails to pause at those points and let their meaning soak in loses much of the real life of the story. The progression of adventures itself is significant. Bilbo gets off to a very bad start in the encounter with the Trolls. Though he and the reader/listener are perhaps surprised by his daring, nonetheless his foolishness and inexperience would have brought his adventures to a quick and violent end if it had not been for the intervention of Gandalf. But even that may be part of the conscious/unconscious intent of Tolkien. In this world and in the vaster world of *The Lord of the Rings* there is the unspoken premise that there always *is* a Gandalf, at least for those who have been chosen.

By the time Bilbo confronts Gollum in the dark tunnels under the Misty Mountains he has grown in both wit and courage. But, as we sense then (or at least learn much later), the most signficant event of that chilling episode is not simply the escape itself. Neither Tolkien, Bilbo, nor the reader could have known the consequences of the quality of Bilbo Baggins' decision to spare Gollum. "A sudden understanding, a pity mixed with horror, welled up in Bilbo's heart," and that pity ultimately saved not only Bilbo but the world of Middle Earth. Whatever may have surfaced when one first experienced that scene, the power is truly in it, and Gandalf's later extraordinary judgment to Frodo of the significance of Bilbo's pity seems entirely justified.

The inner journey is far from complete. In the chapter

called "Flies and Spiders" the courage and ingenuity of Bilbo that belong easily to the surface flow of the story are counterpointed by two less obvious events in the inner life of Bilbo. Of course he will risk his life to save his friends from the Spiders, but Bilbo will also sacrifice a bit of his ego. He reveals (perhaps unnecessarily) the secret of the Ring and risks diminishing his reputation as a hero. Then he even discards the advantage of the Ring itself and fights a huge spider singlehanded. Surely the reader/listener feels, even if he does not recognize consciously, that in the naming of his sword after that fight Bilbo has become one with all the warriors and heroes whose swords were nearly as famous as themselves.

The undercurrent theme of the maturing of the young hobbit in courage and ingenuity continues through many other episodes. While Bilbo stands before the entrance to the tunnel into Smaug's lair, for example, Tolkien reminds us again of the intensely private and personal nature of heroism in the kind of flash of insight characteristic of revelations from the unconscious:

> If was at this point that Bilbo stopped. Going on from there was the bravest thing he ever did. The tremendous things that happened afterwards were as nothing compared to it. He fought the real battle in the tunnel alone, before he ever saw the vast danger that lay in wait. (*The Hobbit,* p. 205)

After this, one can scarcely be astonished by the sudden revelation that Bilbo will give up the most cherished treasure of the dwarf kings, the Arkenstone, to buy peace for those whom he loves, though they may hate him for it. This is the stuff of heroism, the decisions made "in the tunnel alone," not before admiring crowds. And it is experienced quite uniquely and separately by every person who reads or hears it.

If some of Tolkien's purposes in *The Hobbit* are clear, the Rankin-Bass adaptation of that story can be measured against them. That is perhaps the price a filmmaker pays for capitalizing on the success of an original work rather than striking out fresh. The original as it has become familiar to its audience stands in judgment of the imitation. The first questions to be

asked of such an adaptation are how well it conforms to the
original in basic elements of plot and characterization and how
well it retains (if it does not improve on) the power of the
original work to do what in fact it does. In this case what the
original does is to provide a well-plotted adventure story in
which overtones of inner growth for the central character are
capable of moving the reader or listener to emotional identification or empathy.

An examination of the Rankin-Bass animated film with
relation to the chief elements of plot and character in *The
Hobbit* reveals that most of the plot remains intact. Omitted
are the scenes with Beorn, the skinchanger, the river episodes
in Mirkwood in which Bombur was prominent if inert, the
vanishing scenes of the Elves in Mirkwood forest, and, most
conspicuously, the finding and surrender of the Arkenstone.
The changes which the script makes in the original text are
perhaps slight but oddly consequential. The company is not
rescued from the trolls by Gandalf's intervention (through ven-
triloquism) but by crass chance as the trolls are presumed to
have been careless about one of the most important facts of
their survival, the time of the appearance of the sun. In the
goblin tunnels Bilbo actually sees the Ring on the ground, and
thereby removes the significance of Galdalf's exclamation to
Frodo many years later that this was the strangest event of all,
the finding of the Ring in the dark. From this fact and others
Galdalf adduced that Bilbo was "meant" to find the Ring and
thus Frodo, too, was meant to have it. The fact that Bilbo tests
out the powers of the Ring instead of discovering its value by
"accident" further reduces the significance of the event. Almost
as if determined to reduce even further the element of a di-
vinely or otherwise directed "chance," the scriptwriter goes on
to make Bilbo's unintentional question "What have I got in my
pocket?" into a deliberate part of the riddling.

Whatever regrets may be felt for the absence of some of the
scenes of the story, a more serious distortion occurs at several
places because of the pacing of the narrative. The viewer is
almost invited to marvel at how remarkably well the producers
packed the whole of *The Hobbit* into such a brief span of time.
But the triumph of this novel lies in providing exactly what

Tolkien sought in all his story-making—an exciting story that at times deeply moves the reader. Therefore in a dramatized version space must be allowed for the significance of the action at special points to be realized, made conscious. Two episodes were indeed given full weight: Thorin Oakenshield's recounting of the history of the dwarfs' defeat by Smaug was given room even though it did not appreciably advance the immediate narrative. (Perhaps it was played out because it offered an excuse for the kind of fierce excitement that children have come to expect from Saturday morning cartoons.) Another episode which was not hurried was the eminently satisfying mental game Bilbo plays with Smaug, a riddle game in which the now mature hobbit is very much master of himself and, one hopes, of the situation.

The truncation of the scenes of escape from imprisonment by the Elves need not be much regretted. But the Aristotelian dictum that the action of the plot should develop from the essential character of the agents makes unfortunate the speed with which Gandalf is first introduced as if he were nothing more than a plot instigator; the loss of speculation on the Tookish side of Bilbo; the naming of Bilbo's sword; and even the not so hurried deathbed parting of Bilbo and Thorin. The (by contrast) leisurely return of Gandalf and Bilbo to the Shire as they talk of the significance of the adventure almost makes up for the hurried pace of the rest. Almost, but not quite.

A more serious barrier to the full transfer of the impact of the original *The Hobbit* lies in both animation and voice. The dwarfs are a bit too reminiscent of their seven bland counterparts in *Snow White,* and their songs lack the vigor and roughness one might expect from such people. (The songs of the Goblins are a bit rollicking for the full effect of their threat, too.) Any sensitivity and beauty that Elrond's face may be supposed to display is lost forever in a Spockish leanness that momentarily keeps us from knowing whether he is friend or foe. Most unfortunate of all was the producers' decision to provide each character with an already famous voice. The adventitious pleasure of recognition of the voices of Hans Conried, Orson Bean, John Huston, Richard Boone, and others exact a heavy toll from the capacity of losing oneself (or of finding oneself) in the identities of the characters proper to the story. It is an unfortunate and undesirable reminder that this is, after all, only entertainment, like juggling or magic tricks.

Ultimately this production fails of greatness despite all of its genuinely good qualities because its producers never seem to have taken seriously the inner journey of Bilbo and their own opportunity to enable their young audience to participate in it at their own levels and in the context of their own lives. They lost their chance when they failed to perceive the depth and power of Bilbo's capacity to love even the most unlovable; at the most crucial point of the inner narrative of the story they sent him over Gollum's head and down the tunnel to freedom with a flippant "Ta-ta!"

In the Tolkien's *The Hobbit* Bilbo found more than a magic Ring. He found his own instinct for compassion. In the film version he is made to succumb to the temptation to taunt his defeated enemy. He lost more than he found, and we were all made losers in the process.

I Never Met a Rose:
Stanley Donen and *The Little Prince*

JOSEPH ANDREW CASPER

In the literary season of 1943, one of the warmest critical welcomes was accorded Antoine de Saint Exupery's *The Little Prince,* a "parable for grown people in the guise of a simple story for children," as it was appropriately described by the *New York Times* reviewer. Only the *New Yorker's* critic remained aloof, claiming the piece was neither a children's book nor a good book since it lacked the simplicity and clarity all fairy tales need to create their magic. Readers, however, didn't feel that way at all, and they made the book a bestseller. Although the fairy-tale form was a new medium of expression for Saint Ex, *The Little Prince,* like his other works, was a reflection of his own life, personality, philosophy and vision.

Born in Lyons in 1900 into a stuffy bourgeois household where adults mistook his sketch of an elephant swallowing a boa constrictor for a hat, Saint Ex received a thorough schooling in the humanities. Military training ended a bit of bohemia at Paris' École des Beaux Arts. While in the service, he spent all his pocket money and free time in aviation lessons, thus making his childhood dream of flying come true. Taking note, his superiors sent him to flying school in Morocco where he obtained his civilian pilot's license at the age of twenty-one. Writing essays on aviation relieved the boredom of the various jobs that followed his demobilization. In 1926, however, he was hired to fly the mail route from France to her North African colonies and went on to become chief of Juby Airport, where rescue missions were the rule of the day. Antiquated World War I Bréguets planes, dissident Arabs, sand storms, desert

Revised from Joseph Andrew Caspar, *Stanley Donen,* Filmmakers, No. 5 (Metuchen, N.J.: The Scarecrow Press, Inc., 1983) pp. 203-214.

heat and hurricanes made these pioneer days of flying even more treacherous. During his vigils, Saint Ex wrote his first novel, *Southern Mail* (1929), an impressionistic blend of the adventures and romance of an aviator hero—the archetypical Saint Exupery protagonist—subsequently adapted for the screen by French director Pierre Billon in 1937.

In 1929, Saint Exupery joined a new mail line, opening up the first air routes between France and South America. *Night Flight* (1932), his second and much more assured fiction, detailed this hair-raising job. This aesthetic and commercial success underwent MGM's high gloss treatment a year later at the hands of producer David O. Selznick, house director Clarence Brown and stars Clark Gable, Lionel and John Barrymore and Helen Hayes heading an illustrious cast.

As war clouded over Europe, Saint Exupery was charged with various propaganda missions in North Africa—a period which provided the spatial and temporal setting for his *The Little Prince*. With France at war Saint Exupery saw active service on and off. During one of his self-exiles, this time in America, he brooded on his recent reconnaissance missions over Germany and the defeat of France in *Flight to Arras* (1942). Then, confronting the child within—the child which was always part of himself and which, he insisted, must be part of every man—in *The Little Prince* he tweaked contemporary man's callous materialism, pusilanimity and selfishness and went on to assert the significance of man as a spiritual being while defending the values of participation in life, friendship, love, empathy, courage, duty to something beyond oneself, and self-sacrifice.

Henri Peyre, in his study of *The Contemporary French Novel* (1955), predicted immortality for Saint Exupery as a "pioneer who has annexed the virgin dommain of aviation to letters ... and a thoughtful writer who has formulated anew, with force and beauty, some of the baffling problems facing man..." And Peyre's prediction seems to have come true, at least in regard to *The Little Prince*, which has been translated into some thirty languages and kept constantly in print. In addition, from the beginning this slim volume of whimsey has tantalized filmmakers from Walt Disney to Orson Welles—

predictably too, since film, with its phantasmagoric abilities, has always held a natural affinity for fantasy. But it wasn't until the late sixties—when fantasy became, once again, a necessary antidote to the turmoil of the times—that serious work was begun on a film version of *The Little Prince*; the film itself was released in 1974.

A. Joseph Tandet, a theatrical lawyer and sometime producer, who had represented a playwright who had at one time optioned the property, shelled out six figures for the rights owned by Saint Exupery's widow and Paris publisher Gallimard. Because the work was envisioned as a musical film, Alan J. Lerner was approached. An old friend of Tandet's and the celebrated librettist and lyricist of such Broadway hits as *Brigadoon* (1947), *Paint Your Wagon* (1951), *An American In Paris* (1951), *My Fair Lady* (1956), *Gigi* (1958) and *Camelot* (1962), Lerner, at this time, was under contract to Paramount to produce a total of five musical extravaganzas. (The inordinate success of Warner Brothers' *My Fair Lady* (1964), Disney's *Mary Poppins* (1964), and especially Fox's *The Sound Of Music* (1965) convinced Hollywood that the spectacular musical was the newest vein to be mined.) Extremely enthused Lerner wrote a screenplay in the midst of production chores on *Paint Your Wagon* and *On A Clear Day You Can See Forever*.

Recalling that Frederick Loewe, Lerner's former collaborator and now a Palm Springs retiree, had independently expressed an interest in the work, Tandet sent him the scenario. Loewe was hooked immediately and began composing a score with Lerner.

Robert Evans, Paramount's production vice-president, gave Saint Exupery's book to director Stanley Donen, one of the top builders of the Hollywood musical (*On The Town*, 1949, *Singin' In The Rain*, 1952, *Seven Brides For Seven Brothers*, 1954, *The Pajama Game*, 1957, and others). Donen, recently returned to the West Coast in search of projects after having been independently based in London for the past dozen years while fashioning such witty, elegant and deft film comedies as *Indiscreet* (1957), *Charade* (1963), *Two For The Road* (1967) and *Bedazzled* (1968), was quite touched by the Exupery work and equally eager to make another musical. Moreover, he had

already collaborated with Alan Lerner—and quite successfully—when he replaced Charles Walters in the shooting of
Royal Wedding in 1951.

Donen was elated that Lerner's script retained the novel's
narrative form, the day-night format and above all, Saint Ex's
engaging dialogue. The book's first-person point of view became
first-person voice-over narration in the screenplay as the aviator recalled his own childhood, his meeting with the Prince
after his aircraft went down in the Sahara Desert, and then the
Prince's own chronicle of adventures within the aviator's narrative. Throughout the novel and the script, day, regarded as a
time for action, alternated with night, the period of contemplation. And, as in the original, all the encounters in the adaptation were essentially dialogic: ingenuous, concise, poetic
speech. The Frenchman had used words beyond the accepted
range of children, for he believed that children accept and are
tantalized by new and even long words, invariably asking their
meaning and assimilating them with ease. Neither Lerner nor
Donen had difficulty utilizing the vocubulary.

Lerner's adaptation also preserved practically all of the
Prince's major encounters. Recaptured for the screen were his
confrontations with his beloved coquetish Rose on his own asteroid, his meetings on a pilgrimage to other planets with the
power-obsessed Monarch (rewritten as the more visually appealing royal obsession with boundaries), with the Businessman
who keeps account of the stars as if they were his alone, with
the Snake who offered a means to return home, and with the
Fox, the little wanderer's teacher of friendship.

Scratched from the screenplay were the Conceited Man,
always insisting that the Prince applaud him; the Tippler
drinking away the shameful memory of his dependence upon
the bottle; the Railway Switchman sorting out travelers and
sending them on their way; and the Merchant dispensing
thirst-quenching pills to save folks time. Lerner pointed out
that the satire in these episodes was not sufficiently sharp and
Donen concurred. In any case, it was felt that the script contained enough examples of the folly and vanity of modern man.

In an attempt to make the satire more immediately topical,
the novel's Geographer—unable to answer any questions be-

cause he was waiting for an explorer to supply him with the information to fill his volumes—became in the film an Historian who fabricated events. To reflect to anti-war sentiment of the early seventies, Lerner concocted a Militarist who proclaimed that dying was life's *raison d'être*. The character of the Lamplighter, the first the Little Prince does not think ludicrous since he is the only one paying attention to something other than himself, was included in the original screenplay and a sequence was filmed in which he was a life-size puppet on a six-foot planet on which night and day rapidly alternated as the Prince, moon-like, hovered about. However, unsatisfactory optical work forced Donen eventually to delete these scenes from the finished movie.

What Stanley Donen did object to in the script was Lerner's ending in which the Prince returned to the Snake, fell asleep, and merely disappeared. Eager to make all of the fable's points come through, Donen demanded that Lerner keep the author's original ending. Ironically, Saint Exupery himself had had trouble persuading his publishers that the story could end with the Little Prince's death by snakebite. Children accept all natural things, the novelist argued, whereas adults distort the natural. And for Saint Exupery, death was not an end but a means by which the pilgrim may return from whence he came.

The score handed the director by Lerner and Loewe was a mixed bag. On the debit side, it was derivative of their former successes, in particular, *My Fair Lady*, *Gigi* and *Camelot*, and this seemed anachronistic in the seventies. It also failed to capture the poetic charm and rhythm of Saint Exupery's prose. Additionally, it failed to lend itself to dancing—not surprisingly either as Lerner and Loewe wrote in the shadow of Rodgers and Hammerstein who likewise employed little choreography in their productions. This last shortcoming particularly affected Donen whose forte was the dance musical.

As far as the credit side, all the numbers did attempt to dramatize important plot points, vital characterizations, and major motifs as well as they should, since song and dance appear elevated talk and walk. Donen, whose sensitivity to a number's dramatic motivation and function was evident in all his previous musical attractions, proved a catalyst in enabling the tunesmiths to achieve this. After the script's revision and the score's completion, Lerner left the project to concentrate on the musical *Coco* and a revision of *Gigi* for the stage; Donen stepped into his shoes as producer.

The casting of the two leads was a year-long agony for Donen. Frank Sinatra, hearing the score, decided he wanted the Pilot's role. The studio, box-office draw ever on its corporate mind, was agreeable but Donen had misgivings that the star would become lax in the undertaking of the role, and he refused to take such a chance. Richard Burton, Richard Harris, Jim Dale, and many more were subsequently tested before the director decided upon Richard Kiley who had made a sensational Broadway *Man of La Mancha* (1965). Kiley, that rare combination of good actor and proficient vocalist, was a perfect choice. His performance affectingly conveyed the pilot's disillusionment with the world around him, his self-immurement, and his joy at rediscovering the child still within him, while his rich baritone was a perfect vehicle for the score. As for the other male lead, Donen selected Steven Warner, a six-year-old British unknown, quite simply because he couldn't bear to audition any more young children. Under the director's painstaking leadership, Warner's appearance, eye movements, gestures and stride exquisitely capture a child's sense of wonder at things, his matter-of-factness, vulnerability and warm tenderness. So did his unaffected line delivery, when his diction was clear which, unfortunately, wasn't very often. And the faulty lip sync throughout his dubbed passages further exacerbated his often garbled locution.

Donen, filling each supporting role as judiciously and as meticulously as he had the principals, conscientiously sought personalties who could act. As a result, the impressions made by the supporting stars were indelible: the charmingly wicked Snake, Bob Fosse; the Fox, Gene Wilder, brimming with an aching loneliness and an exuberant joy; the pompous Monarch, Joss Ackland; the ossified Businessman, Clive Reville; the absorbed scholar, Victor Spinetti; the British Army General, a vestigial remain from the Great War, Graham Crowden; and the Rose, Donna McKechnie, who kept the character's petulance and guile within the bounds of attractiveness.

After the casting battle Donen went another bruising round over finances. A stickler for authenticity, the director used Saint Exupery's aquarelles, which accompany the text of the novel, as his chief inspiration for the look of the film. The aquarelles had actually been started by the author before the writing, first appearing as a joke in the margin of Bernard Lamotte's original sketch for the illustrations of *Flight to Arras*. (Stories began to grow around these figures. The publisher felt that Exupery's own watercolors would be a selling point and persuaded the writer to include them.) The utilization of the aquarelles, concluded Donen, would necessitate animation to augment the location shooting. Such a concept was judged by the studio to be too expensive, but in the end they acquiesced.

After several locations were scouted, over territory covering most of North Africa, the director, photographer Christopher Challis—a seasoned veteran of Donen productions—and designer John Barry opted for Tozeur in southern Tunisia. On the very edge of the Sahara Desert, it proved a refreshingly exotic setting for a movie musical. (In fact, nearly every Donen production has been gifted with an original look.) The night desert scenes were done at EMI-MGM studios in London. About eight months of testing were necessary to get the approximation just right and to match the location footage with the studio stuff.

Beautifully blended into the locations and recreations were the drawing-board animations, as when the Prince is transported by Escher-like birds from his home on Asteroid B-612 to the various planets, and the Pilot's black-pencil sketches that resembled the author's own.

Throughout the film, Stanley Donen insisted that the decor remain uncluttered, almost spartan, to preserve the adventure's awesome and universal qualities. The frequently unexpected and stark color contrasts also reinforced the narrative's mythic sense, as did Shirley Russell and Tim Goodchild's simple prototypical uniforms which carried through the Pilot-Prince comparison of the plot and narrative device. In addition, Maurice Binder's credits of variously colored cutouts, aping coloring-book figures left uncolored, that floated, twirled and tumbled in and out of frame, were equally thematic and spell-

binding, initially stating the man-child metaphor while sum-
marizing the odyssey to come. The outlines' lyrical motion also
anticipated the director's lyrical staging throughout—for example, the drawing spiralling down in slow motion from the adult's
hand, or Asteroid B-612 revolving toward us—and had much
to do with translating the novel's numinous aura to the screen.

As far as the musical passages go, six out of ten were up
Donen's alley thus witnessing to an imagination at white heat.
"A Matter of Consequence," the Pilot's recitative refusal to
draw a muzzle for the Prince's sheep since he must fix his
airplane, was filmed and later edited out—it didn't play well.
For "It's A Hat," a round conveying the aviator's wry but still
traumatic remembrance of childhood rejection, Donen selected
a quick-cut montage of various obtuse adult reactions to the
child's sketch of a boa constrictor devouring an elephant; it
climaxed with a rapid-fire repetition of these images against a
chorus's crescendo chant. In failing to specify the relation of
the child to the context, these images unfortunately appeared
more akin to decoration than to theme.

To the beats of the melodious expansive "I Need Air,"
Donen effectively alternated long shots, in which the camera's
movements reinforced the 1938 Simoun Caudron monoplane's
with tight shots of the flyer, whom the camera zoomed into
and released, panned across and tilted up and down to, supply-
ing the exhilaration that the Pilot and his creator must have
felt in deciding to make the air their domain.

Anxiety, loneliness and action were the keynotes of "I'm
On Your Side," a twenty-shot montage of the Pilot shouting an
apology and support as he feverishly searches for the runaway
Prince over desert sands. Conflicting screen directions between
and within shots were disturbing as were the extreme changes
of the aviator's form, the racing camera that traced the Pilot's
frantic, even schizoid actions that backtracked upon themselves, the shots' short duration, and the pulsating melody
which approximated someone running breathlessly. The en-
gulfing space—made infinitesmal by some telephoto shots, the
ravine echo, the stark setting, and the color tedium of desert
tan and airman khaki bespoke a solitariness that bordered on
madness. The Pilot's subsequent search for the disappearing

Prince, being highly dramatic and visual, replaced the Prince's reprimand of the adult's insensitivity in the book.

Over a red rose magnified until it filled the frame, the director superimposed the reduced, high-heeled, scarlet wrapped, sensuously alluring Donna McKechnie, suggestively posed with her limbs waving coyly. Though the singsong yet lilting "Be Happy" during which her best wishes for the youth's safe journey turned into a self-pitying lament for her own perceived plight captured the Rose's Gemini character, the business did not. Moreover, the juxtaposition of the female—portrayed as a voluptuous disco queen—and the innocent little boy was disquieting.

Though the quadruple repitition of the King, Businessman, Historian and General's condescending "You're a child" to the Little Prince's queries was boring (and the only time the picture's crisp eighty-eight minutes lagged), the art direction was somewhat arresting. The first and last sections were played in a modern, abstract stage set, while an extreme wide-angle lens made the figures and props of the midsections bulge outward as if stuck to the lens, creating a grotesquely surreal effect.

"I Never Met A Rose," a wistful moonlit ballad in which the flyer understands the Prince's love—though he's never been in love himself—contains an ingenious flower conceit in the lyrics and a twenties' jazz orchestration that keeps the sentiment clear-eyed. Like Saint Exupery, Donen never allows sentiment to spill over into sentimentality. Also leavening the scene are the aviator's self-mocking Rudy Vallee delivery through a scratch-pad megaphone, and the two soft shoes—one on the sand and the other involving his index and middle fingers costumed in flower cutouts upon a miniature mound. Reined-in emotion is the approach similarly selected for "The Little Prince," the plaintive waltz underlining the traveler's death. Saint Exupery would most likely have applauded the mood of quiet pathos conveyed in this finale sequence.

The initial part of "Why Is A Desert?" during the twosome's search for water recalls "I'm On Your Side" in its staging while the slow-motion lyrical montage of their frolicking in a waterfall of the second segment resembled a television shampoo commercial. Yet, the musical passage did invest the book's philosophic line with more action and, on the whole, did illustrate one of the novelist's central themes—the existence and the importance of the spiritual. The lyrics tell that the desert hides a well and the sun; the body, water. The ninety-foot ossified skeleton of a primeval sea monster standing upright in the sands, the sun slipping below the horizon, the lane of dried-out but alive palm trees, and the satiated couple sprawled out on a rock also imaged the theme. Donen even ended on a thematic note as the gurgling of the aviator's stomach pierces the calm.

"A Snake in the Grass," the motion picture's one dance number, was wryly performed and choreographed by Bob Fosse, and so brilliantly staged, photographed and cut by Donen that it ranks among the very best of the director's cine-dances. Fosse's slinky dance metaphor—suggesting the drug pusher bedecked with a python-trimmed black outfit and yellow-tinted specs—sibilant-stressed and self-mocking lyrics, ironic gestures, and a tango heavily orchestrated with hisses, updates the Garden of Eden symbolism while making the snake's sinister ego rather alluring.

In "Closer and Closer and Closer," the business that Donen gave the Prince and the Fox, as well as his mise-en-scène, reinforced the drama of friendship emerging from the song.

Critics loved or hated the film it seemed—no one took the middle ground. And viewers were equally divided. The motion picture was a commercial failure. Paramount didn't know how to market this property efficiently and eventually simply decided to walk away from it. Besides, they had on their financial minds Francis Ford Coppola's big-budget *Godfather Part II*, which was released in tandem with *The Little Prince* during the same Christmas season. They opted to rally one hundred percent behind *The Godfather II* in the hope of filling the tills with greenbacks and the shelves with nominations and possible awards. Since its release, the filmed *The Little Prince*, mirroring its literary namesake, has achieved something of a cult status, frequently appearing on the art house revival circuit and the college campus. This witnesses to an immortality for Antoine de Saint Exupery and his intriguing narrative of an aviator and a little prince who tamed him.

The Screening
of Pippi Longstocking

A. HARRIETTE ANDREADIS

Though early critics felt that the heroine of Swedish writer Astrid Lindgren's *Pippi Longstocking* (1945) was an "outrageous superchild" and inappropriately unconventional, she has proved lastingly attractive to children all over the western world, and her adventures have been continued in two sequels—*Pippi Goes on Board* (1946) and *Pippi in the South Seas* (1948)—a TV series, and four movies. The first of these films, *Pippi Longstocking* (Nord-Art, Sweden, and Constantin Films, Germany, 1969), will be examined here. The initial appeal of the Pippi books is their antiauthoritarianism, as Pippi flouts the conventions of middle-class respectablity. As Mary Orvig, writing in *Horn Book Magazine* attests, "Pippi stands for every child's dream of doing exactly what he or she wants to (regardless of any prohibitions). . . . Pippi is strong, cheerful, and generally happy" (February 1973). "Pippi," observes Marcus Crouch in *The Nesbit Tradition* (1972), "embodies all the dreams of small children who weave fantasies about total freedom from adult supervision, enormous physical strength, escape from the conventions of a civilization invented by grownups."

Lindgren's portrayal of Pippi and her world suffers a gradual deterioration in the two sequels by virtue of the weakening of Pippi's character. In the later books, Lindgren merely suggests this weakening presumably to make Pippi more acceptable to adult book buyers, but in her screenplay for *Pippi Longstocking* she vulgarizes the most engaging characteristics of Pippi and her world to make them palatable to the 151 majority of paying viewers. Her recasting of the *Pippi* trilogy into a screenplay is particularly interesting because it presents an example of an author's vulgarization of her own work, whereas the degradation of the intellectual, aesthetic, and ethical values of a reformulated work can usually be laid at the door of "crass" screenwriters, directors, and producers.

A colorful nine-year-old, Pippi has carrot-red perpendicular braids and freckles; and she wears mismatched stockings, extra-long black shoes, and a patchwork tunic of her own devising. She lives alone in a ramshackle cottage, the Villa Villekula, with her monkey Mr. Nilsson and her horse. Her mother is "in Heaven," having died when Pippi was very small, and her father is king of a South Sea island of cannibals on which he was shipwrecked after a storm at sea. Pippi has a bag of gold pieces given to her by her father to take care of her material needs. She befriends the girl and boy next door, Annika and Tommy, who accompany her on the escapades which make up the narratives of the books.

In *Pippi Longstocking,* the first and best book in the trilogy, Pippi is a thoroughly self-determined child with extraordinary strength. She cooks and cleans for herself, takes care of the yard and two animals, picks up and summarily disposes of two policemen, and lifts her horse on or off the porch. But she also lives in a world imbued with her own logic, generosity, and humanity, a world in which she determines justice and the moral order, a world in which the conventions of adult middle-class life are often exposed as absurd. More than mere strength sustains our interest in Pippi through three books, and her portrait has considerable subtlety. More precisely: "Her pranks are neither stupid nor damaging; she is full of a good-hearted willingness to help people weaker than herself; she is indescribably open-handed and, above all, never boring."[1]

Persuaded by Annika and Tommy to go to school so that she, too, can have vacations, Pippi is disconcerted to find that the teacher already knows the answers to the questions she asks her students, and she can see no reason to know the "pluttifikation" tables, or any other form of arithmetic, since she has no practical use for them. Her day in school is a disaster, and to

[1] Bettina Hürlimann, *Three Centuries of Children's Books in Europe* (Cleveland: World Publishing Co., 1968), p. 82.

the horror of the other children she answers back and exasperates the teacher. When the latter eventually points out her misbehavior, Pippi is unexpectedly contrite: "You understand, Teacher, don't you, that when you have a mother who's an angel and a father who is a cannibal king, and when you have sailed on the ocean all your life, then you don't know just how to behave in school with all the apples and ibexes." Pippi recognizes, in effect, that she is not well socialized, and to atone for her misdeeds she offers the teacher "a lovely little gold watch":

> I think you are awfully nice, Teacher. And here is something for you. . . . You've got to take it; otherwise I'll come back again tomorrow, and that would be a pretty how-do-you-do.[2]

Mistress of the tall tale, in parting from the other children, Pippi tells them that in Argentina no arithmetic is taught in school and that children eat caramels which their teachers thoughtfully unwrap for them—a paradise indeed.

Pippi again has cause to regret her lack of socialization at the coffee party given by Mrs. Settergren, Tommy and Annika's mother. Her anxiety about behaving in a "ladylike" fashion causes her to eat too much and to involve herself inappropriately in the adult women's conversation. When Mrs. Settergren chastises her, "Pippi looked at her in astonishment and her eyes slowly filled with tears. 'That's just what I was afraid of,' she said, 'That I couldn't behave properly. It's no use to try; I'll never learn. I should have stayed on the ocean." Despite this remorse, however, she cannot refrain from a parody of the stuffy and snobbish women whose chief concern is the servant problem. In a *reductio ad absurdum* imitation of them, she relates how her fictive grandmother's maid Malin bit guests in the leg, broke the china, and never swept under the beds, but was beloved because she scorned propriety. "Too bad you don't like your maids," says Pippi, who though aware of her social shortcomings nevertheless retains her own vision of reason and honesty in the world. She has a child's freedom from hypocrisy and social snobbery, and Lindgren lets her have the last word.

[2]*Pippi Longstocking* (New York: Viking Press, 1950), p. 59.

In *Pippi Longstocking*, Pippi's generosity is shown by her heroism, as well as by the way she treats Tommy and Annika. When the burglar-tramps Thunder-Karlsson and Bloom attempt to steal her gold pieces, she first impresses them with her enormous strength and then exhausts them with dancing the schottische. After feeding them, she sends the burglar-tramps on their way—and they are eager to escape from this little girl who has made them work so hard: "As they were going out of the door Pippi came running after them and gave them each a gold piece. 'These you have honestly earned,' she said."

In other episodes, Pippi wins the admiration and affection of Tommy, Annika, and the townspeople by saving little Willie from the bully Bengt and his gang of five, by rescuing (with the help of her monkey) two little boys from a burning building, and by exposing the absurdities of male musclemen by winning the competition with Mighty Adolf at the circus. Thus Pippi, though lacking the conventional social graces of "ladylike" young girls, is loved and respected by both her peers and her elders because she is generous, strong, and clever at both protecting her friends and deflating the mean or pompous. She embodies a simple code of honor and honest values.

In the disappointing final volumes of the trilogy, though Pippi still tells delightful tall tales and plays outrageous but harmless pranks, her heroism and generosity are less prominent. Whereas in the original volume Pippi is portrayed as a free spirit, entirely independent and happy in the Villa Villekula, in the sequels she is increasingly characterized as a somewhat lonely and unruly child. The portrait of Pippi becomes in many respects a judgmental one. It may be that Lindgren responded to the criticism of the initial Pippi book by introducing a more external, more "adult," more "normal," view of her. In *Pippi Goes on Board*, for instance, Pippi returns to observe school:

> "Good morning, little Pippi," said Teacher. Once Pippi had come to school for a whole day, so Teacher knew her very well. Pippi and Teacher had agreed that Pippi might come back to school when she grew a little older and more sensible.[3]

[3]*Pippi Goes on Board* (New York: Viking Press, 1957), p. 40.

And Pippi seems slightly foolish when, at the play at the Fair, she cannot suspend her disbelief and finally leaps up on stage to save the Countess Aurora from the villain. We are encouraged to laugh at her, rather than with her. The shift in tone is subtle but important.

It is also in this second volume that Lindgren introduces explicit sex-role stereotyping. In *Pippi Longstocking*, Tommy and Annika are stereotyped several times by the gifts they receive from Pippi, as when Tommy receives a dagger with a mother-of-pearl handle or an ivory flute and Annika gets a little box with a cover decorated with pink shells or a butterfly-shaped brooch. In *Pippi Goes on Board,* however, this implicit stereotyping becomes more pronounced. Tommy scolds Annika for crying when they think Pippi is leaving on the good ship *Hoptoad* with her father: "Tommy would have liked to cry also, but a boy just couldn't let people see him cry." Worse, however, are the sanctions Lindgren imposes on Pippi. Tommy is finally allowed two tears, but Pippi has this conversation with the Teacher:

> "Listen, little Pippi," she said in a friendly voice, "you want to be a really fine lady when you grow up, don't you?"
>
> "You mean the kind with a veil on her nose and three double chins under it?" asked Pippi.
>
> "I mean a lady who always knows how to behave and is always polite and well bred. You want to be that kind of lady, don't you?"
>
> "It's worth thinking about," said Pippi, "but you see, Teacher, I had just about decided to be a pirate when I grow up." She thought a while. "But don't you think, Teacher, one could be a pirate and a really fine lady too? Because then—"
>
> Teacher didn't think one could.
>
> "Oh, dear, oh, dear, which one shall I decide on?" said Pippi unhappily.
>
> Teacher said that whatever Pippi decided to do when she grew up, it would not hurt her to learn how to behave— because Pippi's behavior at the table was really impossible. (p. 59).

Teacher then proceeds to tell Pippi some of the rules for good manners. Clearly, Pippi is given mutually exclusive options:

she can either have an active, exciting life, or she can grow up to be a well-bred lady. Pippi's understanding of this dichotomy is again illustrated in her gifts to Tommy and Annika. In *Pippi in the South Seas,* she gives Tommy a set of paints and Annika a red parasol for Christmas. Activity, "piracy," is reserved for boys-to-be-men, but young girls who aspire to be ladies must learn to accommodate themselves to being vulnerable and ornamental.

Though Pippi is still clearly outside the social codes, in the sequel volumes she is allowed her eccentricities only with the proviso that she will one day *have* to grow up and put on her proper role. The child reader is thus discouraged from identifying with Pippi and encouraged to identify with Tommy and Annika; Pippi is merely an outrageous child it might be fun to know.

Pippi's freedom is contingent on her childhood, a time when one can be outrageously delightful because one's behavior need not be taken seriously. The last chapter of *Pippi in the South Seas* is called "Pippi Doesn't Want to Grow Up." In it, Pippi elaborates on the fantasy that there are pills which will keep her and Tommy and Annika from growing up:

> "No, that's nothing to wish for, being grown up," said Pippi. "Grown-ups never have any fun. They only have a lot of boring work and wear silly looking clothes and have corns and municipal taxes. . . ."[4]

In this chapter, Lindgren portrays a Pippi who seems to sense that her paradisal time of freedom will be short. Now, Pippi's unconventionality sets her apart and makes her lonely. The closing scene of this last chapter of this final volume in the series is of Pippi seen at her window by Tommy and Annika. She is observed from outside staring dreamily at a flickering candle flame.

> "She—she looks so alone," said Annika, and her voice trembled a little. "Oh, Tommy, if it were only morning so that we could go to her right away!" . . . "If she would only look in this direc-

[4]*Pippi in the South Seas* (New York: Viking Press, 1959), pp. 120–121.

tion we could wave to her," said Tommy. But Pippi continued to stare straight ahead with a dreamy look. Then she blew out the light. (pp. 125–126)

These closing lines of the Pippi series suggest that if Pippi is to be less lonely, she must begin to grow up, that is, assume her proper female role. That there are no further sequels suggests that indeed she has grown up, and that Lindgren has relegated her to the fate of many tomboys: a restricted adolescence and womanhood bound by convention. It seems that, unlike Peter Pan or other storybook children, Pippi is not to be allowed her childhood in perpetuity, for her childhood has become an object lesson in behavior to be avoided by good middle-class children.

The plot of the movie *Pippi Longstocking* is a conflation of episodes from *Pippi Longstocking* and *Pippi Goes on Board*, with the "Spink" episode and closing scene from *Pippi in the South Seas*. The result is a rather arbitrary stringing together of episodes which lacks any unifying principle or idea apart from the presence of the central character herself.

Though she used many episodes from the original *Pippi Longstocking*, Lindgren incorporated into them the flattened character of Pippi and the oppressive role-stereotyping in the sequels. Pippi's humor and strength are also exaggerated and vulgarized; her clever logic becomes pie-in-the-face slapstick and her strength used in emergencies to rescue people and situations becomes a super-child's showing off. The Pippi in the movie is a disruptive, bossy super-child on holiday in a world of bothersome, incompetent adults; she is no longer the free, generous, delightful, noncomformist, yet sensitive and thoughtful child of the first book. Thus, Lindgren's tendencies in the two sequels to make concessions to critics of the original *Pippi,* have in the film been carried out to their logical conclusion.

Many of the changes made from the books to the movie were motivated by considerations of cinematic coherence. For instance, the thieves who are after Pippi's gold in *Pippi Longstocking* are introduced as the town's jailbirds and appear in several episodes throughout the movie, as well as in scenes in which they mill about the town being ominous or comic; they provide continuity. The books, by contrast, use them only once and then have different villains who appear seriatim. Though there is no schoolroom scene in the movie, there is a caricatured "Teacher" who appears throughout to represent adult repressiveness and the town's disapproval of Pippi; she is loud, scolding, and threatening, and Pippi takes pleasure in flouting her authority. The caricature becomes cloying as she carries on a sickening flirtation with Pippi's father in a gratuitous scene (not in the books) whose only intention could be to ridicule feminine opportunism.

In counterpoint to this grotesque creature, Mrs. Settergren, mother of Annika and Tommy, is portrayed as the genteel and appropriately docile person a mother ought to be, and her remonstrances to Pippi are suitably gentle. The other adult women in the movie are caricatured scolds—notably the saleswoman in the hatstore and the women at Mrs. Settergren's coffee party—who react to Pippi with disapproval.

The adult men, on the other hand, are indulgently paternal. The doctor, the salesman in the hardware store, the police, the crew of the *Hoptoad,* and Captain Longstocking, are all benign, if sometimes comic, and benevolent in their treatment of Pippi. Only the apothecary, at first seen through the distorting eye of a wide-angle lens, is made to seem at all ominous. The thieves are too comic and too inept to seem very dangerous. The adult world in the movie is populated by mostly grotesque women and mostly benevolent men. In this way, the movie makes explicit and even embellishes the latent sexism and sex role stereotyping of the two sequel books.

The movie opens with a voice-over of Annika and Tommy describing their friend Pippi as she is shown riding her horse into town. This establishes for the viewer a "normal"—or perhaps normative—point of view. We are encouraged to see the unusual Pippi through the eyes of the two average, good children who are her friends. Certainly children viewing the movie are being encouraged to identify with Tommy and Annika in viewing Pippi as unusual and eccentric. The filmic possibility for voice-over here allows Lindgren to develop the technique of viewing Pippi externally which she uses at the end of the third book. This serves to establish a framework (even though voice-over is not used again) in which to view

Pippi as other—as someone great fun to be friends with, but not someone to be imitated.

The screenplay's attitude toward Pippi is also apparent in the contrast between the fully drawn nuclear family of Annika and Tommy (a scene at the cozy breakfast table with mother and a father who never appears in the books is added), and a Pippi in need of parental presence and who often talks to her mother in Heaven. This contrast extends the loneliness of Pippi which is suggested in the two sequel volumes of the Pippi series.

The closing scene of the movie underscores this motif of Pippi's loneliness. At the end of *Pippi Goes on Board*, Pippi refuses to go to the South Seas on the *Hoptoad* with her father because "I can't bear to see anyone on God's green earth crying and being sorry on account of me—least of all Tommy and Annika. Put out the gang-plank again. I'm staying in Villa Villekulla." At the close of the book, Pippi, Mr. Nilsson, Tommy and Annika are riding toward the Villa Villekulla on Pippi's horse. But for the closing scene of the movie, Lindgren has created a new version of the end of *Pippi in the South Seas*; it leaves Pippi praying to her mother in Heaven, who, she says, will be able to watch over her more easily since she has stayed home. Pippi has given up adventure for friendship and for the protective presence of her mother in Heaven. The effect of this ending in the movie is of course to undermine Pippi's independence and to make it seem that even she, the strongest and most self-sufficient of children, feels a need for the constant watchful presence, albeit fantasied, of parental authority. Pippi's loneliness is thus assuaged and the audience leaves the theater feeling that Pippi is more ordinary than not, and certainly not a role model for a new kind of free-spirited girl child.

In transposing the books into a visual medium, Lindgren has eliminated most of the episodes which involve Pippi's generosity and witty logic in favor of expanding on the potential of some episodes for broad slapstick humor, especially those scenes in which Pippi uses her enormous strength. When she saves Willie from the bullies in the movie, she does it as much to show off her prowess as to protect him. Instead of taking each bully and tossing him over a low-hanging limb as she does in the book, she tosses Bengt very high up into a tree and frightens the bullies away. The movie version is more visually spectacular. But stop-action, which is used to achieve the translation of Bengt from ground to tree, is over-used to demonstrate Pippi's strength. She lifts her horse high into the air; she vaults through a third-story window; she lifts her horse, her friends, her father, and the entire crew of the *Hoptoad* into the air on a door; she carries the policemen along by their belts several feet off the ground; she tosses one of the thieves into the air and onto the top of a wardrobe; she slides around the gables on the roof of her house and then jumps down unharmed; etc. These visual tricks may be entertaining to young children, but to any practiced eye, to the child accustomed to the sophisticated technology of *Star Wars* or *Raiders of the Lost Ark*, they are tiresome and very crude. In fact, the visual trickery in this movie was old-fashioned even in 1969 when it was made; it is little more than a bit of outdated live animation.

Pippi's antics in the movie—unlike those in the book—are not very constructive. Her rescue of the boys from the burning building (in *Pippi Longstocking*) and her chastisement of Mr. Blomsterlund, who is beating his horse (in *Pippi Goes on Board*), for instance, are omitted. Instead, Lindgren inserts numerous pies-in-the-face episodes and adds injury to insult at the coffee party by having Pippi create a melee by pulling the tablecloth and upsetting all the food and dishes onto the floor. Though these and similar added gags might be viewed as adding visual interest to the screenplay, they degrade the humor of the books and do not suggest the redeeming features of Pippi's complex character in *Pippi Longstocking*.

Lindgren has retained those episodes from the books which exploit the materialistic urges of the children in a viewing audience. For example, the inquisitiveness and adventurousness of Pippi, Tommy, and Annika in "thing-finding" and in playing in the hollow tree (in *Pippi Longstocking*) become an episode in which the tree mysteriously dispenses lemonade. A chapter early in *Pippi Goes on Board*, "Pippi Goes Shopping," is expanded into several consecutive episodes in the movie.

The book emphasizes Pippi's innocence about money (she has that bag of gold coins left her by her father, but no idea of its relative value), her generosity and wit (she mixes together the several bottles of medicine she has bought and drinks the mixture to ward off illness: "What one isn't one may become"), and her humor (when she accidentally pulls the arm off the mannikin in the dress shop and buys it to pacify the saleswoman, she says, "Don't people have false teeth and false hair, maybe? And even false noses sometimes? Why can't I have a little false arm?"). While the screen version retains the basic episodes from the chapter of the second book, it expands them into separate episodes, introduces an interlude with the jailbird thieves, and emphasizes the children's greediness for bonbons and toys, rather than Pippi's generosity in treating everyone. The town's children all wait to gobble candy and grab up the toys Pippi has bought. The tenor of the episodes is that of a street holiday for children with nothing in mind but food and toys.

In the movie the children are never shown in school (though they are in school in the first two books of the series), which contributes to the unreality, shallowness, and one-dimensionality of the portrayal of children in the film. This view is confirmed near the end of the movie when a few sentences from the chapter "Pippi Has a Farewell Party" in *Pippi Goes on Board* become a veritable orgy of children stuffing themselves and throwing pies-in-the-face. This introduces a thematic imbalance into the movie, emphasizing not childhood freedom and good spirits but mindless excess.

Two final and significant changes from the books to the screenplay are the addition of an episode with a mouse and Japanese flowers and the omission of the "Pippi is Shipwrecked" chapter from *Pippi Goes on Board* in favor of a new episode of a picnic trip in a flying balloon. The first addition adds nothing but cuteness; it is basically silly. The episode of the flying balloon adds the adventurous and the spectacular— and affords the opportunity for more trick photography. It also offers a motive for the continuing antics of the inept police chasing the jailbird-thieves and, thus, creates some suspense and more slapstick. These changes are like the others described here in that though they may provide visual amusement for children they sacrifice the subtleties of the books.

The movie version of *Pippi Longstocking* may well be an entertaining and colorful extravaganza for children—its three sequels attest to its success—but it lacks the substance, subtlety, and appeal of the books. The consistency of the changes made indicates that Lindgren flattened the characters, enhanced the sexism, degraded the humor, emphasized conventionality and materialism, and relied overly on visually surprising and spectacular material in the screenplay. The result is a pallid and charmless reflection of the uniqueness of the original *Pippi Longstocking*, which not even the delightful performance of Inger Nilsson as Pippi could change. Lindgren's increasing tendency to give her audience (in this case, probably the parents of the children she was originally writing for) what it wants produces its inevitable result—more pablum for children's minds.

Aslan in Filmland:
The Animation of Narnia

DONNA J. HARSH

*T*he Lion, the Witch and the Wardrobe, first of the seven books in the Chronicles of Narnia, has transported child readers to an imaginative world for the past three decades. Written by C. S. Lewis, English scholar, theologian, and literary critic, the book has become a classic modern fairy tale, acclaimed by adults and eagerly read by children on both sides of the ocean. Some adults consider the book, often accepted as a religious allegory, too frightening for children because of its constant shifts from reality to a make-believe world, its bloody battles, and its repeated threats of evil. Other adults argue as did Lewis himself, that children read the book as an adventure that has something important to say about life and the world, and that whether or not they understand the underlying message about Christianity depends on their religious background.

The influence of Lewis' life is seen in the book in various ways. During his childhood he was allowed free access to his father's library, and at an early age he began writing his own stories. Lonely during the years his brother was away at boarding school, the young boy enriched his own life by using his lively imagination to concoct a medieval Animal-Land history and geography. The medieval ideas and the "geography" in *The Lion* may have sprung from these early roots.

Lewis's boyhood home, which he says became almost a character in his stories, must have been much like the Professor's house in *The Lion*, with high ceilings, mysterious passages, and enticing places to explore. It is an ideal setting for

163

the adventures of the Pevensie children, who discover the strange land of Narnia.

The Christian themes of the book undoubtedly emerged from Lewis's desire to convey in a children's story his own conviction of the importance of religion. He chose the fairy tale genre because it seemed the best vehicle for what he wanted to say to children. The choice of this genre also reflected Lewis's childlike qualities as a grownup. He retained a freshness that was much like that of children who experience things for the first time. Quotes from his autobiography in *Something About the Author* (1978), give a glimpse of this characteristic of Lewis with this description of a rainy day. "How nasty the sugar cottage in 'Hansel and Gretel' must have been in wet weather."

In *Surprised by Joy* (1955), Lewis summed up his writing philosophy in a letter to an American child: "Don't use adjectives which merely tell us how you want us to feel about the thing you are describing. I mean, instead of telling us a thing was 'terrible,' describe it so that we'll be terrified." Because of his ability to do this in his writing, the book provided material for filmmaker David Connell to do the same in his 1979 animated film adaptation of the story.

The "sense of place" in the book is well reproduced in the film. When Lucy enters Narnia through the wardrobe, the reader moves from one world to the other with her as she feels "something crunching under her feet" and discovers snow in the woods at night, even though she can still look back through the crack in the wardrobe door and see a daytime scene, bright and real.

The home of Mr. Tumnus, the Faun who is Lucy's first contact in the magical world, is shown in the film just as described by Lewis. The viewer recognizes the scene in the cave where Mr. Tumnus and Lucy have tea. One even sees Lucy reading the same book titles from the shelves of his library. By using the filmed device of animating the picture of an old Faun on the wall, the producer allows the viewer to see the scenes of Narnia as Mr. Tumnus described it to Lucy. The home of the Beavers, minutely outlined by Lewis, is also faithfully reproduced in the film.

When first viewing the animated film, one may question

the appropriateness of this technique for a story with a religious theme, but on reflection Connell's choice is better understood. The story takes children from a setting in reality to a world with "a separate time of its own," where good and evil battle for dominance and where a witch's magic turns animals to stone. Animation works quite well to cast such spells.

Although both the book and the film are seen from the point of view of the children, they are less well developed as characters than the White Witch and Aslan. One knows the exciting actions in which the children are involved but little is known about them as individuals. Edmund, who betrays the others, is the best developed child character.

Aslan, who represents good, is a prominent character in both the book and film. Peter, Susan, and Lucy first see him when they leave the home of Mr. Beaver to flee from the White Witch. The first sight of the Christ-like Aslan is briefly described in the text and extended into a powerful scene in the film. The awe felt by all of the children is apparent in their facial expressions, in their dialogue, and in the stirring music that builds the scene to a peak of emotion. The benevolent aspect of the characterization is shown in the film by the tenderness Aslan demonstrates as the creatures of the woods gather around him.

The episode with Aslan reappearing to Lucy and Susan is the most apparent link between Aslan and Christ and is more powerfully stated in the film than in the book. Lucy and Susan, mourning the death of the great beast at the hands of the evil White Witch, feel the cold of their night of sorrow as they realize they can do little for him but remove the muzzle and stroke his poor violated body. Suddenly the scene shifts from showing the girls shivering in the gray early morning to one that bursts into a dawn that promises a miracle. Pinks, blues, and yellows light the sky and the background music changes from a slow, woeful melody to one of excitement and exultation. The effect is heightened when a loud, resounding crash, accompanied by jagged lightning, moves the earth, and the Stone Table on which Aslan was crucified splits in half. Simultaneously Aslan appears and almost "floats" in the meadow as the girls realize what has happened. Aslan is back with them.

This scene clearly evokes a feeling of reverence and awe by using colors, lighting, sound effects, and music in a most effective way.

Some critics have complained that Lewis's portrayal of Aslan is often inappropriate and in the word's of Margery Fisher tends to make him "more like Tigger than like Christ." Others accept this aspect of Aslan's character as part of the joy of the resurrection. The film builds on this feeling as Lucy and Susan climb on Aslan's back and ride off to the Witch's castle, leaping over the wall, to find many of the forest creatures turned into stone statues and waiting for Aslan to breathe life into them so that they can be released from the Witch's spell. The scene is full of movement, color, music, and joy, as Aslan's touch changes Mr. Tumnus (who could still cry although turned to stone) back into a Faun who would never be in the pay of the White Witch again.

In Lewis's story the White Witch is a major character representing evil, and she cunningly entices Mr. Tumnus and Edmund to work in her behalf. Her power over the seasons prevent Spring from coming to Narnia—for if Spring comes, so would Christmas, i.e., the birth of Christ.

The Witch is the most compelling of Lewis's evil creatures, and the film plays this up by showing her as both larger than expected and sharp featured. Her chin is tapered to a thin tip, her eyes look evil with pointed corners, her lips are thin and blood-red, her hands have elongated fingers and nails that look dangerous. The razor-fine lines of her dress give a power to her being. She is pictured in white, grays and shades of blue, and she communicates a feeling of inevitable bleakness. Her castle has sharp lines and pointed towers that suggest evil and danger. Even the windows convey this feeling by means of shapes that recall the eyes of the Witch.

One of the reasons the film works is that the voices for the characters were chosen with care. The voice of the Witch sounds sharp, grating on the ear as she drives Edmund through the snowy forest to find the other children. It causes Edmund to cringe when she is angry with him for coming to the castle without the other children, and it becomes triumphant when she taunts Aslan before she binds him and plunges her knife into him as he is lying on the Stone Table. When she speaks, lightning and thunder crash through the atmosphere.

Another evil character is the Wolf, Maugrim, who guards the door to the evil castle. Although he is scarcely mentioned by Lewis, until the battle with Peter, he achieves more importance in the film because of his fierce portrayal. He is large and shaggy, with long, prominent, wicked-looking teeth, glowing yellow eyes that penetrate through the screen, and a low, gravelly voice that causes Edmund to quiver in dread.

The voices of the characters representing evil contrast with the voice that represents good, that of Aslan. When the children see him for the first time, they tremble as they contemplate this great creature so vividly described by Mr. Beaver. When he speaks, his voice is strong and reassuring, and it's low, soothing tone calms them. His power is shown when he gives a mighty roar as he and the Witch struggle for dominance. The quality of Aslan's voice when he reappears to the children fittingly suggests resurrection though a quality that is light but nevertheless strong, vibrant and full of tender concern.

Lewis uses the character of Father Christmas both to signify the weakening of the White Witch's magic and to indicate that the power to ward off evil comes from Christ. Connell does not show Father Christmas in the film but refers to him in the episode in which the sledded White Witch drives Edmund, bound and shivering, through the forest in an attempt to overtake the Beavers and the children. His presence is felt in both the book and the film when the snow begins to melt, flowers bloom, and the Witch's journey is slowed. Lewis describes the gifts Father Christmas gives the children: a shield and a sword for Peter; a bow, a quiver full of arrows, and a little ivory horn for Susan; a dagger and a little bottle of cordial for Lucy. In the screen version, it is Aslan who gives them these gifts as they prepare for the battles, and the switch suggests that Aslan and Father Christmas represent the same religious concept.

Connell's film version retains Lewis's basic plot, most changes being necessitated by the medium and the need to condense the tale enough to "fit" into the two hours allowed for its original television premiere. The major change concerns the story's beginning. In the book, the children, bored on a rainy day when they are staying with the Professor, explore an interesting old house. Lucy, intrigued with the possibilities of the wardrobe as a place in which to hide, finds that it leads to the land of Narnia. She shares this secret with Susan, Peter, and Edmund, and when they greet her tale skeptically she urges them to see for themselves. The film begins with Lucy coming out of the wardrobe to tell the others of her adventure and to invite them to explore Narnia with her. The preceding episodes are telescoped through a flashback as Lucy, disgruntled because the children do not believe her, remembers the enchanting place she had entered through the wardrobe door.

After Lucy discovers Narnia, the structure of the book gives us one chapter telling of the adventures of Peter, Lucy, and Susan, and the next following the actions of Edmund. This antiphonal pattern continues until Edmund is rescued from the White Witch by the children, Aslan, and the rescue party of "centaurs and unicorns and deer and birds." The film carries out the pattern of alternating stories by letting the viewer follow Edmund's actions and then switching to the involvement of the other children. This movement from one story to another also gives the effect of building suspense and working toward a peak of excitement.

In the film, the book's moods, tone and emotions are faithfully reproduced, the addition of the pictures and sound often heightening the effects. The mystical feelings developed in the episode in which Aslan is introduced, the sorrow felt at his death, and the joy experienced when he is seen again are all encountered in the film in most satisfying ways.

There are episodes in both the book and the film that are melodramatic. The White Witch is preparing to kill Edmund when she realizes that her plan to overtake the group is not working. The knife is being sharpened—when suddenly, like the cavalry in action, the rescue party appears.

> At that very moment he heard loud shouts from every direction—a drumming of hoofs and a beating of wings—a scream from the Witch—confusion all round him. And then he found he was being untied. Strong arms were round him and

he heard big, kind voices saying things like—'Let him lie down—give him some wine—drink this—steady now—you'll be all right in a minute.' Then he heard the voices of people who were talking not to him but to one another. And they were saying things like 'Who's got the Witch?' 'I thought you had her.' 'I didn't see her after I knocked the knife out of her hand—I was after the dwarf—do you mean to say she's escaped?' '—A chap can't mind everything at once—what's that? Oh, sorry, it's only an old stump!' But just at this point Edmund went off in a dead faint.[1]

The filmed version of this episode uses humor to provide a relief from the tension previously built. Melodramatic effect is again used in the film, although not so noticeably in the book, when Peter, Edmund, and the rest of Aslan's army fight against the crowd of wicked creatures and the Witch. The film shows the wild confusion of the battle, with the Witch using her magic to "zap" various animals and turn them to stone, and Edmund barely escaping death.

Often Lewis talks directly to the reader, rather than through the characters or as the omniscient author. For instance, as Mr. Beaver whispers, "They say Aslan is on the move—perhaps has already landed," the author speaks directly to the reader.

And now a very curious thing happened. None of the children knew who Aslan was any more than you do; but the moment the Beaver had spoken these words everyone felt quite different. Perhaps it has sometimes happened to you in a dream that someone says something which you don't understand but in the dream it feels as if it had some enormous meaning— either a terrifying one which turns the whole dream into a nightmare or else a lovely meaning too lovely to put into words, which makes the dream so beautiful that you remember it all your life and are always wishing you could get into that dream again. It was like that now. At the name of Aslan each one of the children felt something jump in its inside. Edmund felt a sensation of mysterious horror. Peter felt suddenly brave and adventurous. Susan felt as if some delicious smell or some

[1](New York: Macmillan, 1950), pp. 133-134.

delightful strain of music had just floated by her. And Lucy got the feeling you have when you wake up in the morning and realize that it is the beginning of the holidays or the beginning of summer (pp. 64-65).

By describing the ways in which the children sense the significance of the whispered statement, the author catches the reader up in the same mystical feelings the children experience.

The film uses this author's statement to the reader as a basis for extending the scene in which Mr. Beaver tells the children about Aslan. The emotional reactions of the children to his speech are a part of the visual presentation. The viewer is allowed to know the thoughts and feelings of the characters, sometimes conveyed with words and sometimes with facial expressions.

The same technique is used by Lewis in the episode where the children are having tea with the Beavers and discover that Edmund is missing. As the author moves from the story of one character to that of another he writes, "And now of course you want to know what happened to Edmund." In this direct statement he prepares the reader to become involved in Edmund's journey to join the White Witch, an extended passage that is very well done in the film. We see Edmund's facial expressions and his thoughts as he goes to the White Witch with the intent of betraying the other children and Aslan. The scene is built directly from Lewis's text, and much of Lewis's dialogue is reproduced.

The ending of the film follows the original story closely, and the final scene is one of golden triumph in which as trumpets play and crowds cheer the children are crowned Kings and Queens by Aslan. Quick shots of the children, ruling in great joy, show that they are maturing and growing older. Then, as they are riding to catch the White Stag, who can grant wishes, they discover a familiar looking lamppost that leads them back to the wardrobe and reality. Connell's skillful interpretation of this episode is a beautiful climax to a successful filmed version of a classic story for children.

Charlotte's Web:
Flaws in the Weaving

MARILYN APSELOFF

When the film adaptation of *Charlotte's Web*[1] first reached the public in 1973, audiences and critics for the most part greeted it with enthusiasm. Nevertheless, E. B. White himself did not particularly care for the screen adaptation written by Earl Hamner, Jr. and directed by Charles Nichols and Iwao Takamoto. Why not?

George Bluestone pointed out in his preface to *Novels into Film* (1957) that literature and film are "marked by such essentially different traits that they belong to separate artistic genera. . . . the novel is a linguistic medium, the film is essentially visual." The filmist, he notes later "becomes not a translator for an established author, but a new author in his own right." The result is that "on the screen there is inevitably more King Vidor and John Huston than Tolstoy and Melville." If such is the case, it is not surprising that E. B. White was disappointed with the filmed *Charlotte's Web*. White had had reservations about adaptations of his book from the time of its publication twenty-one years earlier, in 1952.

In *Letters of E. B. White,* collected and edited by Dorothy Lobrano Guth (Harper & Row, 1976), White reveals how *Charlotte's Web* originated, the changes he made while writing it, his concerns about the illustrations that were to accompany it, and his fears that possible film adaptations might not capture the true spirit and nature of the original. It was those fears and White's insistence upon having the right of approval that de-

---

[1] *Charlotte's Web* (New York: Dell, 1968). All references are to this edition.

layed the book's adaptation into film for more than two decades.

White's letters reveal that when he first wrote *Charlotte's Web* "the story did not contain Fern" (*Letters*, p. 648). He was ready to submit the manuscript to Harper's when he had second thoughts about it, felt that something was not right. "I set the thing aside, and then gradually rewrote the whole book— this time with the little girl. It was a lucky move on my part, a narrow squeak" (*Letters*, p. 469). Earlier, he had further explained,

> The idea of the writing in Charlotte's Web came to me one day when I was on my way down through the orchard carrying a pail of slops to my pig. I had made up my mind to write a children's book about animals, and I needed a way to save a pig's life, and I had been watching a large spider in the backhouse, and what with one thing and another, the idea came to me. (*Letters*, p. 375)

The spider he had been observing he had already named Charlotte. "I used to watch her at her weaving and at her trapping and I even managed to be present when she constructed her egg sac and deposited her eggs" (*Letters*, p. 633). In his barn White also had geese, sheep, a pig he had named Wilbur, an old rat, and spiders. Once he had the idea for his story, he read about and studied spiders for a year and then took another year to write the book. Still unsatisfied, he put it aside for a while, then rewrote it, which took another year; he would not rush his work.

Garth Williams was chosen to do the illustrations and the dust jacket. Concerned that Williams would not portray the animals and Charlotte properly, White specified, "the book must at all odds have a beguiling Charlotte" (*Letters*, p. 361). To be sure that Williams knew his subject thoroughly, White sent him a book on American spiders and a New York Public Library slip for another three-volume set on the subject. When White saw the illustrations for his book, he made suggestions for improvements which Garth Williams obligingly heeded. The results are immensely satisfying.

The novel begins with the spotlight on Fern Arable who, learning that her father is about to kill the runt of the pig litter, intervenes and is given the pig, whom she names Wilbur. In the second chapter the omniscient narrator gradually shifts his focus from Fern to Wilbur, preparing the reader for Wilbur's move to Zuckerman's barn. Here White is richly descriptive of the environment, not only of its physical features but also of the marvelous mixture of smells of manure, hay, the sweat of horses, the breath of cows, etc. White obviously loves to list objects: "ladders, grindstones, pitchforks, monkey wrenches, scythes, lawn mowers, snow shovels, ax handles, milk pails, water buckets, empty grain sacks, and rusty rat traps" (p. 14). Such lists occur elsewhere in the story (and in some of his letters) along with various descriptions, filling the reader visually and sensually.

Except for the episode at the Fair, Zuckerman's barn becomes the center of Wilbur's universe, with Fern appearing less frequently as Charlotte becomes Wilbur's best and loyal friend. It is she who saves Wilbur from the traditional fall butchering by writing words in her web ("Some Pig," "Terrific," "Radiant," "Humble"). Only Mrs. Zuckerman observes that "we have no ordinary *spider*" (p. 80); everyone else, believing the words in the web, thinks Wilbur is extraordinary. When Charlotte eventually dies alone at the deserted Fair, the reader's grief is assuaged by the knowledge that Wilbur has her egg sac. White also offers the reader the continuity of the changing seasons as life goes on until spring arrives once more in the barnyard and Charlotte's eggs hatch. There is another tense moment when the baby spiders take to the air leaving Wilbur devastated below, but all ends happily when Wilbur awakens to find that three of Charlotte's daughters have remained in the barn with him.

Like all prominent novelists, White was faced with repeated questions about the message of his book, and he gave the same response to all queries: "'Charlotte's Web' is a tale of the animals in my barn, not of the people in my life. . . . Any attempt to find allegorical meanings is bound to end disastrously, for no meanings are in there. I ought to know." (*Letters*, p. 373) Later, in a letter to Gene Deitch who was working on a film adaptation of the novel, White again commented, "there is no symbolism in 'Charlotte's Web.' And there is no political meaning in the story. It is a straight report from the barn cellar, which I dearly love." White goes on to note that while his book celebrates life, it is essentially amoral, because animals are essentially amoral. "I respect them, and I think this respect is implicit in the tale (*Letters*, p. 613)." White's emphasis is on the barn and the animals, on nature. The characterizations of the people, especially such adults as the Arables, the Zuckermans, and Lurvey, the hired hand, are not as finely drawn as those of the animals.

E. B. White was skeptical of and cautious about film versions of *Charlotte's Web*. After his book's publication in 1952, various people tried to get the rights to handle the adaptation, including Disney Studios. White wrote,

> My feeling about animals is just the opposite of Disney's. He made them dance to his tune and came up with some great creations, like Donald Duck. I preferred to dance to their tune and came up with Charlotte and Wilbur. (*Letters*, p. 614)

He was determined that an adaptation would not violate "the spirit and meaning of the story" (*Letters*, p. 649); therefore, he wished

> to have a look at the screenplay, see sketches of the principal characters, and hear the principal voices. . . . I want the chance to edit the script wherever anything turns up that is a gross departure or a gross violation. (*Letters*, p. 650)

Because of those stipulations, Hollywood turned down the offers made by John and Faith Hubley, who had the book under option.

> Just as soon as a Hollywood producer stumbles on the clause in the contract that gives the author the right of approval, he chucks up his dinner and abandons the deal. The standard procedure in the movies is to knock off the author with one clean blow, and then proceed with the picture. (*Letters*, p. 585)

He reiterated that attitude in a letter which was written about a television production of *Stuart Little* but applies equally to the attempts to film *Charlotte's Web*:

> It is the fixed purpose of television and motion pictures to scrap the author, sink him without a trace, on the theory that he is incompetent, has never read his own stuff, is not responsible for anything he ever wrote, and wouldn't know what to do about it even if he were. . . . the only way a TV person or a movie person can become a creator is to sink the guy who did it to begin with. (*Letters*, p. 540)

There were several attempts, in addition to Disney's, to get *Charlotte's Web* under contract. When an unanimated version by Arthur Zegart fell through, White proposed to Louis de Rochemont (who wanted to try an adaptation) that a live-action picture was possible with some intermingling of animation *if* the transitions were smooth. He also felt that "the key lies in narration—in particular, narration by Fern herself." Since Fern does relate some of the barn happenings to her parents in the book, White felt that she would be especially appropriate as the film narrator "speaking directly to the audience, using words from the book." His greatest fear was that Charlotte would be humanized; he believed that a filmmaker would "have . . . good results by sticking with nature and with the barn. . . . I saw a spider spin the egg sac described in the story, and I wouldn't trade the sight for all the animated chipmunks in filmland" (*Letters*, p. 482). In 1969, Les Davis asked about film possibilities. Later, the Sagittarius company proposals were accepted by White over those by Joel Katz and a contract was signed, but trouble developed with Gene Deitch, the director, and the enterprise was finally turned over to Hanna-Barbera Productions. *Charlotte's Web* had gone to Hollywood after all.

Many of White's fears came to pass. Although he was sent Earl Hamner, Jr.'s screenplay and made careful annotations, most of his suggestions were ignored. As William Kittredge and Steven M. Krauzer observe in their introduction to *Stories into Film* (1979): "The business of adapting literature into film becomes a process of translation from one kind of language into another; . . . the faithful translation is often a betrayal of the original."

When the translation takes liberties with the original, even more of a betrayal may result. In the film, for example, Henry Fussy's role is enlarged and a new character, his mother, is introduced. The resulting episodes detract from the story. As White stated, *Charlotte's Web* is not a boy-girl story, it is a study of miracles, tinged with the faint but pervasive odor of the barn. It will stand or fall on the barn. Henry Fussy can't save it" (*Letters,* p. 629). Furthermore, Charlotte *has* been humanized, as Colin L. Westerbeck observed in his review of the film for the March 23, 1973 issue of *Commonweal*: "If there is a deficiency in Charlotte's portrayal, it is that she looks a bit too much like Debbie Reynolds rather than that she sounds like her." White's desire to have "the storyteller say the words that announce the death of Charlotte" (*Letters,* p. 629) accompanied by Mozart's "Quartet in F Major" for oboe and strings also goes unfilfilled, for in the film version Charlotte dies while Wilbur is still with her at the Fair; this lessens the impact of her death. In addition, most of the dialogue relating to her death is omitted, so that much of the foreshadowing is lost.

The animated film opens at predawn with a panning óf the New England-type countryside as a general narrator tells about the miracles of springtime on a farm, the new births. As dawn comes up the camera moves to the Arable home and the pig family where the runt of the litter is squeezed out of the nursing. Then John Arable is introduced with the foreshadowing of the necessity to kill the runt. As Fern Arable carries eggs to the house, she passes her father holding an ax; then she learns from her mother what her father is planning to do with it, which is where White's book begins.

Although the opening scene in the book is more dramatic and emotional, revealing quickly the characterization of Fern, her parents, and her brother, Avery, the film version works well since it establishes setting, creates an idyllic mood— suddenly altered by the ax—and emphasizes White's hymn to nature and the barn.

However, the film quickly begins to add cartoon elements that detract from White's tone. For example, when Avery is introduced he is carrying a frog that jumps out onto the table and into the food—typical Saturday-morning cartoon fare; in the book, Avery carries an air rifle and a wooden dagger, and he disparages Fern's new pet. In the film when Wilbur is put outside to live, Fern gives him a blanket which, as White says, "is not in the spirit of *Charlotte's Web*" (*Letters*, p. 628). Wilbur's pen had plenty of straw in it in White's version, for he never treats Wilbur as anything but a pig who loves his slops and manure pile, a pig who burrows under straw, not under a blanket, to keep warm.

The Hollywood people could not resist giving the film added treatment to correspond to Henry Fussy's last name: they created his fussy mother and episodes for her and Henry, emphasizing the boy-girl relationship between Henry and Fern from the very beginning. The scene at Henry's house where Wilbur is running loose has taken the place of the escape at Zuckerman's farm in the book, again shifting the emphasis from Wilbur's pig-like characteristics to cartoon-like features. The film also draws considerable attention to Wilbur's ability to speak as the goose (well-voiced by Agnes Moorehead) tells him to try. When he succeeds, he bursts into song ("I Can talk") using words such as "articulate" which are uncharacteristic of Wilbur's simple vocabulary (Henry Gibson is Wilbur's voice, a good selection).

Some changes work very well. The "Loneliness" chapter has been moved forward, coming right after Wilbur is sent to Zuckerman's farm, which is very effective as Wilbur mourns his loss of Fern. Although there is no rain in the filmed episode, which would have helped to emphasize Wilbur's gloom, that omission does not seriously detract. Other changes are not for the better, especially turning Wilbur into a "fainter." The early fainting spells lessen the impact of the climax at the Fair instead of building up to it; such episodes are more in a cartoon style than in one that should be stressing animal characteristics. Another alteration goes against nature itself, for it is Wilbur who is made nearsighted instead of Charlotte. Later, when the goslings hatch, in the film one of them is a runt called

Jeffrey who wants to be like Wilbur, and a song follows ("We've Got Lots in Common Where It Really Counts"). This moralistic Wilbur-Jeffrey friendship weakens the bond between Charlotte and Wilbur, blurs the focus. It is not true to the nature of White's book.

As George Bluestone has noted, "changes are *inevitable* the moment one abandons the linguistic for the visual medium." The author and the audience can only hope that the changes will be suitable. Earl Hamner, Jr., has used much dialogue and narration from the "Talk at Home" chapter—although he has Mrs. Arable ask all of the questions—and the spirit of the original remains. White informs the reader through the goose's *thoughts* that Wilbur is being fattened for slaughter; in the film, Wilbur and the audience learn about his intended fate together, an acceptable change. Later, however, when Templeton's boasting about the egg that saved Charlotte's life is deleted in favor of his pleasant remarks to Charlotte that night, his characterization is distorted. In the novel, Templeton "starts out as a rat and he ends as a rat—the perfect opportunist and a great gourmand" (*Letters,* p. 613). He also does not end up with a wife and family in the novel. The omission of the "Dr. Dorian" chapter does not harm the film, although its inclusion would have reinforced White's emphasis on the miracles in nature to go along with Mrs. Zuckerman's earlier observation about the miracle of the words in the web and the spider who created it.

The directors/writers have added a scene in which Charlotte gets Templeton to go to the fence where a cat is skulking, quite out of character for Charlotte. The sheep, knowledgeable in the book (revealing Wilbur's fate to him and talking Templeton into getting words for the web), has his dialogue and characterization usurped by the goose, who is supposed to be empty-headed, a characteristic emphasized by her repetitive speech. Yet in the film, it is *she* who convinces Templeton to go to the Fair. The result is inconsistent characterization. Wilbur's reiteration of his need for Charlotte at the Fair is omitted, but a scene is added in which Wilbur tells her to release a bug she has just caught because he cannot stand to see her kill her food. Such an addition disrupts the narrative because Charlotte's eating habits had been carefully explained when they first got acquainted, and Wilbur should have accepted them by now.

The first fainting episode in the book has been omitted in the film, which had Wilbur fainting earlier and more frequently. At the Fair only the film Avery goes off to sample the Fair's delights while Fern stays behind with Wilbur until Henry Fussy shows up—this time without glasses and looking a little more filled out and tanned. Fern's colloquialism, "I'm mad with you," must have made E. B. White shudder when he heard it. Lacking in the film are the many references to Charlotte's tiredness and age, and when she sends Templeton out for a word, she does not foreshadow her death by tellng him that she will be writing in the web for the last time. Instead, the focus shifts to Templeton and to his gorging through the song "A Fair Is A Veritable Smorgasbord."

Much of White's narration and dialogue from "The Egg Sac" are used, although Charlotte's comment that she will never see her children is omitted (the filmmakers were obviously trying to de-emphasize her death as much as possible). There are no remarks by Templeton about pork, ham, and bacon when he discovers that Uncle, the pig in the next pen, has already won the blue ribbon, the hoped-for lifesaver for Wilbur. Although White had wanted the award scene at the Fair played "for all it's worth," he did not have in mind the band scenes or the song and dance routine that follows the announcer's speech. Because of the emphasis on Wilbur's earlier fainting spells, the climactic fainting scene in the book— with Templeton's biting Wilbur's tail to revive him and Avery's antics on stage—has been deleted, dampening the strong impact found in White's story. As White says, "The Blue Hill Fair . . . has become a Disney World, with 76 trombones" (*Letters,* p. 646).

There are a few more discrepancies before the film ends. Charlotte says that she will be staying behind at the Fair because she has no strength left to climb into the crate, yet she descends on her spinneret to talk to Wilbur before she dies. The following spring when her babies hatch, they leave immediately, contrary to their nature, instead of staying for several days and nights. When they do fly off in the film, those who remain are three little runts "too small to fly," a rather heavy-handed approach. Wilbur also asks the baby spiders if they are writers, too, and tells them to write about their mother in their webs; this lessens the miracle of Charlotte's ability to weave words. The film then ends with the narrator saying the last paragraph of the book.

What has been lost most in the film is the sensory richness of the book and the emphasis upon its spirit, "a paean to life, a hymn to the barn, and an acceptance of dung" (*Letters,* p. 614). The movie captures that spirit in part, but too often the cartoon tradition intrudes. Furthermore, although a substantial amount of White's dialogue and narration have been used in the screenplay, his love of lists and his skill as a wordsmith are sorely missed. White's story was one of "friendship, life, death, salvation" (*Letters,* p. 645). Such serious matters can be treated with humor as White does successfully in his book because he keeps the barnyard sharply in focus. "I discovered that there was no need to tamper in any way with the habits and charac-teristics of spiders, pigs, geese, and rats. No 'motivation' is needed if you remain true to life and to the spirit of fantasy" (*Letters,* p. 613).

White did feel that *Charlotte's Web* could be made into a successful musical: "Which can be done by music of the right kind" (*Letters,* p. 613). Many of the songs written by Richard and Robert Sherman are catchy and lively but do not accu-rately portray characters. White wrote of Wilbur's "I Can Talk" song: "I regard this song as not only out of key with this story but embarrassingly suggestive of Rex Harrison. . . . If a song is needed in this spot, it should be Fern's song: she sings, very quietly, 'I can hear him. He speaks'" (*Letters,* p. 633). The most memorable tune for children from the film is undoubt-edly Templeton's at the Fair during his gluttonous orgy, vis-ually accompanied by his overindulgence; the song encom-passes much of White's dialogue. The late Paul Lynde voiced Templeton, obviously relishing the part. White's favorite song is the haunting one sung by Charlotte, "Mother Earth and Father Time": "It stayed with me and seemed on the right track and in the right spirit" (*Letters,* p. 634). Interestingly, the Mozart quartet referred to earlier and the one lullaby that White himself wrote—"Deep in the Dung and the Dark"—were not included in the film.

Andrew Horton and Joan Magretta, in their Introduction to *Modern European Filmmakers and the Art of Adaptation* (1981), have argued that "adaptation can be a lively and creative art, and that attention to this art will enhance our understanding of film." They believe that "the study of adaptation is clearly a form of source study and thus should trace the *genesis* (not the destruction) of works deemed worthy of close examination in and of themselves." If one accepts that approach, the film *Charlotte's Web* can stand on its own as an entertaining, rather skillfully animated musical for children and adults, well voiced, with distinctive characters and some memorable songs and visual effects. It is when the adaptation is compared with the book and the book's *intent* that its divergence from White's work is realized.

Survival Tale
and Feminist Parable

ELLEN E. SEITER

Scott O'Dell's *Island of the Blue Dolphins* (1960)[1] is a survival tale, an animal story, and a feminist parable. It is the account of a girl's passage into adulthood and her achievement of a rare maturity and wisdom. The author based this children's novel on an historical figure, "The Lost Woman of San Nicolas," who was left behind by her tribe on an island off the coast of Santa Barbara and lived alone there between 1835 and 1853. The heroine, Karana, narrates this simple, Robinson Crusoe-like tale of her adjustment to a solitary existence on the island. The story is episodic in structure and takes on the quality of a diary: full of the details of her day-to-day survival, her frustrations and loneliness, her triumphs and joys. The immediacy and poignancy of the account make *Island of the Blue Dolphins* a compelling book for readers of all ages. Though the film version, directed by James B. Clark for Universal in 1964, suffers from the limitations of translating into film a novel whose interest lies primarily in its strongly subjective point of view, and from the poverty of the film's images compared to O'Dell's descriptions, it is nevertheless an important children's film thanks to its sensitive treatment of the relationship of people to the environment, the struggle for life amid the ever-present danger of death, and the singular experiences of a capable, sagacious young woman.

In presenting challenges to the human will and spirit, survival tales have enormous appeal. They speak to the fantasy of

---

[1](Boston: Houghton Mifflin, 1960). All references are to this edition.

living in a state of complete independence, alone with nature and free of all social responsibilities. For children, this fantasy is particularly powerful because of the dependent and subordinant nature of children's relationships to parents and teachers. The presence in children's literature of so many juvenile protagonists who are orphans contributes to this mythology of facing the world alone. In *Island of the Blue Dolphins,* Karana experiences none of the social constraints children face at home and at school. She is entirely self-sufficient and free of supervision. The price which she pays for her independence is loneliness and the threat of physical danger, and this provides the compensatory aspect of the fantasy. Few of us would be able to survive physically and emotionally under such circumstances and this gives a strong element of anxiety to our interest in survival tales as well.

Abandoned on the island and threatened by a pack of wild dogs who have killed her brother, Karana must immediately confront a series of problems: finding and building a shelter, gathering and preparing her food, and defending herself from attack by the wild dogs. In the film we see Karana making a bow and arrow, then, in a series of short shots, practicing with it until she can shoot with strength and accuracy. She is also shown building a shelter with whale bones, teaching herself to use the canoe, fishing and gathering food. Karana's routine of subsistence activities is established early in the film—shots of Karana going to or returning from her fishing trips in the canoe bracket most of the film's scenes of narrative action. The actress, Celia Kaye, has a strong, graceful body and the long shots of her walking around the island have considerable charm.

The book, of course, presents Karana's activities in much greater detail and conveys a great deal of practical information about survival skills. Every challenge which Karana encounters is described as a problem to be solved. The heroine discusses her needs and each potential alternative for meeting them. Every step in the survival process is logically thought through; each success or failure is carefully evaluated. These passages in the book convey Karana's intelligence and the strength of her will. One of her most striking characteristics is her continual ability to plan ahead. In her moments of despair, she invents another project to occupy her days and test her skills: hunting a sea elephant, capturing a devilfish, sewing clothes of otter skin or cormorant feathers.

As a story of emotional survival, *Island of the Blue Dolphins* is unusual because Karana's isolation is never depicted pathetically. The character describes her loneliness and the process of mourning candidly and without self-pity. At the beginning of the story, Karana's father, chief of the tribe, and most of the men on the island are killed wantonly by a group of Russian traders who have come to the island for otter pelts. In the book, Karana describes the grief of her people:

> . . . more than the burdens which had fallen upon us all, it was the memory of those who had gone that burdened our hearts. After food had been stored in autumn and the baskets full in every house, there was more time to think about them, so that a sort of a sickness came over the village and people sat and did not speak, nor even laughed (p. 28).

Such a frank and unsentimental treatment of depression is rare in children's fiction. The book also treats her feelings of anger and vengeance in response to the death of loved ones. When Karana's brother is killed by the wild dogs, she vows revenge. Planning a way to kill the dogs preoccupies her during her first days alone on the island, forcing her to take action rather than mourn passively.

A turning point in Karana's emotional adjustment to her solitude occurs when she attempts to escape from the island by canoe—a part of the narrative which does not appear in the film adaptation. She explains her motivation for taking such a risk:

> . . . whatever might befall me on the endless waters did not trouble me. It meant far less than the thought of staying on the island alone, without home or companions, pursued by wild dogs, where everything reminded me of those who were dead and those who had gone away (p. 61).

After three days on the ocean, the canoe begins to leak dangerously and Karana, exhausted and heavyhearted, decides she must turn back. The following morning, she realizes that she has achieved on the journey a new acceptance of her situation:

> I felt as if I had been gone a long time as I stood there looking down from the high rock. I was happy to be home. Everything I saw—the otters playing in the kelp, the rings of foam around the rocks that guarded the harbor, the gulls flying, the tides moving past the sandspit—filled me with happiness (p. 69).

Reconciled to life on the island, she begins building her new home. Her love for and appreciation of nature make her life a joyful one. While Karana misses her family and her people, living alone is not a tragedy for her.

In the film adaptation of *Island of the Blue Dolphins,* Karana's solitude is treated more conventionally and sentimentally. The film character seems younger and less mature than the narrative voice in the book. The actress does not age during the course of the film; she appears to be permanently fourteen years old. She cries often, and Celia Kaye's recitation of lines frequently verges on whining. When she finally succeeds in wounding the wild dog who killed her brother, Karana runs in a frenzy down to the beach, vainly tries to push the canoe in the water and then bursts into tears. Later in the film when the same dog, Rontu, whom she has now befriended, leaves her to return to the pack, she reacts bitterly. After repeatedly calling the dog and begging him to return, she says aloud, "All right, go with them. You stay with them! You dare come back now and I will throw stones at you. I don't need anybody." The immaturity of this outburst stands in striking contrast to the even temperament of the book's character.

Toward the end of the film, Karana makes friends with Tutok, a young woman in the service of the fur traders, who have temporarily returned to the island. When the time comes for Tutok to leave, Karana begs her to stay and cries pitifully after their good-bye scene. When the dog Rontu dies in the film, Karana falls sobbing over his body. Author Scott O'Dell, however, treats the dog's death matter-of-factly:

> I buried him on the headland, digging for two days from dawn until the going down of the sun, and put him there with some

sand flowers and a stick he liked to chase when I threw it, and covered him with pebbles of many colors that I gathered on the shore (p. 160).

In the film we see Karana standing at the grave; the emphasis is on her emotional reaction. It is the same place where her brother, Ramo, is buried, and she says aloud by way of eulogy: "If you had known him, Ramo, you would have loved him, too."

The film version of *Island of the Blue Dolphins* is a more straightforward animal story than the book. Karana's relationship to Rontu is the main narrative interest in the film; it takes up only a fraction of the book's plot. As a strategy for adaptation this is understandable because it allows the interaction of two figures in the shot-reverse shot construction which is conventionally so central to narrative film. The relationship between the girl and the dog also provides the basis for the film's only moments of comic relief. Rontu, played by a golden retriever with a strong resemblance to Old Yeller, turns in the most entertaining performance in the film. The camera favors the dog in most sequences; Rontu seems to get more and closer close-ups than the humans.

The animal story in O'Dell's *Island of the Blue Dolphins* is more than just an account of the companionship between a child and a dog, however. The relationship of Karana to Rontu functions as a metaphor for the human capacity to accept, appreciate and live in harmony with nature. When the wild dogs kill Karana's younger brother, she develops a fierce hatred for them and promises to kill them. She succeeds in injuring the leader (Rontu) with her bow and arrow. When she discovers the dog later, wounded and near death, she inexplicably begins to help him. At considerable risk, she approaches the dog, removes the arrow, treats the wound with herbs, leaves food and water for the dog and finally takes him into her home. In the beginning the two are extremely wary of each other, but they gradually develop a strong bond of trust and affection. Karana learns through her relationship with Rontu to appreciate the fellowship animals can provide, and she comes to realize the senselessness of violence against them. When Karana forgives Rontu and nurses him back to health, she begins to live more harmoniously with her whole environment.

In the course of the film, she befriends not only Rontu but also Rontu's puppy, a pair of birds and a young otter. Rontu is the only animal we see Karana hunt in the film. In the book, however, Karana initially has no qualms about killing animals and hunts many of them. Eventually, her relationships with animals bring her to the decision never to kill any kind of animal again. She comments on how strange this resolution would seem to her family:

> Yet this is the way I felt about the animals who had become my friends and those who were not, but in time would be. If . . . all the others had come back and laughed, still I would have felt the same way for animals and birds are like people, too, though they do not talk the same or do the same things. Without them the earth would be an unhappy place (p. 156).

The reasoning behind her decision is compelling in its simplicity and its compassion. Karana's respect for nature gives *Island of the Blue Dolphins* a powerful ecological message.

The most unique aspect of *Island of the Blue Dolphins* is its strength as a kind of feminist parable. The novel's diary-like quality is significant since diaries have traditionally been one of the primary forms for women's self-expression. As a courageous, capable and stalwart character, Karana offers an exceptionally positive role model for girls. A new range of possibilities open up to Karana when she is left alone on the island. Existing outside of traditional social and familial roles, her ego, identity and world view develop in an unusually individual way. Ramo's death has left her in solitude but it has also freed her from the duty of her maternalistic, big sister role.

In both the book and the film the change in Karana's character after her little brother's death are obvious. In the beginning, Karana is more subdued and restricted. She always has Ramo with her, and is constantly busy taking care of him or worrying about him. Her feeling of responsibility for Ramo is epitomized when, having sailed away from the island with her people, she realizes that Ramo has been left behind, dives into the water, and swims back to the island. Karana's isolation is also her liberation, allowing her to create her own world, concentrate on herself, and discover the power of her own self-reliance.

Karana re-creates her environment on the island and adapts the culture she has learned as a child to suit her own purposes. She burns the circle of huts which constitute the village she was reared in and builds her own home high on the rocks, from which she has a view of the entire island. When Karana meets each of her animal friends the first thing she does is name them. The process of naming takes on great significance for her; it is her way of understanding and claiming the world around her. In the novel, she describes her first night in the place she has chosen for her home: "The stars were bright overhead and I lay and counted the ones that I knew and gave names to the many that I did not know." She carefully chooses the names for her dogs, birds and otter. When she tells Tutok, the girl working for the traders, her secret name, it is her greatest token of friendship. Inventing language and naming things in the physical world are Karana's means of creating her own culture.

Island of the Blue Dolphins has an explicitly feminist message about restrictions on female activity. Karana faces a serious problem in reconciling her cultural heritage with her immediate needs on the island: it is traditionally forbidden for women to make or use weapons. The taboo is established early in the film (a scene which does not exist in the book). Sitting with her father and Ramo while they are making spears, Karana instinctively reaches over to help Ramo. Her father stops her and scolds her harshly for this, explaining she must never touch weapons. In the book, Karana discusses her fear of breaking the taboo; she has been repeatedly told that weapons will always fail in the hands of women at the crucial moment. Recognizing the necessity of weapons, Karana does not let the taboo intimidate her. In making the spears and the bow and arrow, she must remember what she has observed but never been taught. Karana takes over such "man's work" easily and naturally. Having mastered these skills, she has the wisdom to avoid anything which she sees as harmful to the environment or an unnecessary waste of life. The book offers a rare vision of feminine understanding and love of nature. Its theme is very different from the man *against* nature motif found so often in literature. Instead, we are shown a woman in peaceful, harmonious coexistence with the environment. Karana feels no need to "conquer" the environment.

Karana's physical strength is underplayed in the film, which tends to rely on more conventional and more sexist representations. When swimming back to the island to join Ramo, Karana is shown in a series of shots gasping and weakly stroking the water as though she is nearly drowning. In the book the same incident is described this way: "I could barely see the two rocks that guarded the entrance to Coral Cove, but I was not fearful. Many times I had swum farther than this, although not in a storm." The film turns a scene in which Karana sprains her leg while hunting into an accident in which she simply drops the canoe on her foot. Trapped under the canoe and approached by the pack of wild dogs, she is at the last minute rescued by Rontu. This scene owes more to Lassie and Rin Tin Tin stories than it does to the spirit of the novel. In the comparable scene in the book, the pack of dogs attacks Rontu, and Karana stands by, ready to intervene with her bow and arrow to save the dog.

Adapting *Island of the Blue Dolphins* to film must have been a difficult task. The screen has no devices other than voice-over for conveying the interior first-person narration, and since this technique is not used here, Karana is left talking aloud to herself or the animals. The language of the novel is spare and formal; the simplicity of its style is perfectly suited to the episodic story. The film translates this into visual simplicity—compositions and camera angles are unobtrusive to a tedious degree. The film is shot almost entirely in long shot, with symmetrical compositions taken from eye level or overhead camera positions. The photography suggests the assumption on the part of the film's makers that children cannot or would not appreciate striking or visually complex imagery—a common error among children's filmmakers. The physical distance of the camera from the actress throughout the film and the tendency to shoot her from high angles breaks our identification with her and diminishes her character. The film does nothing to replicate the sense of intimacy with Karana developed in the book. It also fails to suggest cinematically the island's potentially spectacular landscape, and this fault is aggravated by the color fading of the print. Reading the novel, one imagines a visually richer world than what we actually see in the film—shot on location in California. The movie viewer always has the sense of being on a shore, not an island. The costumes and sets fail to add any sense of historical realism. Though the film opens with a title announcing the time to be around 1800, Karana and her world have a distinctly modern look.

However, the film version of *Island of the Blue Dolphins* does have some powerful moments. The killing of Karana's tribesmen by the fur traders is more shocking on the screen than in the book. The opening sequences are unusual for a children's film in their portrayal of the exploitation of the Native Americans by the white traders. At the end of the film, Karana walks down the cliff at sunset to meet the missionary priest and the men who have finally come to rescue her. The final shot shows Karana walking in silhouette toward the water. She is dressed in her cape of cormorant feathers, carries her bird cage in hand, and walks with her dog at her side. The image conveys a sense of a world lost as much as the narrative resolution accomplished by Karana's rescue.

The Bittersweet Journey
from *Charlie* to *Willy Wonka*

RICHARD D. SEITER

Published in 1964, Roald Dahl's *Charlie and the Chocolate Factory* has remained one of the most widely read children's fantasies, and its immense popularity inspired Paramount Pictures to produce a musical film version. Dahl wrote his own screenplay, and in interpreting his story for a visual medium took the opportunity to revise and refine the original narrative to meet earlier critical objections.

Both book and film depend heavily on the excitement generated by the search for five golden tickets hidden under the wrappers of five Wonka candy bars scattered among the millions dispersed in the world. These tickets admit five children to a tour through the chocolate factory conducted by Mr. Willy Wonka, its wacky owner. Wonka cuts a dashing figure with his "plum-colored tail coat, bottle-green trousers, gold-topped cane and twinkling eyes." His eccentric dress matches his behavior, which borders on insanity and includes a sadistic sense of humor that makes his eyes twinkle when the children in his charge run into difficulties. Because his irrational presence dominates the fantasy, his name was used in the film title: *Willy Wonka and the Chocolate Factory* (1971). Gene Wilder's portrayal of Wonka commands the film viewer's attention and catches the dazzling and deranged spirit of this character as his gold-topped cane cuts and whistles through the air, narrowly missing those children who try to precede him through the factory.

The tour is immensely significant because many years before Wonka temporarily shut down his factory when he discovered that spies in his work force were stealing his recipes and passing them on to competitors named Slugworth, Prodnose, and Fickelgruber. (These caricature tag names reveal Dahl's fondness for a technique made famous by novelist Charles Dickens.) When the factory reopened no workers were rehired from the outside world, and how Wonka was running the factory became "one of the great mysteries of the chocolate making world." The search for an explanation adds suspense and sustains the narrative pace in both book and movie.

The descriptions of the factory rooms resemble those of fantasy palaces and enchanted castles found in many magical folktales. A chocolate river flows through the huge chocolate room and a chocolate falls makes it "light and frothy." The grass at the edge of the chocolate river is a "new kind of soft minty sugar" dotted with edible buttercups. However, what should be a delightful outing becomes a survival course for the five children as they discover the hazards of this confectionary world.

Four of them are spoiled greedy brats who fall into dilemmas because they will not heed Wonka's warnings. Augustus Gloop, an obese child, tries drinking the chocolate river, falls in, and becomes stuck in one of the glass tubes that directs the chocolate to other factory rooms. Veruca Salt, a spoiled child who is given everything she wants, tries to grab one of the one hundred squirrels shelling nuts for the Wonka Nutty Crunch Surprise Bar. The squirrels grab her instead, tap her on the head, determine she is a bad nut and dispatch her down the garbage chute. Violet Beauregarde, an incessant gum chewer, pops a piece of experimental gum into her mouth and discovers that it actually tastes like a three-course dinner. As she chews through the blueberry pie dessert flavor, she comes to resemble a ripe blueberry and is rolled off to the juicing room. Mike Teavee, a television addict, insists on being transmitted by Wonka's invention called Television Chocolate and is turned into a Tom Thumb miniature as he steps out of the television screen.

It is the bitter misadventures of the four spoiled kids that give the episodic plot its momentum and unfortunately play to the reader's sadistic nature; these kids can justifiably be punished since they are ill-mannered and greedy. The fifth child, Charlie Bucket, kind, quiet, obedient, and *passive*, is described in the original text as the hero. He is given the chocolate factory at the end of the book because he is good and does not disobey Wonka's instructions. These one-dimensional characters are similar to folktale characters; they are rewarded and punished according to the strict moral outlook found in the traditional world of the cautionary folktale.

Essentially the movie retains the obnoxious traits in these children by graphically portraying their misadventures. Since the film is live action, live geese laying chocolate eggs replace the squirrels in the Veruca Salt sequence. There is appreciably no difference in being judged a "bad egg" instead of a "bad nut" and Veruca is dispatched with equal speed down the garbage chute. This substitution does not disturb the continuity of the plot and if anything alligns the narrative more closely to the folk-fairytale world, since a magical goose laying special eggs is a familiar folk motif.

Dahl's most extensive revision of a child character for the filmscript comes in the added temptation scenes involving Charlie and his Grampa Joe, who accompanies Charlie on the tour. To get this added depth in Charlie, Dahl borrows from his original fantasy the tag name of Slugworth, the candy competitor, and develops a minor character who in the film works under this disguise for Wonka and tests the honesty of each child who finds a golden ticket. Every time this shadowy character appears, he whispers a message that the movie audience does not hear. This aids in sustaining suspense and mystery, and at the end of the film Wonka divulges that this message has been a bribe. Each child is promised riches if he or she will smuggle from the factory an unreleased Wonka candy, so the other candy competitors can get the jump on the market.

As it happens, the four obnoxious brats have no chance to smuggle out any candy because they become stuck in their own dilemmas long before the end of the tour. Charlie becomes the sole remaining child and he does have a newly created everlasting gobbstopper hard-ball candy—given him earlier by Wonka—tucked in his pocket. In a climactic scene, an enraged, omniscient Wonka has just informed Charlie (Peter Ostrum) and Grandpa Joe (delightfully played by Jack Albertson) that he knows they have disobeyed him by sampling the fizzy lifting drinks. This sampling nearly cost Charlie and Grandpa their lives as the carbonated gas lifts them off the factory floor and draws them toward the whirling blades of an exhaust fan. Fortunately they remember Wonka's remedy for gas—"a great big rude burp, and *up* comes the gas and *down* goes you." Wonka abruptly dismisses them for this transgression, and if Charlie were a spiteful kid he could have easily walked out of the factory with the gobbstopper. Instead he places the candy on Wonka's desk and prepares to leave; instantly Wonka rejoices and embraces Charlie exclaiming he has passed the test by proving his honesty. He is given the candy factory as his reward.

In the book Charlie is rewarded for his obedience and passiveness; in the movie Charlie *proves* his worth by action: though he is shown to be a typical kid, capable of mischief and burping his way out of it, he returns the gobbstopper. Peter Ostrum gives to this role the "all boy" dimension that Dahl adds in the screenplay. In the film Charlie becomes a more complex and interesting character.

The most obvious change in film characterization came from pressure applied by the critics on the original text. The great mystery of the new factory workers is solved when Wonka introduces the Oompa-Loompas, described in the original text as pygmies from Africa. Critics sensed racism in Wonka's patronizing attitude toward the Oompas, especially since the Oompas' freedom is restricted and they are paid in cacao beans supplied by the boss—a proceeding which smacks of the company store. Although Wonka states he rescued the Oompas-Loompas from a starvation diet of caterpillars and from certain death from large jungle beasts, he willfully uses the Oompas as experimental subjects for his new sugary concoctions, "sometimes with unfortunate effects." (See Lois Bouchard, "A New Look at Old Favorites: Charlie and the Chocolate Factory" in *The Black American in Books for Children: Readings in Racism* (1972.) In the film the Oompas are changed into fantasy creatures with green faces, red hair, and rotund dwarflike bodies reminicent of John Tenniel's Tweedledum and Tweedledee. When Dahl revised his book in 1973 the new and more realistic Oompas became little white-faced men with long hair and flowing beards from Loompaland. Joseph Schindleman, the illustrator, revised his pen and ink sketches for this edition so the new Oompas look like diminutive hippies.

The Oompas-Loompas' function as group commentators is retained in both book and movie. Like the chorus in Greek tragedy, the Oompas comment through rhymed chants (in the book) and songs (in the movie) after each spoiled child falls into difficulty; however, the tone in the chants is more caustic than the songs. Rhymed name calling is used consistently in the chants: Augustus Gloop is called a "nincompoop" and Violet Beauregard is labeled "a little bum" because she chews "gum." Veruca Salt is called a little "brute" which rhymes with her fate of falling down "the garbage chute." After Mike Teavee is shrunk through Wonka-vision, these chants climax when the Oompas surrealistically describe the typical contemporary child as obsessed with television.

In almost every house we've been,
We've watched them gaping at the screen.
They loll and slop and lounge about,
And stare until their eyes pop out
They sit and stare and stare and sit
Until they're hypnotised by it [television]
It rots the senses in the head
It kills imagination dead
His brain becomes as soft as cheeze
His powers of thinking rust and freeze
He cannot think—he only sees.[1]

This mindless generation of children is not far from the apparitions found in Huxley's *Brave New World* and Orwell's *1984*.

In the film, the lyrics sung by the Oompa-Loompas are not as dark and threatening, and their content emphasizes the cause for this mindless, gluttonous, spoiled, gum chewing, TV-addicted generation. The blame is placed on parents who neglect to set limits for their offspring. The Oompas' song

[1]*Charlie and the Chocolate Factory* (New York: Knopf, 1964), pp. 145-146.

about Veruca Salt's tantrums pinpoints the source of the problem.

> Who spoiled her, then? Ah, who indeed?
> Who pandered to her every need?
> They are (and this is very sad)
> Her loving parents, MUM and DAD.

Dahl expands this view of the adult world in the film through added visual sequences (or sidebar incidents), which capture and gently satirize the mindless preoccupations of the general public. These scenes come early as the public catches chocolate fever after learning of the golden tickets through a hyped press. Newspapers carry huge headlines when a new ticket is found. As the number of tickets dwindle, schools are closed and even the cranky headmaster Turketine dismisses classes. Even heads of state succumb to chocolate fever in two juxtaposed scenes: in one a van loaded with Wonka bars turns into the White House driveway; the next scene switches to an exclusive London auction house where the last case of Wonka bars has been sold for 5,000 pounds. As the auctioneer brings down the gavel and looks up to the buyer, he bows deeply and says, "Thank you, Your Majesty." Similar zaniness coupled with upbeat songs like "The Candy Man" sprinkled throughout the soundtrack, replace the bitter aftertaste that lingers after reading the original fantasy with a lighter more palatable tone.

Fleming's Flying Flivver Flops on Film

MARK WEST

Early in the nineteenth century many authors, critics, and parents felt that if children were exposed to fairy tales and other forms of nonrealistic literature, they would become incapable of accepting or even of perceiving reality. Gradually these prejudices against the fantasy genre eased, and by the second half of the century an ever increasing number of adults had decided that certain sorts of fantastic literature did not harm or confuse childhood values. However, though approval was generally given to fanciful children's literature in which the fantastic elements were confined to a secondary world, many adults still frowned upon juvenile authors prone to interject otherworldly components into otherwise realistic settings.

Although there is no longer strong adult objection to children's books in which the line between fantasy and reality is not clearly drawn, this literary genre still engenders discomfort in some parents and critics. This uneasiness surfaced when Ian Fleming's only children's book, *Chitty Chitty Bang Bang* appeared in 1964. The novel about the adventures of the magical car immortalized in the title received overwhelmingly positive reviews; but even in their praise some critics expressed once familiar reservations about Fleming's use of fantasy. Rex Stout, for example, in reviewing the novel for the November 1, 1964, *New York Times Book Review*, commented, "If I understand children at all, . . . my guess is that four out of five of them would love this book. The danger is that many of them might love it too much; they might want to trade in their family car for one like Chitty Chitty Bang Bang, the magical car."

197

Such remarks were apparently well heeded by the makers of the 1968 musical film adaptation. Producer Albert Broccoli, and director Ken Hughes, who along with novelist Roald Dahl (*Charlie and the Chocolate Factory*) coauthored the screenplay, seemed intent upon sidestepping the controversy surrounding Fleming's blend of fantasy and reality by confining the fantastic elements to a clearly defined secondary world. In so doing, however, the filmmakers considerably altered both the plot and the tone of Fleming's original story.

Fleming sets his tale in the England of the early 1960s. Here the readers become involved in the antics of Commander Caractacus Pott, a retired officer of the Royal Navy turned rather eccentric inventer, his wife, Mimsie, and their eight-year-old highly adventurous twins, Jeremy and Jemima. At the beginning of the book Commander Pott invents a candy that makes a whistling sound when eaten. The newly invented confection strikes the sweet tooth of Lord Skrumshus, the owner of a large candy factory, who pays handsomely for the manufacturing rights. With the transaction complete, the Pott family finally has enough money to buy their first automobile. They end up purchasing a rusty, 1920s vintage racing car. Commander Pott spends the whole summer repairing the vehicle and in August it is ready for its first drive. The family christens the machine "Chitty Chitty Bang Bang" because of the sound its engine makes. An initial excursion is decided upon and next day the Potts head for the beach to have a picnic. Caught in a massive traffic jam, they fear they will never make it to the beach. Suddenly a knob on the dashboard illuminates with instructions for Commander Pott to pull it. When he does so the auto magically sprouts wings and, to the amazement and delight of all, flies the family to a stretch of uncrowded seashore.

Screenwriters Hughes and Dahl have taken extreme liberties with the adaption of this initial sequence. While the story is again set in England, the film's time frame has been moved back to around 1910. In the 1968 United Artists release Caractacus Pott (Dick Van Dyke) is a widower. Jeremy (Adrian Hall) and Jemima (Heather Ripley) generally take care of themselves while their father works on his inventions. The movie introduces Caractacus Pott's father, Grandpa Pott (Lionel Jeffries), who lives with the family.

The opening shots are of Jeremy and Jemima learning that the local junkman plans to sell a wrecked racing car in which the children often play. Unable to bear the thought of being without it, they decide to ask their father to purchase the auto before the other buyer takes it away. On the way home, the children are nearly run over by a young woman named Truly Scrumptious (Sally Ann Howes), who drives them home, and after meeting Caractacus and observing his Rube Goldberg-like inventions, attempts to convince him to send his children to school more regularly. An argument ensues and Truly departs in a huff. When the children ask their father to purchase the automobile they are told he cannot afford to. His attempt to raise enough money to purchase the vehicle, through the sale of his musical candy to Lord Scrumptious (James R. Justice), coincidentally Truly's father, is in the screen version, unsuccessful. The filmmakers relegate Caractacus to dancing in a carnival act (a more visually stimulating alternative) to earn the purchase money. Once he repairs the machine, he decides to take his children to the beach for the picnic and along the way they encounter Truly, who joins the outing. After playing on the beach for several hours the children ask their father to tell them a story.

In the novel, the Potts take an afternoon nap after their picnic, and while they are sleeping the tide rises; they awaken to find themselves surrounded by water. Running to the already partially submerged auto, they start its engine, but are unable to escape to safety. Fortunately, another knob lights up, and when turned it converts the car into a hovercraft. The vehicle skims across the English Channel and ends up in France on a desolate beach boardered by cliffs. Driving Chitty into a large cave, they discover a huge vault used by a notorious criminal, Joe the Monster, to store his guns and explosives. After blowing up the weapons, the Potts drive off, but they are overtaken by Joe the Monster and his cohorts. The criminals are about to attack the captives when the Commander pulls the knob that releases Chitty's wings, and the family soars away amidst a hail of gunfire.

The film makes a complete break with Ian Fleming's plot structure after the picnic sequence. Caractacus begins to tell the children the story which in turn becomes the focus of the rest of the movie. In this version, Chitty Chitty Bang Bang is endowed with magical properties. Baron Bomburst (portrayed by the suitably menacing Gert Frobe, no stranger to Fleming films), the maniacal leader of the mythical land of Vulgaria, has heard of the car, and he wants it for himself. He sends his henchmen to capture the car or its inventor, but unable to find Chitty Chitty Bang Bang, they abduct Grandpa Pott, whom they mistake for Caractacus. Grandpa is transported in the Baron's Zeppelin to the baronial castle high in the mountains of Vulgaria. The Baron greets Grandpa as Caractacus and commands him to build a duplicate of the magic automobile. Meanwhile, Caractacus, Truly Scrumptious, and the twins fly to Vulgaria aboard Chitty, which they hide before setting out to rescue Grandpa Pott. The Baron's toymaker (Benny Hill) gives them shelter and warns them that Baroness Bomburst (Anna Quayle) has outlawed children. Soon Vulgaria's child catcher (Robert Helpmann) shows up, but he is fooled by the fact that the children have been disguised as toys. Once he leaves, the search for Grandpa Pott is resumed by Caractacus, Truly and the toymaker. Jemima and Jeremy are cautioned to remain in the safety of the toyshop.

In the Fleming original, the Pott family decides to spend the night in a quiet French hotel after making their daring escape from Joe the Monster. While they are sleeping, Joe the Monster discovers their whereabouts, and with the help of his cronies, he kidnaps Jeremy and Jemima. Fortunately, Chitty Chitty Bang Bang realizes what is happening, and using a miniature radar screen hidden in its hood it homes in on the hideout where the gangsters have taken the children. In the morning, Chitty sounds its horn and wakes Commander Pott and Mimsie who, becoming aware of the kidnapping, jump into the car and set out to rescue Jeremy and Jemima. The miniature radar screen points out the way by swiveling either left or right to indicate a turn. Meanwhile, the children are being held captive in a deserted Paris warehouse. Joe the Monster wants them to aid in his holdup of Le Bon-Bon, a famous Parisian candy shop, but the twins succeed in warning Monsieur Bon-Bon, who locks his store and calls the gendarmes before Joe and his thugs can carry out their scheme. Chitty Chitty Bang Bang arrives on the scene and crashes into the Monster's getaway car. The gendarmes show up and arrest the thieves, a number of French mechanics repair Chitty, and after spending a day with Monsieur Bon-Bon and his family, the Potts pile into their magical machine and soar away in search of new adventures.

Not a bit of this scenario appears in United Artists' cinematic adaptation of the same name!

In the film version, the child catcher returns to the toyshop while the children are alone and lures them into his wagon with promises of candy and ice cream. He then locks them in a cell in the Baron's Vulgarian castle. There is a crosscut to the Baron's soldiers finding Chitty Chitty Bang Bang, taking it to the castle, and presenting it to the Baron. Grandpa Pott is commanded to take the Baroness and Baron for a flight in the machine, but he is unable to make the car take off. Cutting back to the toyshop, the filmmakers show Caractacus, the toymaker and Truly returning to discover that the twins are missing, and they immediately begin making rescue plans. The toymaker leads them to an underground cavern, in which they find all of the children of Vulgaria, who have for years been waiting for liberation. These children agree to help overthrow Baron Bomburst and rescue Jeremy, Jemima and Grandpa Pott. The next day as Baron Bomburst celebrates his birthday, Caractacus and Truly attend the royal party disguised as mechanical dolls. While Caractacus and Truly are dancing for the Baron's entertainment—another convenient vehicle for the interjection of a musical number—hundreds of children sneak into the ballroom and trap the Baron and his followers. The people of Vulgaria join in the rebellion, the Baron and Baroness are overthrown, Caractacus and Truly find Jeremy, Jemima and Grandpa, and all our heroes climb into Chitty Chitty Bang Bang and fly home.

The film then cuts back to the seashore—Jeremy and Jemima thank their father for telling them this story and ask if the story ends with Caractacus marrying Truly Scrumptious.

This of course causes some embarrassment for he feels that he is too poor to marry Truly. However, in typical Hollywood fashion, when they return home they find Lord Scrumptious waiting there with an offer to buy Caractacus's long ago forgotten musical candy. Thanks to his newfound wealth, Caractacus feels free to pop the inevitable question to Truly, who of course readily agrees. It must be presumed they will all live happily ever after.

In addition to seriously tampering with Fleming's story-line, Broccoli, Hughes and Dahl significantly altered the overall tone and feel of the novel. The fantastic elements in the book are smoothly integrated into a fast-paced adventure. The motion picture on the other hand plods along unmercifully for over two and one half hours, the fantasy elements absent until the last hour. In the narrative the car plays the pivotal role, but for much of the film it stays in the background. Instead of focusing on the automobile, the movie often centers on the romantic relationship between Dick Van Dyke and Sally Ann Howes. Also, in this screen version much of the car's original appeal is stripped away. Only in the film's fantasy shots does the auto exhibit any magical traits, and even in these sequences it sadly lacks the personality that Fleming so conscientiously gave to it. The fact that the film is set in the early 1900s also detracts from the auto's distinctiveness. In the novel the racer is unique because it is so much older than the other vehicles on the road, but in the movie Chitty Chitty Bang Bang looks (to the audience) much like the other old-fashioned autos.

Broccoli, Hughes and Dahl just as consciously reduced the importance of Jeremy and Jemima. Author Ian Fleming allows the children to serve as active participants in the development of his narrative: they make decisions on their own, and in the end prove utterly superior to a gang of professional criminals. Their screen counterparts, however, are usually relegated to the positions of passive onlookers. The one time they are entrusted with responsibility, they fall prey to the child catcher.

In addition, the villains of the film are much less threatening than the gangsters of the novel. Fleming meticulously develops Joe the Monster and his thugs into ruthless criminals.

Baron Bomburst on the other hand is presented cinematically as being no more than an overgrown child who rides around his castle on a toy horse. While the fear of enhancing the already villainous criminals into an overly scary visual portrayal was undoubtedly the screenwriters' reason for softening the Baron's villainy, this film alternative is such a watered down antagonist that even to the young he is by and large of little threat and of even less interest. All these changes tend to create a film less satisfying and far more superficial than its narrative namesake.

Rather than attempt to remain as true as film could allow to Fleming's original, or at least to utilize its recognizable skeletal structure to build upon for a more filmic richness, the film's executives clearly attempted to pattern their adaptation after Walt Disney's successful *Mary Poppins* (1964). Both creations star Dick Van Dyke, both films are set in pre-World War I England, and both feature the songs of Richard M. and Robert B. Sherman. However, *Chitty Chitty Bang Bang* did not meet with the same tremendous commercial success and rave reviews that greeted *Mary Poppins*. Despite an expensive promotional effort, audiences stayed away from the United Artists feature, and most film critics gave *Chitty Chitty Bang Bang* resoundingly negative reviews. In her piece for the *New Yorker* (January 4, 1969), for example, Pauline Kael wrote: "This ten-million-dollar musical fantasy for children has a desperate jollity; everybody has been doing his damnedest and everything has gone hopelessly wrong." The *Time* reviewer in his telling "Chug-Chug, Mug-Mug" (December 27, 1968) complained that the movie has "enough saccharine to sweeten the Sargaso Sea."

Given the reception that greeted Disney's *The Love Bug* in 1969, it seems likely that Broccoli, Hughes and Dahl seriously misread the taste of the public when they decided not to adhere to Fleming's original story. In many ways *The Love Bug* more accurately captures the underlying spirit of Fleming's book than does this purported film version of *Chitty Chitty Bang Bang*. Both movies are about magical automobiles, but *The Love Bug* is set entirely in the primary world. The car in the Disney feature not only possesses a myriad of magical properties but has a personality. *The Love Bug* motors along in high gear and the film's characters find themselves in numerous exciting situations—the sorts of situations chronicled by Ian Fleming and ignored by the United Artists trio. It is quite conceivable that if Broccoli, Hughes and Dahl had had faith in (or possibly merely understood) the original Fleming creation, their cinematic adaptation of *Chitty Chitty Bang Bang* might have succeeded both with the critics and at the box office. It is certain that lessons learned here were remembered when Roald Dahl adapted his *Charlie and the Chocolate Factory* into the *Willy Wonka* musical three years later.

As the adapters of Ian Fleming's more notorious adventure novels readily realized, Fleming knew how to create interesting and potentially cinematically captivating narratives—the astute filmmakers could retain basic plot concepts while enhancing their screen effectiveness with the wonders of filmic potential rather than ignoring or working against them. This lesson was too late realized it seems to salvage the integrity of this pedal-to-the-floor fantasy thrown jarringly into reverse as it hit the silver screen.

"Different on the Inside
Where It Counts"

PRISCILLA A. ORD

As children, most of us have at one time or another considered running away so that our parents would miss us, realize how important we were to them, and appreciate us more when we returned. Of course, to be truly successful at running away, one must have a place to which to run.

In my own family, at the first announcement of such intentions my mother would immediately volunteer to help us pack, and she would calmly ask us where we were going and how we intended to get there. That stopped me every time, but it never would have stopped Claudia Kincaid and her brother from traversing the wonderful hideaways of New York's Metropolitan Museum of Art.

The 1973 screen adaptation of Elaine L. Konigsburg's *From the Mixed-up Files of Mrs. Basil E. Frankweiler*, scripted by Blanche Hanalis, directed by Fielder Cook, and produced by Westfall, is an artful recreation of the 1968 Newbery Medal-winning novel. For the most part, adaptation to the film medium required only minimal changes. Perhaps the greatest, and yet most necessary, alteration was the shift in the point of view from that of Mrs. Frankweiler in the book to that of the actual viewer of the movie.

The entire novel is presented from the perspective of Mrs. Frankweiler herself and is set within a somewhat improbable frame story of a letter from the eccentric, eighty-two-year-old art collector to her lawyer, Saxonberg. In the letter she directs him to make arrangements for several additional bequests in

205

her will as a result of her encounter with two special children. In revealing her reasons for the proposed legal changes, she tells the story of Claudia Kincaid, age eleven, and her brother Jamie, age nine, who following serious deliberations and careful planning, run away to live in the famed New York Metropolitan Museum of Art. Her narrative provides a complete explanation for Claudia's reasons for running away, relates the detailed plans for her escape with particular emphasis on who would accompany her, and describes the significant incidents of the children's adventures away from home. Unfortunately the narrative is punctuated by Mrs. Frankweiler's intrusive admonitions to Saxonberg, on the one hand, and appreciation of Claudia's or Jamies's thoroughness, cleverness, or perception on the other. In the end, as the finishing touches are added to the frame story, it is revealed that Saxonberg is in fact more improbably, the children's grandfather. Credibility is stretched to the breaking point.

Fortunately, most children who read the book or have it read to them are able to ignore the frame story. It is similarly fortuitous that this method of presenting the children's extraordinary adventure is one of the story's main features that could not survive in transition to the screen.

The film's opening shots show Claudia Kincaid (Sally Pradger) sitting in a tree and singing the haunting folk song "Pretty Saro." Later she is even running home through a sunlit field. Despite these idyllic suggestions, Claudia is dissatisfied with her lot in life. As the oldest child and only girl, she is expected to help her mother (Madeline Kahn) more than her brother Jamie (Johnny Doran) is. Among the injustices she feels oppressed by is the task of emptying all of the family's wastebaskets each week and being expected to watch her youngest brother when her mother is busy. Claudia decides to run away—not forever, but long enough to make those at home appreciate her. She also hopes that while she is away something will happen to make her different—that she will become *someone* or learn *something* that will set her apart and make her special in her own eyes, as well as in those of her family. She therefore plans her escape carefully and judiciously selects Jamie as her companion.

In the novel Claudia has three brothers: Steve, who is closest to her age and purposely, she believes, annoys her by emptying his pencil sharpener into his wastebasket to make it messy; Jamie, who is somewhat younger than she is; and Kevin, a first grader who must be shepherded to and from the school-bus stop by one of his older siblings. The necessity for simplification in the film version causes the elimination of Steve altogether, and the lowering of Kevin's age to that of an infant. In both versions, Jamie's inclusion in Claudia's plans is based on three factors: first, he could be counted upon to keep her plans a secret; second, he was, by juvenile standards, rich, for he saved almost every penny of his weekly allowance as well as his ill-gotten winnings from his ongoing game of war with his best friend, Bruce; and, last, he owned a potentially necessary transistor radio. The details of Claudia's plan are simple but masterful, and it is its detailed visual presentation that fills the dramatic interlude between the revelation of Claudia's intentions and the children's actual exodus.

"I've decided to run away from home, and I've chosen you to accompany me,"[1] Claudia tells Jamie. They must leave on Wednesday, the day of their music lessons. She will pack her violin case and her book bag with her clothes and underwear, and Jamie is to do the same with his book bag and trumpet case. Finding her father's accidently discarded commuter pass with one remaining adult fare, or, for their purposes, two half-fares, when she empties her parents' wastebasket on the Saturday before their departure is considered a good omen and adds to the excitement of waiting for the designated day to arrive. Jamie, along with the viewing audience, likes the complications of waiting for Claudia's final instructions, which he finds pinned to his pajamas under his pillow the night before they leave.

Reading about the injustices, real or imagined, from which Claudia Kincaid is fleeing is, understandably, more convincing than its screen portrayal. Claudia's mother does not appear to be as unloving or uncaring as one would have imagined her to

---

[1]E. L. Konigsburg, *From the Mixed-up Files of Mrs. Basil E. Frankweiler*. (New York: Atheneum, 1967), p. 14. All subsequent references will be noted internally.

be. The suspense and excitement that the undertaking produces, however, more than makes up for what the film version fails to evoke in empathy.

On Wednesday morning, according to plan, the two children take the bus to school as usual, but that is where the ordinary leaves off and the extraordinary begins. Claudia's scheme calls for them to sit in one of the back seats of the bus. When they arrive at school, they are to duck down, pull up their feet, and remain hidden from view until the other children leave the bus and the driver returns the bus to the school parking lot. From there, when "the coast is clear," they will be able to walk to the train station.

The reality of the situation as it is presented, coupled with the excellent shots inside the school bus, is so convincing that few child viewers dare to breathe or even move while Claudia and Jamie Kincaid are crouched in their seats waiting for the bus to empty and be driven to the parking lot, or during the seemingly interminable period of time until it is deemed safe for them to attempt to leave the bus. In fact, the tension relaxes somewhat only after the children have successfully avoided detection while boarding the train and are headed safely for New York. The signs of relief from the audience are audible.

Upon their arrival in New York, not everything proceeds according to Claudia's envisioned plan. While it is she who wanted to run away and formulated the plans to do so, it is Jamie who, as chancellor of the exchequer, has the final say on what means will be employed to achieve their end, if expenditure of any kind is required. Where would Claudia be without Jamie's twenty-four dollars and forty-three cents—mostly in small change. As Mrs. Frankweiler notes, Claudia "was cautious (about everything but money) and poor; he was adventurous (about everything but money) and rich" (p. 17). For example, in the book Claudia, who had looked forward to taking a taxi from the train station to the museum, is forced to walk the forty odd blocks when Jamie declares that even the bus fare would be an extravagance. She is similarly forced to yield to his better financial judgment concerning where they eat, what they eat, and whether they can afford a newspaper.

Although Jamie would probably find camping out in Central Park more to his liking, he is noticeably impressed and pleased with Claudia's selection of the Metropolitan for their "hideaway." Her choice—or Mrs. Konigsburg's—coincides with a fantasy that many children and adults must share—having a store, a park, or a museum entirely to oneself to shop in or to visit without the inconvenience of crowds, the restraints of rules and regulations, or the constraints of time.

Claudia's thoroughness in her research and advance planning is commendable. She knows how they are going to enter and re-enter the museum and how they will be able to remain there, undetected, even during the crucial period of the museum's opening and closing each day. She has even planned that they would live in one of the rooms of French or English period furnishings, and soon after their arrival, she leads Jamie in search of the ideal sleeping accommodations.

> "At last she found a bed that she considered perfectly wonderful, and she told Jamie that they would spend the night there. The bed had a tall canopy supported by an ornately carved headboard at one end and by two gigantic posts at the other. . . . Claudia had always known that she was meant for such fine things. . . . "State bed—scene of the alleged murder of Amy Robsart, first wife of Lord Dudley, later Earl of. . . ." (pp. 37–8)

To create the proper degree of authenticity, the reader is provided with reproductions of the actual floor plans of the museum as well as several pages of illustrations from within the museum. Since for security reasons the museum was naturally reluctant to divulge information about cleaning schedules, etc., when she was working on the book Mrs. Konigsburg and her children gathered much of this information themselves, as guards looked on suspiciously. The result was a reasonably authentic account.

The film, of course, has no need to verify the authenticity or attempt to justify the verisimilitude of the setting. The majority of the footage for the eighty-seven minute movie was filmed on location at the Metropolitan Museum of Art. The screen is filled with frame after frame of carefully selected, sensitively photographed long shots and close-ups of famous paintings, sculpture, and furnishings as seen both during the hours that the museum is open to the public and the hours that are "reserved" for Lady Claudia's and Sir James's private viewing. The movie audience is skillfully made to share their awe, and only the very real fear that the children will be discovered detracts from the visual smorgasbord of art and artifacts.

Since getting there is often half the fun, it would not have been surprising to some if Claudia and Jamie, having achieved their aim, had grown bored with their existence after a day or two, thought better of their plan, and contritely returned home to their nearly frantic parents. Elaine Konigsburg, however, knows and is out to prove that getting there *is* only half the fun. The other half must be a real adventure, something unplanned and unexpected that will require an expenditure of wits before a successful conclusion can be achieved.

On their very first day in residence, following a quite mature decision to make the most of their opportunity to learn and to study everything about the museum, the children discover a very special acquisition in the Hall of the Italian Renaissance.

> . . . now they reached what everyone was standing in line to see. A statue of an angel; her arms were folded, and she was looking holy. As Claudia passed by, she thought that that angel was the most beautiful, most graceful little statue she had ever seen; she wanted to stop and stare; she almost did, but the crowd wouldn't let her. (p. 52)

Claudia is practically bewitched by the statue, and both children have their curiosity piqued when they read in a stolen issue of the *New York Times* the next day that the statue may be the work of the Italian Renaissance master Michaelangelo. Now the real adventure begins. In between their planned schedule of joining visiting school tours and enjoying their independent nocturnal tours, Claudia and Jamie begin an earnest research project to determine the true identity of Angel's creator. By day they read about Michaelangelo and his work at the New York Public Library, and at night and on Sunday morning when the museum opens late, they unhurriedly study Angel and look for clues.

Their diligence does not go unrewarded. Finding a significant clue to the statue's origin, they decide to share it with their host, the museum. But how can they do it discretely? They ultimately decide upon a letter, which they write on the typewriter in the office for the museum shop—the children in the book use one in front of the Olivetti store on Fifth Avenue, but keeping to a minimum of shots outside the museum eliminated that from the script—and sign "Friends of the Museum." After renting a box at the Grand Central Post Office, under the name of Angelo Michaels of Marblehead, Massachusetts, they wait impatiently for their moment of acclaim and recognition.

The eventual answer to their letter proves to be courteous but disappointing, and they are tempted to return home immediately, without even retrieving their belongings from the museum; however, Claudia stalwartly refuses to accept defeat. She has to return home on her own terms; she somehow has to be different. "An answer to running away, and also going home again, lay in Angel. . . . Finding out about Angel will be that difference" (pp. 95 and 98). In a moment of daring, the two children decide to take the train to visit Mrs. Frankweiler–the statue's previous owner—who in the film version lives in Essex Fells, New Jersey. The closer she gets to Mrs. Frankweiler's home, the better Claudia feels—especially when the only way to reach the house from the train station is by means of a long-hoped-for taxi ride.

Filmviewers are at last to meet Mrs. Basil E. Frankweiler, and unlike readers of the book they have not been exposed to the acerbic comments with which she larded her narrative of Claudia's and Jamie's escapades. They are therefore free to hope that she will furnish Claudia with the information she desperately needs in order to return home with dignity.

The movie Mrs. Frankweiler is not the Hansel and Gretel witch readers may have imagined. She is a shrewd lady who having amassed a sizable and enviable collection of priceless art objects intends to enjoy disposing of them. However, she is not about to allow others, including two children or the curators of the Metropolitan, to obtain without effort the information it has taken her a lifetime to collect on her various pieces of art—especially and particularly the statue of the angel.

In the original story Claudia and Jamie are permitted to use her "mixed-up" files for one hour in an attempt to find a conclusive answer to the mystery. In return, they are to give her a complete account of their adventures, which she records on tape. As further compensation for their making her the first to know all the details of their adventures, she will have her chauffeur drive them home; they are now penniless—their last seventeen cents has been given to the taxi driver as a tip.

The movie audience is not quite as apprehensive as the reading audience about the outcome, for Mrs. Frankweiler is an elderly and charming woman as portrayed by Ingrid Bergman. In the screenplay Mrs. Frankweiler, sensing Claudia's need to know the secret of the statue even if, as it turns out, she will not be permitted to reveal the information to anyone until after Mrs. Frankweiler's death, takes Claudia down to her room of files and, without actually permitting her access to them, allows Claudia to discover the secret for herself through a series of logical deductions. She knows intuitively that Claudia will keep her secret for the same reason that she herself has kept it all these years. "Simply because it is a secret. It will enable her to return to Greenwich [The film version has transplanted the Kincaid home to Madison, New Jersey] different" (p. 149). Jamie, in the meantime, is upstairs cheating the butler, to whom the name Saxonberg has been transferred, in a game of war.

Surprisingly enough, in neither version do Mrs. Frankweiler's files appear to be particularly mixed-up; they are no more idiosyncratic than most filing systems. It is, no doubt, this fact, as well as the late appearance of the character in the title role—to say nothing of the title's length—that has caused the movie to be reissued as *The Hideaways*.

In the final analysis it is secrets, not mixed-up files, that are the key. Elaine Konigsburg, through Mrs. Frankweiler, says it herself:

> Of course secrets make a difference. That is why planning the runaway had been such fun; it was a secret. And hiding in the

museum had been a secret. But they weren't permanent; they had to come to an end. Angel wouldn't. She [Claudia] could carry the secret of Angel inside her for twenty years just as I [Mrs. Frankweiler] had. Now she wouldn't have to be a heroine when she returned home . . . except to herself. And now she knew something about secrets that she hadn't known before." (pp. 150–151)

The screenplay and actual movie present a superb adaptation of a recognized children's classic that goes beyond a mere translation of a work from one medium to another. The message is clear and direct, the point of view is just right, and the means for achieving a mood through both photography and accompanying musical score are masterful. The child actors who play the parts of the children provide an even portrayal of their designated characters that is not only faithful to the intent of the original author but believable to the intended viewing audience. Ingrid Bergman is the very kind of person that Claudia and Jamie would want to adopt as their grandmother. The true treasure of this film, however, is not the angel but the cinematography itself. The shots and scenes within the museum are exquisite. Everyone is able to return home "different" for having seen it—"different on the inside where it counts," as Mrs. Konigsburg observed in her Newbery Award acceptance speech.

The Named and the Unnamed

LEONARD J. DEUTSCH

The book and film versions of *Sounder* are both artistic triumphs but each has a somewhat different story to tell. The novel about a Negro boy in search of his identity was written by a white man; the screenplay about an irrepressible black family was written by a black man—but the differences between the two works can be ascribed as much to artistic vision as to racial considerations.

The narrative outlines for both novel and film are essentially the same. In each, a black family of sharecroppers faces starvation. In order to feed his family, the father pilfers some meat and while he is being arrested, his dog, Sounder, is shot when he heroically attempts to protect his master. The father is incarcerated and the dog disappears into the woods. Sentenced to hard labor, the father is sent to an undisclosed location. The boy never finds him despite a dauntless search throughout the state. But Sounder—named for the mighty bark he once brandished during the possum hunt—returns, now a crippled remnant of his former self. He maintains a quiet vigil until one day the reverberating sound of his mighty voice announces the return of his master.

William Howard Armstrong's 1969 novel, illustrated with James Barkley's black-and-white sketches, won both the 1970 John Newbery Medal and the 1970 Lewis Carroll Shelf Award. Based on a story the author had heard from an old black man many years before, it retains the central incident—the coon dog's remarkable fidelity. However, Armstrong enlarges the story until it becomes much more than a tale about a dog possessing admirably superior "human" qualities. With the author's shift in focus, *Sounder*, applauded by many as a master-

piece of children's literature, reaches beyond the usual boundaries observed in juvenile fiction and transcends its genre. In
tackling concerns not conventionally associated with children's
literature, it demands a mature audience. Ironically, a medita-
tive novel for mature children was converted into an action-
packed film aimed primarily at an adult audience.

The novel confronts the issue of racism head on; the theme
of social injustice is developed through many instances of dis-
crimination concretely rendered in the text—especially as perceived by the eldest boy in the family (who, like the other
characters in the book, is never named). From the boy we learn
that no mailman passes his house and that his family does not
even own a mailbox; that he has never looked out of a window
with curtains on it; and that he has smelled ham bone only
twice in his life, "once when he was walking past the big house
down the road." We learn that when his father helped to
butcher hogs at the big house he was allowed to bring home
"lots of sowbelly, but not much spareribs." The boy doesn't get
on a soap box and denounce the injustices all around him;
rather, these experiences implicitly define the inequitable caste
system that invariably relegates blacks to the have-not category. When the boy observes the prisoners at work, the scene is
described in a manner that makes didactic comment superfluous: "None of the men whitewashing the round rocks that lined
the path stood up and walked. They crawled the few feet from
stone to stone, and crawling, they all looked the same." The
strongly etched image of dignity and individuality denied requires no further commentary. As in Mark Twain's *The Adventures of Huckleberry Finn*, ideas are not abstractly argued, but
weighty moral issues are confronted. This is serious subject
matter for a "children's" novel.

When acts of violence occur, they are handled much more
graphically in the novel than in the film—as though young
readers are assumed to have stronger stomachs than middle-
aged moviegoers. Two instances of shockingly candid reportage
in the book come to mind. When Sounder is shot, we are told:

> A trail of blood, smeared and blotted, followed him. There was
> a large spot of mingled blood, hair, and naked flesh on one
> shoulder. His head swung from side to side. He fell again and

pushed his body along with his hind legs. One side of his head was a mass of blood. The blast had torn off the whole side of his head and shoulder.[1]

The boy finds Sounder's severed ear, puts it in his pocket and that evening places it under his pillow so he can make a wish upon it. When the "living skeleton" of Sounder eventually reappears, he is described in terms that are unsparingly brutal: "One front foot dangled above the floor. The stub of an ear stuck out on one side, and there was no eye on that side, only a dark socket with a splinter of bone showing above it." The other instance of graphic description occurs when a guard smashes the skin of the boy's fingers with a piece of iron: "Drops of blood from his fingers dripped down the fence from wire to wire and fell on the ground." The book's realism prompted the reviewer for the *New York Times* to note warningly: "I am not sure children should read this book. If so, perhaps parents should loiter nearby, ready to enforce their child's revulsion from violence so truly and so well described." The novel, clearly, is strong stuff for its young readers.

Though violence is more uncompromisingly depicted in the novel than in the film, paradoxically, the novel is by far the more subdued and contemplative work. In terms of externalized action, relatively little "happens" in the novel because so much occurs inside the mind of the boy. The film's objective camera eye makes the father, the mother, the boy, and the dog all equally important as characters. But Armstrong, in utilizing the third-person limited point of view, focuses on the boy and makes *Sounder* the story of *his* maturation (this authorial strategy also invites greater identification between the reader and the young hero). In the Harper Trophy edition which runs 116 pages, the father disappears on page 26 and does not reappear (except for the brief jail visit scene, pages 61 to 64) until six years later on page 104; Sounder disappears on page 28 and does not return until page 70. Their absence places the spotlight on the boy; *his* feelings, *his* yearnings, *his* psychological development are emphasized as he is propelled into early maturity.

Like a window, the boy looks both outside and inside at the

[1]W. H. Armstrong, *Sounder* (New York: Harper & Row, 1969), p. 28.

same time. But, by and large, Armstrong does not concern himself with the physical aspects of the boy's experience (for a children's novel, the narrative is surprisingly devoid of adventure); instead, the author concentrates on the psychological significance of experience as it is filtered through, and transmuted in, the mind of the introspective boy.

Whether he's lying in bed at night or walking all over the state searching for his father, the boy is always *thinking*, because while he cannot find his father in fact, he can possess him in memory. The boy, always trying to sort out the mystery of life's meaning, is often confused and ambivalent in his feelings (as when he wants to see Sounder and at the same time doesn't want to see him). Unlike his counterpart in the film (who is given the name David Lee Morgan), he is not a paragon of virtue. He entertains gory fantasies of revenge: he visualizes the deputy who ruined his mother's cake being decapitated like a bull with blood oozing out of its mouth and nostrils, and he imagines the sadistic guard who smashed his fingers with a piece of iron being dismantled by his father like a scarecrow. The boy may be pensive but he is not placid or preternaturally perfect. His hatred is keen at times and finds full expression in his resourceful mind. He is a much more complex character than the children in the film, all of whom seem a little too good to be true.

When the father finally returns, the family reunion is more somberly portrayed in the novel than in the film. Having been mutilated by a dynamite blast which left him buried under an avalanche of limestone, the father's deformity exactly parallels Sounder's infirmities:

> The head of the man was pulled to the side where a limp arm dangled and where the foot pointed outward as it dragged through the dust. What had been a shoulder was now pushed up and back to make a one-sided hump so high that the leaning head seemed to rest upon it. The mouth was askew too, and the voice came out of the part farthest away from the withered, wrinkled, lifeless side.

Instead of running to meet him, his wife sits on her rocker, "suffocated in shock." Crushed in body but not in spirit, the father has an invincible will that perfectly mirrors Sounder's will: like the dog, "he resolved he would not die, even with a half-dead body, because he wanted to come home again." Within a few pages, however, the father, having achieved his purpose in returning home, dies. The boy, going off to school, realizes that before he will have time to come home again Sounder will be dead. He is right; when he returns his mother simply tells him: "He just crawled up under the house and died."

The novel then, unlike the film with its relatively happy ending, concludes on a sad note: both the father and the loyal dog die. Consolation is provided by philosophy; citing Montaigne's belief that "only the unwise think that what has changed is dead," the teacher reassures the boy that Sounder and his father will always remain living forces lending their strength to his spirit. The boy has learned how to endure; the secular view he comes to embrace at the end of the novel— "Everything don't change much, the boy thought"—is not all that different from his mother's religious acceptance of fate.

When the movie, *Sounder*, was released in the fall of 1972, critics generally hailed it as a welcome relief from the spate of "blaxploitation" films such as *Superfly* (1972) and *Shaft* (1971) that glorified mean macho studs reveling in pointless sex, rampant brutality, and reverse racism (directed at maniacally mindless Caucasian stereotypes). Shot on location in East Feliciana and St. Helena Parishes, Louisiana, on a budget of slightly over $900,000, *Sounder* was a relatively inexpensive undertaking. The movie was directed by socially conscious Martin Ritt (*Long Hot Summer* (1958), *Hud* (1963), *The Spy Who Came in From the Cold* (1965), *The Molly Maguires* (1970), *The Great White Hope* (1970), and *Norma Rae* (1979); Charles Washburn, a black man, served as assistant director; black playwright Lonne Elder III (*Ceremonies in Dark Old Men*) wrote the screenplay; and Robert Radnitz produced the film. Minor roles were played by amateurs but the movie starred Cicely Tyson as the mother, Rebecca Morgan; Paul Winfield as the father, Nathan Morgan; and thirteen year old Kevin Hooks as the boy, David Lee Morgan. Characters

original to the film include Mrs. Boatwright, the white liberal
who tries to help David locate his father, played by Carmen
Mathews; Ike, played by Taj Majal; and Camille Johnson, the
black teacher who befriends and inspires David, played by
Janet MacLachlan.

Not only are the characters in the film individualized by
having been given particular names but the setting and time
period of the story are explicitly identified by a caption that
superimposes "Louisiana, 1933" on the screen. The film, about
the Morgan family during the Great Depression, achieves the
effect of a documentary while the novel featuring nameless
characters and set in an unspecified locale (presumably the
South but an area that is so cold in October that the ground is
already frozen and the coons are said to migrate to a warmer
climate), takes on the air of a timeless, universal tale.
Barkley's illustrations with their indistinct, blurred brush-
strokes reinforce this impression. According to one critic, the
characters in the novel "are a symbol of all the poor, black or
white, who face indignity with courage."

Armstrong's *bildungsroman* has been transformed by Ritt
and Elder into a paean to the resilience and fortitude of the
black family. In the film we watch members of the family de-
riving spiritual sustenance and strength from one another. The
force that cements all of their relationships and ensures their
survival is familial love. The film's family has been diminished
in size (one less child than in the novel) but its importance has
been magnified. Whereas in the novel only the boy, traveling
alone, delivers the cake to his imprisoned father, in the film
the whole family walks to the jail together. The cardinal point
seems to be that black strength is derived from a strong family
(and, when the father is absent, from a supportive black community, represented by Ike and his wife).

While the novel treats the boy as the protagonist and develops his character more fully than the film, the movie gives
more substance to the father and the mother. Tyson's Rebecca
is a commanding figure totally unlike Armstrong's religious
fatalist who surrenders herself wholly to the will of the Lord
and whose passive philosophy is contained in lines such as:

" . . . you must learn to lose child. The Lord teaches the old to lose. The young don't know how to learn it. Some people is born to keep. Some is born to lose. We was born to lose, I reckon" and "There's patience, child, and waitin' that's got to be." In the film, Rebecca, a dynamic woman with a desire to win, utters neither of these speeches.

Armstrong's character has two standard responses: she sings hymns softly through big, warm lips when she is happy, and she hums through lips that "seemed to be rolled inward and drawn and long and thin" when she is worried. Tyson's Rebecca does not retain these mannerisms. Moreover, she more outspokenly attempts to defend her husband when the police come to arrest him: "You know what kind of man he is and the troubles we've been having in these hard times." By way of contrast, in the novel the mother remains motionless and silent until after her husband has been taken away; then she stoically tells the boy: "Come in, child, and bring some wood." With her husband gone, the film mother heroically takes on the strenuous job of "croppin'" in the hot fields "because we owe all that money." The mother in the novel merely takes in more laundry. Rebecca is also more obviously proud of her son's ability to read and write—"a good fine letter" she encouragingly nods to David when he writes to the black teacher—and she is more demonstrative in her affection for her husband: she embraces him frequently and lovingly offers him coffee in the morning, and she enjoins her son to "Tell him I love him" if he should find the prison camp to which his father has been assigned.

The father, who is gone for six years in the novel, is gone only one year in the film. When he is absent, David imaginatively projects him back into the picture: in his one fantasy scene (a wish-fulfillment dream in contrast to the novel's revenge fantasies) the boy runs through the cane fields into the arms of his laughing father; when he looks around the next second, his father isn't there. The camera cuts to a close-up of a sweating David in bed at night. When Nathan *is* present, he and his son have a more fully realized relationship. Whereas in the novel's jail visit scene the father punctures the "awful quiet

spell" with a total of twenty-eight words, in the film Nathan
and David communicate freely and at length. Nathan comforts
his son by promising him that Sounder will return one day; he
tells David: "I love your mama"; they smile at one another;
together they eat the mother's cake—"a few knife holes ain't
gonna destroy the soul she done put in this cake," Nathan
reassuringly tells David; and at the end of the visit they shake
hands warmly. In other parts of the film we see Nathan as an
affectionate and sensuous man, as a hero in his family's eyes
(when he tosses the winning pitch in a baseball game, for
example), as a man audacious enough to kick at the deputy's
gun in a futile attempt to keep Sounder from being shot, and as
a father who has taught his son a tough lesson in life: "You
sometimes lose what you go after, but you always lose what
you don't go after"—all of which scenes never occur in the
novel.

When Nathan returns home after a year's confinement, the
film's storyline takes off in a direction different from that of the
novel. With Nathan's return the family is regenerated and
hope is restored. One of the dominant cinematic images of the
reunion scene—the hands and arms of every member of the
family intertwining—suggests a magnetizing and electrifying
chain of human love. Although Nathan is knocked down by the
draw-bar of the cane press because his leg is still weak, he is
effusively optimistic: he's ready to work and to go hunting
again; he's proud, he says to David, "of the way you helped your
mama keep this place goin'"; he teaches his son how to pitch a
ball; and he has recuperated enough to insist that the boy go to
school—despite David's protestations that he stay home and
help out with the work.

The endings of the film and novel offer a study in contrasts.
As a case in point, in the latter, the mother (usually the only
parent around) actively discourages her son from going to
school: "Give it up, child," she says early in the story; later,
with a tinge of sarcasm, she suggests: "Maybe [the teacher]
will write letters to the road camps for you . . .'cause you'll be
so busy with schoolin' and cleanin' the school house . . . that
you can't go searchin' [for your father] no more." When the boy

reiterates his determination to go despite her opposition, the mother capitulates in her characteristically resigned way: "it's the Lord's will." In the film, Rebecca asserts that it is her husband's will, not the Lord's, that counts: "If it's all right with [Nathan], it's all right with me." It is not merely "all right" with Nathan, he is anxious and adamant that David Lee attend school because he wants a better life for his son and he sees education as a political tool. Whereas in the novel the boy wants to learn how to read so "he wouldn't be lonesome even if his mother didn't sing," in the film Nathan sees education as "a way out," the road to salvation for David: "I want you to beat the life they have laid out for you in this place, 'cause they ain't nothin', ain't nobody here but them bastards . . ."

The basic difference, however, centers on the upbeat ending of the film version. In one of the concluding scenes Nathan follows David into the woods to persuade his son to go to school. When the father's will prevails, the spirit of peace and understanding seems to descend upon them. The two figures are cinematically framed together as they sit by a sparkling stream. The low-angle shot emphasizes the father's height and suggests his authority. When he assures David that "whatever you is, I'm gonna love you. I love you, son," the boy reaches his hand toward his father; they shake hands, and while they hug one another, a close-up of David's face on his father's chest captures the comfort and strength he finds there; then the camera pans to a close-up of Nathan's loving face. In the long shot that concludes this scene, the camera is behind Nathan and David; we see them sitting close together with the sparkling river before them (representing, rather obviously, the promise of a hopeful future).

In the final scene of the film, David (in a suit and tie) joins his father and Sounder in the wagon that will take them to the school. David Lee says: "I'm gonna miss this place but I'm sure not gonna worry about it," and the camera in a tracking shot depicts father and son, arm in arm, laughing. Then in a final shot, while laughter still fills the soundtrack, the camera jump cuts to David, now back in his overalls, engaging in camaraderie with his father as they walk into the distance together—suggesting that their close relationship will survive both in spiritual and physical terms.

Sounder as fiction differs dramatically from the filmed *Sounder* in terms of its informing sensibility. The literary tradition Armstrong draws upon is essentially the so-called Western tradition: Greek myth, the Bible, and classic Western writers. In the introduction, for example, Armstrong mentions Sounder in the same breath with Argus, the faithful dog of Odysseus. The account of Joseph from the Bible is the boy's favorite from among the stories his mother tells; and while his fingers are smarting from the guard's blow, he fancifully compares himself to the Biblical David in his confrontation with Goliath. Secular wisdom in the novel is personified by the reference to Montaigne. In the film, on the other hand, the traditional spirituals are supplanted by Taj Majal's music; the white schoolteacher reads from *The Adventures of Huckleberry Finn*—Would such an anti-slavery novel been taught in a predominantly white Louisiana school in 1933?; and the black teacher (female in the film, male in the novel) reads not from Montaigne but from W. E. B. DuBois. The ideological stance of the film is pointed up when the teacher points out volumes on her bookshelf that deal with black hero Crispus Attucks and black heroine Harriet Tubman, and when she reads a passage from *The Souls of Black Folk* in which DuBois admonishes: "The longing of black men must have respect: the rich and bitter depth of their experience, the unknown treasures of their inner life, the strange rendings of nature they have seen, may give the world new points of view and make their loving, living, and doing precious to all human hearts."

The DuBois lecture on racial injustice makes explicit what had remained implicit in the novel, prompting one reviewer to criticize "the film's stagy moral simplicities and self-conscious ideological instruction." Although this is an overstatement, the film strives more insistently than the novel to make a political statement, as when Ike sardonically jokes: "Good Lord said: 'You doin' better than me 'cause I've been trying to get into [that white church] for two hundred years and I ain't made it yet"; also, when Nathan attacks the sharecropping system during a conversation with Rebecca; and when the Morgans discover that the police, in broad daylight, have entered their house without a search warrant during their absence. Still, despite the bitterness that is hinted at in the movie, the film's characters are hardly more militant than Armstrong's characters. Far from being black power advocates (which would have been anachronistic, at any rate), they draw upon their fund of decency and face adversity with dignity and composure.

Each of the two works makes rich and effective use of the properties inherent in its own art form. The novel, for example, exploits the resources of ruminative and literary language to capture, alternately, the questing spirit of the boy when he ransacks his mind for answers to the meaning of life, and the poetry in his soul when he achieves understanding. The boy's loneliness for example is described in noncinematic terms: "It made the boy's tongue heavy. It pressed against his eyes, and they burned. It rolled against his ears. His head seemed to be squeezed inward, and it hurt." Here an abstraction (loneliness) is embodied in a concrete figure of speech. The poetic description of Sounder's bark provides another example of the bark's linguistic largess: "it was not an ordinary bark. It filled up the night and made music as though the branches of all the trees were being pulled across silver strings." Such a description would be difficult to transfer to the screen, and Ritt and Elder do not even attempt it. Throughout the novel, a fairly simple style is employed: "From one of the [jail's] windows there came the sound of laughter. Now and then a door slammed with the deep clash of iron on iron. There was a rattle of tin pans. The boy felt very lonely. The town was as lonely as the cabin, he thought." Such short sentences, with a preponderance of monosyllabic words, are not only appropriate for young readers, they capture the way the world is perceived by the boy and how his mind operates.

In the film, the cinematic aspects of the story are evidenced from the very outset by the exciting scene that introduces Sounder, Nathan, and David Lee. The mobile camera captures the frenzy of the hunt by alternating quick close-up shots of the dog and possum with vertiginous tracking shots as the camera attempts the impossible task of keeping the animals in focus. A point of view shot from the treed possum's perspective as he looks down on his pursuers foreshadows the victory he is soon to achieve by eluding them. After hearing Nathan's rifle shot that is wide of the mark, we see, in close-up, a smug possum escaping into his snug hole. Later, when Rebecca walks by the prison we are struck by the visual contrast between her dark skin and the white walls of the prison that threaten to overwhelm her. Shortly thereafter we see her approaching Mr. Perkins's store; the camera, positioned inside the store window, is trained down on her (a high-angle shot) as she is almost hit by an automobile. Despite all efforts to beat her down and diminish her humanity, however, Rebecca remains a strong and imposing person. When the family (minus Nathan) is working in the fields, the print has a brownish-yellow tint that suggests the trying conditions—aridity and scorching heat— under which they labor. The boy's arduous search for his father is efficiently conveyed through a montage showing David Lee and Sounder in a variety of locations as scene after scene dissolves into the next. Though the scene in which Nathan returns from prison has become a cinematic cliché, it works: the camera cuts back and forth between Nathan and Rebecca as they run toward one another; at the same time, the long shots evolve into medium shots until their hugs and kisses are captured in a poignant close-up. The movie may produce a documentary *effect* but, as all of this artful camera work implies, it is not filmed in an entirely documentary style.

Sounder is such an elegiac, sad, and sensitive book that it is a wonder anyone thought to film it. And yet both versions are worthy works of art, even if of a different order and shaped by different media requirements and artistic visions. Both are affirmative works: the film affirms the black family; the novel affirms the invented family that inhabits the recesses of one's mind (a family that may include a dead father and a dead animal reclaimed by the imagination).

The film, then, although more doctrinaire and more perceptibly stamped by the spirit of Hollywood (in its pacing, its camera-eye point of view, its happy conclusion), nevertheless succeeds as a rousing celebration of black strength, and audiences have been deeply moved by it. But the novel, so spare and spartan in its telling that it is entirely devoid of sentimentality, is perhaps even more moving. Despite the more pronounced tenor of its violence, it is a quiet novel in which injustices are all the more appalling because they are so understated by the unassuming boy. The novel, after all, is his story, and telling it more or less from his introspective point of view produces a work of supreme delicacy, beauty, and dignity.

Breaking Away from the Warren

TOM JORDAN

A well-written book demands a slow reading pace if the reader is to develop the proper complex, reflexive relationship to the material. There is a great deal to be assimilated, and we experience a conscious desire to luxuriate in the imaginative details or repeat the pleasure of affective experiences. The richness and depth of response in such cases can be considerable and rewarding.

As filmgoers, we are allowed no such freedom. Once a film begins, it cannot be stopped without loss of meaning. Each frame, shot, and scene is related syntagmatically. Since the rate at which its information is received cannot be altered by the viewer, the editing rhythm established forms the basis of the audience's acceptance of the material. Variations in rhythm, either longer or shorter than the average shot length, produce an immediate change in the mind's ability to receive and process information and to generate a communicative response. As film is, in a sense, a theme with variations, the major emotional moments being controlled so that our sensory channels are in a constant ebb and flow with regard to the amount of information they receive.

Watership Down (1972) came into being as a brief, whimsical tale of rabbits told to amuse Richard Adams's daughters. Its popularity with them was such that finally he was forced to work out the ramifications of his simple story, and the novel took shape. A labor of love, it was inspired by the desire to tell a good story. The tone of the story reflects this attitude.

If a color tone were ascribed to *Watership Down*, it would necessarily be golden yellow, for the color runs rampant through the story. The central character is named Hazel, which evokes a yellow-brown color, and the first and last sentences in the novel refer to primroses, more often light yellow than any other color. A number of scenes are set in the early evening, when the sun is gold and the rabbits are enjoying their evening feeding. Their new warren is named the Honeycomb. And so forth.

Gold pervades the book, and lends itself to the tone of the writing, creating an atmosphere of warmth which in turn creates an empathy in the reader. Gold is the color of heroes, but it serves as easily as the color of nostalgia, calling forth sunsets and pleasant experiences in an atmosphere of serenity and security. Consider, for example, this passage from the end of the book:

> He saw more young rabbits than he could remember. And sometimes, when they told tales on a sunny evening by the beech trees, he could not clearly recall whether they were about himself or about some other rabbit hero of days gone by.
>
> The warren prospered and soon, in the fullness of time, did the new warren on the Belt, half Watership and half Efrafan—the warren Hazel had first envisaged on that terrible evening when he set out alone to face General Woundwort and try to save his friends against all odds.[1]

But the issue of color is, of course, purely ancillary to the more important point concerning overall response to the tone, a tone which draws us into the story and makes us live the lives of heroes. The color is only a beginning of our feeling for the story.

We deal exclusively with rabbits, toward whom most people find themselves well disposed. Their image at large connotes softness, gentleness, and an absence of violence. They may even have struck us as the inhabitants of another world, for our encounters with them leave us often with no more than a glimpse of a scurrying animal in the twilight. We see them in a positive, albeit less-than-heroic, light.

Perhaps the first problem for the author to overcome attaches itself to the image of the rabbit story. Certainly we have

[1]Richard Adams, *Watership Down* (New York: Avon, 1975), p. 473.

the traditions of Peter Rabbit and his peers, Brer Rabbit, Aesop's Hare, and even Bugs Bunny. Literary rabbits have been with us throughout history, but always as a vehicle for a moral or a source of whimsical fun—never as credibly real rabbits living in their own environment. The deliberate, slowly paced opening of *Watership Down* may in large part stem from the necessity to eliminate our conception of rabbits in previous stories and replace it with a new image that reaches into the world of complex relationships and realistic dangers. By the time the story begins to pick up narrative speed, we are a wholehearted part of a rabbit world that exists within our own world—though no doubt our sensation is rather that of a fourth-dimensional fantasy world just out of sight. The author even creates a small language for the rabbits to remind us of their point of view regarding events and things for which we have no names or for which they have no way of knowing our names—for example, "hrududu" for "automobiles" or "silflay" for "feeding." Such occasional words serve to keep us aware of their world.

Customarily, the best fantasy comes to grips with significant problems of the human character and existence. A two-dimensional story will give us joy at a victory without engaging more than our reservoir of stock attitudes toward heroes and villains. Naturally, in such circumstances, the heroes will win and the villains will die or disappear. A perfectly human desire is thus fulfilled.

But what great fantasy does not require a smashing of the stock vessels and their replacement by genuine feelings groping dimly toward half-recognized goals? The result, a satisfying ending, is superficially the same, yet the processes by which it is arrived at are part of a different literary and emotional plane. For the tone of the golden ending to ring artistically true, it must be preceded by despair, hunger, moral and emotional confusion, physical danger, and the imminent presence of death. *Watership Down* takes us into such a world where the only goal is a comfortable and happy life, and its achievement is in doubt until the final chapters. The story of Hazel and, particularly, the intuitively gifted Fiver, presents us with nonreflective minds that are capable of feeling and sensing a great deal regarding their situations but lack the ability to analyze and work into a coherent pattern abstract information, such as character motivations or social mores. What analytical powers these characters do have are pragmatic, dealing with immediate physical problems.

Much of our major literature deals directly with the signal difference between reflective and nonreflective minds. In a reflective story, the reader is intended to sympathize with the protagonist but to retain a detachment that allows an objective understanding of the issues at hand. For example, Shakespeare's tragedies consistently focus on the development of the reflective mind. We become fascinated by the spectacle of Hamlet coming to grips with the incredible situation in which he finds himself, of Lear fumbling from obtuseness to clarity during his transition from king to beggar, and so on. By the end of these plays, the protagonists have learned much about the human character—and we have learned through them. Thus, the greatest strength Homer ascribes to Odysseus is his growing wisdom.

By contrast, comedies are normally nonreflective; virtually no one learns much consciously because the emphasis is on the action. From Aristophanes to Archie Bunker, comic heroes have been mere symbols of reality, acting in ways no rational persons could act, yet striking very genuine chords of response in the audience that recognizes a common bond with their fallibility. Fantasy is similarly nonreflective, at least inasmuch as its central characters generally do not concern themselves with the growth and development of their understandings of the world around them. Because fantasy normally tells an adventure story, the characters must concern themselves with the often perplexing but thrilling matters at hand. The job of organizing the experience of the characters into a coherent statement is left to the reader, for the characters can rarely articulate what they have learned on their adventures.

We empathize with these characters, for they live largely through feeling, intuition, and occasional flashes of insight—a condition of life thoroughly recognizable to us all. For example, at no point in J.R.R. Tolkien's *The Hobbit* does the indomitable Bilbo Baggins ever seriously attempt to understand why or how he was chosen for a hair-raising series of adventures with a band of dwarfs. Yet our pleasure is not diminished because he does not ask the questions we might almost certainly ask. In fact, we may like him even more because of the imprecise manner in which he muddles to victory. For many readers, a slight, perhaps unconscious, vein of superiority is evoked by such a character, and we often want to protect, pity, and cheer for a protagonist unable to see patterns clear to us. In terms of perception, in *The Hobbit*, we align ourselves with Gandalf, who sees much further than the hobbit or the dwarfs. And if that seems questionable, merely ask yourself with whom you, a critical reader, would rather spend an evening talking, Gandalf or Bilbo? Hamlet or Fiver? The point is not that we do not enjoy some of these characters—presumably we enjoy them all—but that the processes by which their authors present them differ widely, and our empathetic responses often spring from the realization that the characters could use our help.

Watership Down falls in the tradition of nonreflective, empathetic characters, and, because our level of artistic involvement is so intense, we finish reading the book with a profound sense of satisfaction at having lived in the midst of such adventures, and sorrow that they have concluded. We may not feel like crying when Hamlet dies, but we certainly do when Hazel meets a strange rabbit who asks, "You know me, don't you?"

> "Yes, of course," said Hazel, hoping he would be able to remember his name in a moment. Then he saw that in the darkness of the burrow the stranger's ears were shining with a faint silver light.
> "Yes, my lord," he said. "Yes, I know you."

The scene reaches a climax several lines later with one of the most poignantly understated sentences in the book, "It seemed to Hazel that he would not be needing his body any more, so he left it lying on the edge of the ditch. . . ."

Because a film is a strongly visual, rhythmic, emotional experience that cannot be fully analyzed until it has finished running, an obvious problem is created when a book is being adapted. If the film tries to compete with the original in terms

of complexity and density, the audience will be unable to process the incoming information fast enough to keep pace with the
on-going syntagmatic development. However, since plot alone
is rarely the reason for a book's success, the film is often left
with the impossible task of conveying those "extraneous" elements that added to the significance and success of the original
work.

Even if a picture is indeed worth a thousand words, a film
cannot compress all the elements of a major novel into ninety
minutes. That the animated *Watership Down* (1978) is one of
the few really successful translations of a novel into a movie is
a tribute to director Martin Rosen's understanding of how film
could be used to recreate the tone of the book. Moving through
Watership Down with a deft touch, he faithfully preserved only
the core material of the plot. When he elaborates he does so in
terms of emotionally stimulating visual detail—the strength
of the cinema. Through a handsome combination of artwork,
camera work, and editing, the story unfolds to produce a moving experience and a remarkably faithful retelling of the novel.

The striking animation employs a variety of artistic styles
to influence mood. Working from a basic style reminiscent of
Holman Hunt and the Pre-Raphaelites, who emphasized a feeling of lushness through immense detail and full, rich colors,
the film moves occasionally into expressionism (as in Fiver's
Field of Blood vision), Native American symmetrical designs
(as in the opening sequence introducing Frith), and the three-
dimensional, Disney-like multiplane images that provide the
rare animation treat of a shallow depth of field by throwing
foregrounds and backgrounds out of focus. Inside the stylistic
variations are color changes that match the strong colors
Richard Adams uses in the novel. The emotional impact of
strong colors aids in the forwarding of the story by forcing the
audience unconsciously to modify its mood to suit the current
action.

In animation, the camera is so closely tied to the art that
the two are virtually functioning as one in the creation of effects. While in a normal film, the camera serves as the audience's point of view and creates through its placement emotional reinforcement, in animation the camera photographs

every frame from a fixed position. Thus, apparent camera movement is really just a series of shifting drawings. However, the final effect is to provide a sense of motion, as in a live film.

The point of view all through this movie is involved, taking us along with the action and moving to underscore emotional points. Of particular note are the long shots, not common in animation because the central figures become dwarfed by the landscape; however, in *Watership Down*, this is a desirable effect. The long shots effectively focus our attention on the rabbits' environment by employing a combination of colors, visual composition, focal points, exceptional detail in vegetation, and stressing camera motion. Thus, very small rabbits exist in a very large and complex world, and the seeming realism of their story is reinforced.

Camera angles are invariably used here to assist characterization. General Woundwort and significant Owsla members are normally seen from a low angle that makes them appear even more fearsome and overpowering than they already are, while the Watership Down rabbits are generally seen from a slightly high angle that makes them seem very small and ordinary. This increases the tension in tight spots, since we can't be sure that the Good Guys will win; by the same token, when they do win, they have struck a blow for ordinary people everywhere.

A particularly effective motion technique involves the characters' movement to and from the camera. This changing of relationship to the camera not only holds our attention on the character moving but serves to involve us more directly in the action. Characters who move across the field of vision remain generally two-dimensional and less interesting, while characters who move toward us or away from us demand visual attention. This is demonstrated nowhere better than when Kehaar flies, and the camera takes flight with him.

Editing in a film provides pace and helps control the emotional tone by arranging the flow of information. Despite the number of thrilling sequences in *Watership Down*, the editing pace is slow. Through a median shot-length of nine seconds, a pleasant, thoughtful atmosphere is established, and it sustains the tone of the book, much of which is devoted to the virtues of the peaceful life. A slow editing pace automatically directs the audience to absorb the details of the images, and because of the fullness of the frame, we almost unconsciously appreciate the pleasant pace of life on the Down. Even the action scenes are paced relatively slowly so that we can enjoy the complexity of the pictures and keep the various participants straight by picking out their identifying marks. The ability of the book to weave two story lines simultaneously is well duplicated by the editing of the movie, especially in the finale when the Honeycomb Warren is under attack by the General, and Hazel is off for the desperate effort to lead the farm dog up the hill to rout the Efrafan army. The crosscutting in this scene builds fine tension as we know the events are occurring simultaneously.

The editing reinforces emotional tone, but the music generally stays in the background, pushing us to respond more vividly to the development *of the story*, on which it comments through the employment of motifs. In particular, there is a travel theme that invariably sets them on the road for new adventures and makes us march right along with them. Only once does the music become the dominant element and then to less effect than might be hoped for. A song, "Bright Eyes," is actually included, and while it is being sung several minutes are given over to establishing the beautiful tone of life on the Down. While there is a certain attractiveness to the scene, the segment seems too much like padding or a hope on the part of the producers that the song might make the hit parade.

A major feature of the book, the dialogue, was correctly whittled down in the film. Obviously, in the novel the dialogue markedly assists characterization, and Adams devotes a great deal of space to pleasant conversation and storytelling. Rosen establishes this "conversational tone" by making use of the more emotionally oriented elements of film. However, even though the dialogue is pared to the strictly informational level—and the storytelling eliminated completely—the rabbit language still causes trouble.

In the book, a small rabbit vocabulary serves to remind us that our protagonists are rabbits. The words are introduced slowly, and we come to enjoy this reminder of point of view. In the film, the rabbit language is simply confusing. Because we can never stop to think about anything, we don't have time to translate the rabbit words from context before new impressions are calling for our attention. Since we have before us visual evidence of who is doing the talking, the language has no function in the film, whereas in the book it reminds us that our heroic characters are rabbits.

Both the book and film succeed, a rare accomplishment, because both follow the strongest features of their media. The book weaves a complex verbal atmosphere with many diversions, literary devices, and rhetorical flourishes, while the movie is resolutely visual, making its emotional pitch through art, cinematography, editing, and music. The urge to tell a good story is paramount in both, and as readers and viewers we can all be thankful for the results.

A Hero for the Movies

ELBERT R. HILL

The important differences between novels and films become particularly apparent when the same author treats a story in both media, as Alice Childress did when she wrote the screenplay for *A Hero Ain't Nothin' But a Sandwich* (1978), based on a novel she had published five years earlier.

Like other novels directed at an adolescent audience, the story has an adolescent, Benjie Johnson, as its central character. Benjie, who lives in Harlem with his mother Rose, with his grandmother, and sometimes with his "stepfather" Butler, has a heroin habit. The novel follows him through his, initially, casual flirtations with drugs, his insistence that he can always kick the habit—that he, in fact, does not really have a habit—his grudging recognition of his addiction, to an indeterminate but hopeful ending in which he has at least a good chance of getting off drugs. The story is told in a series of first-person narratives, several by Benjie himself, and others by ten other characters, including members of his family, his teachers and friends. Newspaper clippings regarding events mentioned by the narrators follow the appropriate chapters and lend accent or emphasis.

The mood of the novel is stark, and the reader shares Benjie's hopelessness. He does not know where his real father is and agonizes over this fact. Because his mother is busy with her job and her new love, he feels excluded from her life. Butler makes efforts to be a father to him, but Benjie is unable to relate to him and feels that he has stolen Rose's love from him.

In school, Benjie encounters such diverse role models as

Nigeria Greene, a fiery black nationalist who makes racial pride the main study in his classes; Bernard Cohen, a Jewish teacher who worries about the decline of traditional learning in general and about the influence of Greene's teaching methods in particular; and the principal, who is just trying to hold on until his retirement three years hence.

Besides narratives by these characters, we also find various other points of view represented. Benjie's grandmother believes that her particular brand of religion-superstition is the answer to his problem; a neighbor woman has designs on Butler and thinks Rose is foolish to let Benjie or anyone else come between her and such a fine man; a pusher, Walter, denies that he is doing anything particularly bad and maintains that if he didn't supply his customers someone else would. Several boys Benjie's age are portrayed in the book, including his only real friend, Jimmy-Lee, who has broken the dope habit, and with whom Benjie must then break if he is to rationalize his own heroin dependence. There are also some "dope friends," Carwell and Kenny, and another pusher, Tiger.

The first-person narration form is particularly effective in bringing out the uncertainty and ambiguity the various characters feel about their own identities; their stories provide an effective parallel to Benjie's own confusion and uncertainty.

The book is extremely powerful, and Benjie is a character we care about. Though he indulges in considerable adolescent self-pity, he is not without saving graces. His fear of allowing himself to look up to anybody lest he later be disappointed is expressed in the title statement: "A hero ain't nothin' but a sandwich."

We also care about Rose, who longs to express her love for her son but finds herself only able to criticize, and about Butler, who sincerely loves Rose and is fond of Benjie but who though he works hard to support both them and Benjie's grandmother is keenly aware that he has no official status in their lives.

The novel's ending offers no easy solutions to Benjie's problems, but it leaves us hopeful. As Butler waits for Benjie to show up at the Drug Rehabilitation Center, he says: "Come on, Benjie, I believe in you. . . . It's nation time. . . . I'm waiting for you." We do not know for sure that Benjie will actually come, but the understanding that he and Butler have begun to achieve suggests that he has at last begun to have a hero in his life, and it strongly implies that if he does not come that day he will come soon.

Both the problem portrayed and the characters are clearly realistic, and what might easily have been a preachy or sentimental book becomes in Childress's hands a sensitive, honest view of life, the way things are today. Because of her skillful use of first-person narrations, the characters—and not just the problem (drugs)—are important. This is not always true of "problem novels" for young readers.

The film based on the book is a Robert Radnitz production, directed by Ralph Nelson and released by New World Pictures. The character of Benjie is played by Larry B. Scott, with Cicely Tyson as the mother, Paul Winfield as Butler, Glynn Turman as Nigeria, and David Groh as Cohen.

The first change one notices is that the setting has been changed from Harlem to Los Angeles, presumably because it was cheaper to film location shots near the Hollywood studio. Obviously, a drug problem such as Benjie's might as easily be found in Los Angeles as in Harlem since no locale or level of affluence is immune from drugs today, but, the effect of moving Benjie from what is clearly an ugly, threatening environment, as portrayed in the novel, to the movie's world of beautifully landscaped parks, palm trees, and beachfront, is to mute the dreariness that characterizes Benjie's environment in the book. In addition, Benjie's home as depicted in the movie, while not elegant, is clearly no tenement. It is comfortable and livable, and there is even one scene of Benjie and Butler talking in the back yard, with the sky showing through the leaves of a vine arbor overhead.

Even more significant than the shift in setting, however, is the change from the multiple first-person narration form of the book to the dramatic objective viewpoint of the camera eye. The power of the novel in illuminating the characters' inner frustrations and confusions is largely lost through this change. Nowhere is this more evident than in the characters of Nigeria and Cohen, who seem much weaker in the film than in the novel. The very sharp, deep conflict between them and their values—as well as the genuine concern for their students that forms a mutual bond between them—is reduced in the film to a superficial playground confrontation that does little except establish the fact that there is a school drug problem—something already apparent to the viewer. In the case of Benjie and Butler, however, the characters are both so well developed that we do not miss having their first-person narrations.

The roles of some characters are given either greater or lesser emphasis in the film than in the novel. Rose seems more of a real person in the film than in the novel, where she was a rather shadowy figure. The principal does not appear in the film, and we do not particularly miss him. The grandmother and her religion are given somewhat less prominence in the movie, the neighbor woman is completely eliminated; both changes work well in the film. The four characters of Benjie's dope world acquaintance are effectively combined into two in the movie, each being given enough of a role to make him seem real.

Butler's role is significantly increased in the film—so much so that he seems almost equal in importance to Benjie. This may give the movie a real problem with respect to its intended audience. The book is clearly aimed at young adolescents who—to use the filmmakers' term—would be "pre-sold audience," the carryover audience from a popular book. The movie, with its "PG" rating, is apparently trying to appeal to the whole family, thus the greater emphasis on Butler and Rose and their problems. However, a young adolescent would likely not be able to relate to Butler's problem of establishing his role as the father, for instance. The movie is almost *too* much Butler's story, and there is a mild schizophrenia in point of view. The book, in spite of the multiple first-person narration form, is very clearly Benjie's story.

One of the outstanding points about the movie is the excellent quality of the acting. Larry B. Scott as Benjie successfully conveys the adolescent vulnerability hidden beneath a superficial teen-age swagger. Cicely Tyson captures Rose's full range of emotions, from her girlish excitement about a night on the town with Butler to her despair over Benjie's drug problem.

The scene in which Rose desperately tries to wash Benjie's drug problem away in the indigo bath is one of the most touching in the movie. Winfield's portrayal of Butler has quiet strength and great sensitivity. In fact, from the very beginning of the film Butler seems so clearly concerned about Benjie that it is difficult for the viewer to understand why the boy holds him at arm's length for so long. In the book, this side of Butler is far less apparent until late in the story.

The plot of the novel moves more or less straight forward in normal chronology, though there are some overlaps in time because of the changes in narrators, who frequently comment on the events already mentioned and commented on. In the book, this effectively brings out the various viewpoints and is not really distracting or confusing to the reader. Nevertheless, the movie's straightforward presentation may be somewhat easier for young people to follow.

There are several changes in the sequence of events from novel to film. For instance, the encounter between Benjie and Jimmy-Lee in which the latter declares that he is not going to use dope any more because "I got somethin' better for a dollar to do," takes place early in the book. This is a signal to the reader that despite his protestations to the contrary Benjie is becoming so addicted to heroin that he prefers to break off this important relationship, since Jimmy will no longer join him in his habit. In the movie, this scene appears almost at the very end and therefore only indicates that Benjie is continuing in what we already know is a serious drug habit. Its usefulness in helping us follow Benjie's descent into drugs is lost in the movie.

In fact, the movie never makes it sufficiently clear how or why Benjie becomes addicted to drugs. To show that Benjie is becoming hooked, the filmmaker resorts to the device of repetitive scenes showing him using the drugs and earning money for this habit by delivering drugs. In the movie, the whole time lapse from Benjie's first use of marijuana to when we know that he is, in fact, unable to quit heroin, seems altogether too brief and unrealistically sudden. And the question of *why* Benjie takes drugs remains quite puzzling. Though bothered by the fact that he does not know where his real father is, he appears to have no other problem. Because of the shift in setting and some other changes as well, Benjie's environment seems neither hostile nor threatening. At home, he is surrounded by people who care about him, even though they have their own needs and preoccupations too. And in school he even seems to be something of a star. There is a scene in Nigeria's class in which Benjie is able to amaze the whole class, teacher included, with his knowledge about a particular black leader. And in Bernard Cohen's class, he is asked to read aloud a composition for which he is publicly praised and given an "A".

The scene is apparently used to show two things: first, assigned to write about a member of his family, Benjie has selected his mother, thus revealing her importance to him as his only remaining parent. Second, when as part of his praise Cohen says, "Keep this up and some day you'll be somebody," Benjie replies, "I'm somebody now." We are confronted with a common adolescent problem: the feeling that adults don't give them credit for being someone *now*, and focus too much on what they *may* grow up to be. The scene thus fulfills some valid functions in the movie, but combined with the scene in Nigeria's class it also suggests that Benjie's school provides a generally supportive atmosphere. In the book, the praise Benjie receives for the paper about his mother is said to be something that happened years before the time of the book, and it is not typical of his school career. There is no equivalent in the book of the scene in Nigeria's class.

In addition, the Benjie of the novel tells us several times that one of his problems is that he feels betrayed by Nigeria Greene, who, along with Cohen, has turned him in for drug use. Though the movie does show the two teachers taking him out of class when he is obviously stoned, it does not emphasize for us the importance that this betrayal has for Benjie because it has not made sufficiently clear how he has idolized Nigeria.

A time shift that is even more troublesome than the one involving Benjie's encounter with Jimmy-Lee concerns the change in the relationship between Benjie and Butler. In the book, after Butler has saved his life, Benjie writes "Butler is my father" one hundred times. This indicates that Benjie finally realizes that Butler does indeed care for him, and suggests to the reader that the boy is accepting Butler's role in his life. Also, because Benjie slips this paper into Butler's coat pocket, where Butler is sure to find and read it, Butler is given more justification for taking off work to meet Benjie at the Drug Rehab Center. In the movie, Benjie writes "Butler is my father" much earlier, *before* Butler has saved his life—and so far as we know Butler never sees the piece of writing. Thus, the movie Benjie's motivation for trying to get off drugs—like his motivation for getting on them—is not fully clear, and the movie Butler does not have the same motivation to wait for Benjie at the Rehab Center.

Several scenes and elements in the movie do not appear in the book, and some of these are extremely effective. Although the encounter group scene in the hospital, in which other patients bombard Benjie with their views about drugs, seems to add little, Nigeria's oration at Carwell's funeral is touching and effective. The still photographs of Benjie as he goes through the various stages of withdrawal in the hospital are a brilliant directorial choice and heighten our horror at Benjie's predicament.

Moving pictures, however, are clearly better at vividly portraying some scenes than are either stills or word pictures. For instance, the rooftop scene in which Benjie's life is in danger gets our adrenalin flowing far better in the visual medium than in Childress's novel. Along with Benjie, we hang precariously by one hand as Butler strains to pull us up.

The ending of the movie is revealing of the overall differences between the two forms. In the movie, when Butler waits for Benjie at the Rehab Center, the boy actually appears; in the book Butler only waits and hopes. The movie ending is weaker in consequence, but the change is necessitated by the differences in chronology and motivation mentioned earlier. The reader was led to believe that Benjie will appear, because this would be the logical result of his realization of Butler's love for him and of his acceptance of the older man as his hero. But since moviegoers have not had this clear motivation for Benjie to change, they need to be shown that the boy does indeed intend to change.

The experience of viewing a movie based on a book need

not—cannot—be the same as that of reading the book. Whereas the book is more subtle in its portrayal of people and uncompromising in its presentation of the environment in which they live, the movie sharpens the individual portraits but softens the environment. However, we care deeply about the people in both book and movie, and that is one of the important tests of any story presentation, whether verbal or visual.

NOTES ON THE CONTRIBUTORS

LUCIEN L. AGOSTA is an Assistant Professor of English at Kansas State University and a specialist in Victorian literature. His research has been seen in *The Literary Chronicle, The Times Literary Supplement, The Pre-Raphaelite Review, Studies in Short Fiction,* and other publications.

A. HARRIETTE ANDREADIS, as an Assistant Professor at Texas A&M University, initiated and currently instructs in programs both in Film and Women's Studies. Her academic credits include work in women and the media, and in film as literature. Research into definitions of self among nineteenth-century Texas women has culminated in her soon to be completed *Voices of Texas Women.*

MARILYN APSELOFF teaches in the English Department at Kent State University. Her articles and reviews on children's literature and related fields have appeared in *Children's Literature* and in *Children's Literature Quarterly.* She is also a past president of the Children's Literature Association.

CAROL BILLMAN is an Assistant Professor of English at the University of Pittsburgh where she teaches courses in children's literature, film and literature, and popular culture. Her work has appeared in such journals as *Literature/Film Quarterly, Studies in American Fiction, The Journal of Popular Culture,* and *Children's Literature.*

PHYLLIS BIXLER, an Assistant Professor of English at Kansas State University, is a specialist in children's literature and was awarded the Children's Literature Association prize for the outstanding piece of literary criticism published in the field of 1979. Her articles have appeared in *Research About Nineteenth-Century Children and Books,*

Selma K. Richardson editor; *Perspectives on Children's Literature*, Anita K. Moss, editor; and both *The Lion And The Unicorn* and *Children's Literature*.

WILLIAM BLACKBURN is a member of the English faculty at the University of Calgary where he teaches children's literature and science fiction. He is co-editor of *A Manual of Children's Literature in England, 1200–1900*, and has published in *Children's Literature Quarterly*, *Canadian Children's Literature*, *Resources in Education* and *English Studies in Canada*.

JOSEPH ANDREW CASPER is Associate Professor of Cinema at the University of Southern California. His writing and performance credits for television and film are numerous. He is the author of *Vincente Minnelli and the Film Musical* and *The Style of Stanley Donen*.

LEONARD J. DEUTSCH is Associate Professor of English at Marshall University, where he chairs the Black Literature program and teaches courses in Film and Fiction. He is co-founder of *Penumbra* and an advisory board member of *MELUS*. His work has appeared in *Negro Literature Forum*, *Obsidian* and other journals.

CAROL GAY published articles on children's literature, children's drama and pre-Civil War American literature while a member of the English faculty at Youngstown State University. She is currently an Associate Professor and Coordinator of English Graduate Studies. Her work has appeared in such journals as *American Literature*, *Essays in Literature*, *American Literary Realism* and *Children's Literature Quarterly*.

GENE HARDY is a Professor of English at the University of Nebraska-Lincoln and a founder of that department's program in Children's Literature. A force in curriculum development in the Plains region, he was coordinator for the Nebraska Curriculum Center Project, the Tri-University Project at Nebraska, and the Training Teacher Trainers program during the early 1970's. In 1982 he received the University Award for Teaching Excellence.

DONNA J. HARSH has administered programs in language arts, reading and children's literature as an Assistant Professor of Education at Fort Hays State University. Since 1970 she has coordinated her annual Conference on Literature for Children and Youth, and has conducted seminars on Internationalism in Children's Literature in the U.S. and twenty-five foreign countries including the U.S.S.R. and The People's Republic of China. Her work on *The Reconstruction of a Culture*, detailing efforts in China to improve the state of children's literature, is being readied for publication.

ELBERT R. HILL is Professor of English at Southeastern Oklahoma State University, where he teaches a variety of topics in literature and ethnic studies. He has researched and published in areas of Native American Literature and Studies, focusing on the children's tales and traditional tales of the Winnebago. He has taught English in the Vietnamese Refugee Program in Oklahoma, and has acted as director for the Oklahoma Humanities Committee's project in Cultural Awareness in Oklahoma.

TOM JORDAN is the film and arts critic for television station KDFW in Dallas, Texas, and has taught various courses in film studies. His publications include *The Anatomy of Cinematic Humor*.

RUTH K. MACDONALD is currently Assistant Professor of English at Boston's Northeastern University. Her articles and reviews on nineteenth-century American children's literature have appeared in *Children's Literature* and *The New England Quarterly*. The author of *Literature for Children in England and America, 1646–1774* and *Louisa May Alcott*, she is also a past president of the Children's Literature Association.

RODERICK MCGILLIS is Assistant Professor of English at the University of Calgary. He has written on children's literature, film, fantasy studies, and Victorian fiction criticism for journals such as *English Studies in Canada*, *The English Quarterly*, *Canadian Children's Literature*, and *Mythlore*.

PERRY NODELMAN is a member of the faculty of English at the University of Winnipeg, where he teaches Children's Literature, Modern Drama, and Victorian Literature. He was a founder and president of Winnipeg's Cubiculo Theatre and currently serves as an editor for the *Children's Literature Quarterly*. His articles have appeared in *Modern Drama*, *The Journal of Canadian Fiction*, *Children's Literature in Education*, and *Children's Literature*.

KEITH C. ODOM is Director of the Honors Program and Associate Professor of English at Texas Christian University. A specialist in the English romantic Period, the British novel, and fantasy, he is at present working on a book about the Brontës and Romanticism. His articles have appeared in *Descant*, *Studies in the Novel*, and in other journals, and he has written a full-length study of the English novelist Henry Green.

PRISCILLA A. ORD is a linguist and children's literature specialist currently on the faculty of English at Iona College. She has previously served as Administrative Assistant at Pennsylvania and American

University and is currently the editor of *Proceedings of the Children's Literature Association* and an associate editor of *Children's Literature Quarterly*.

ELLEN E. SEITER is an Assistant Professor of Film at the University of Oregon. She has been co-editor of *Film Reader* and lectured on avant-garde film and women in film and video. Her work has been seen in *Film Reader* and *Jump Cut*. As an experimental filmmaker, she has had screenings in both the U.S. and Canada and possesses film awards from two international festivals.

RICHARD D. SEITER is an Assistant Professor at Central Michigan University. He has taught Children's Literature and has created special courses in film versions of children's books, children's picture books, and special children in children's literature.

W. M. VON ZHAREN has written and lectured on film production and analysis both in the United States and Europe. She has been a regular film critic for several newspapers, and has also published studies of Ingmar Bergman and the image of American Indians in film. A Fulbright Lecturer in Film and American Studies in Denmark, she currently lives and teaches in West Germany.

MARK WEST is currently a teaching fellow in the American Culture Program of Bowling Green State University. A specialist in children's studies and children's popular entertainments, he has published in both *Young Children Magazine* and in *The Journal of Social History*.

VIRGINIA L. WOLF, whose writings have appeared in *The Wilson Library Bulletin*, *Children's Literature*, and *The Wisconsin English Journal*, is a writer and critic whose teaching experience has included instruction in children's literature, writing for children, fantasy, and science fiction. She is an Assistant Professor on the faculty of the University of Wisconsin–Stout.

THE EDITOR

DOUGLAS STREET has taught both in English and in Theatre while serving as chairperson for the Children's Literature Program in the English Department of Texas A&M University. His articles on film adaptation and children's fiction and on current child taste in cinema have appeared in special issues of *Children's Literature Quarterly*. His analyses of children's literature, children's theater, and American Studies, have appeared in *Children's Theatre Review*, *The Journal of*

Philosophy and Social Science, The Prairie Schooner and *Southwest Review*. His overview of American children's literary history, 1880–1980, is included in *Dramatic Literature for Children: A Century in Review*, and his book-length study of Bram Stoker is being readied for publication.

FILM CREDITS

Films are listed in order of discussion within this volume.
CODE: *Prod*: Production Company/Producer (if appropriate).
Dir: Director. Scr: Screenplay. Photo: Director of Photography. Anim: Animated.
(Rental sources are included in the Filmography.)

Tom Brown's Schooldays (1940). Prod: RKO/David O. Selznick. Dir: Robert Stevenson. Scr: Walter Ferris, Frank Cavell. Photo: Nicholas Musuraca. Music: Anthony Collins. Cast: Freddie Bartholomew, Sir Cedric Hardwicke, Billy Halop, Jimmy Lydon, Gale Storm, Josephine Hutchinson.

Tom Brown's Schooldays (1951). Prod: Renown-United Artists/Brian Desmond-Hurst. Dir: Gordon Parry. Scr: Noel Langley. Photo: C. Pennington-Richards. Music: Richard Addinsell. Cast: John Howard Davies, Robert Newton, James Hayter, John Charlesworth, John Forrest.

Alice In Wonderland (1933). Prod: Paramount. Dir: Norman Z. McLeod. Scr: William Cameron Menzies, Joseph L. Mankiewicz. Photo: Henry Sharp, Bert Glennon. Music: Dimitri Tiomkin. Cast: Charlotte Henry, Richard Arlen, Gary Cooper, Colin Campbell, W. C. Fields, Cary Grant, Sterling Holloway, Edward Everett Horton, Mae Marsh, Jack Oakie, Edna May Oliver, May Robson, Charles Ruggles, Ned Sparks, Ford Sterling.

Alice's Adventures In Wonderland (1972). Prod: 20th Century-Fox. Dir & Scr: William Sterling. Photo: Geoffrey Unsworth. Music & Lyrics: John Barry, Don Black. Cast: Fiona Fullerton, Michael Crawford, Peter Sellers, Dudley Moore, Flora Robson, Robert Helpmann, Michael Hordern, Ralph Richardson, Michael Jayston, Spike Milligan.

Little Women (1933). Prod: RKO/David O. Selznick. Dir: George Cukor. Scr: Sarah Y. Mason, Victor Heerman. Photo: Henry Gerrard. Music: Max Steiner. Cast: Katharine Hepburn, Joan Bennett, Frances Dee, Jean Parker, Paul Lukas, Douglass Montgomery, Edna May Oliver, Henry Stephenson, Spring Byington.

Little Women (1948). Prod: MGM/Mervyn LeRoy. Dir: Mervyn LeRoy. Scr: Andrew Solt, Sarah Y. Mason, Victor Heerman. Photo: Franz Planer. Music: Adolph Deutsch. Cast: June Allyson, Margaret O'Brien, Janet Leigh, Mary Astor, Peter Lawford, Elizabeth Taylor, Rossano Brazzi, C. Aubrey Smith.

Toby Tyler, Or, Ten Weeks With A Circus (1960). Prod: Walt Disney. Dir: Charles Barton. Scr: Bill Walsh, Lillie Hayward. Photo: William Snyder. Music: Buddy Baker. Cast: Kevin Corcoran, Henry Calvin, Gene Sheldon, Bob Sweeney, Richard Eastham, James Drury, Barbara Beaird, Edith Evanson, Dennis Joel, Tom Fadden.

Pinocchio (1940—Anim). Prod: Walt Disney. Dir: Ben Sharpsteen, Hamilton Luske. Scr: Ted Sears, Otto Englander, Webb Smith, William Cottrell, Joseph Sabo, Erdman Penner, Aurelius Battaglia. Music: Leigh Harline, Ned Washington, Paul J. Smith. Voices: Dickie Jones, Cliff Edwards, Evelyn Venable, Walter Catlett, Frankie Darro, Don Brodie.

Treasure Island (1934). Prod: MGM/Hunt Stromberg. Dir: Victor Fleming. Scr: John Lee Mahin. Photo: Ray June, Clyde de Vinna, Harold Rosson. Music: Herbert Stothart. Cast: Wallace Beery, Jackie Cooper, Lionel Barrymore, Otto Kruger, Lewis Stone, Nigel Bruce, Douglas Dumbrille.

Treasure Island (1950). Prod: Walt Disney. Dir: Byron Haskin. Scr: Lawrence Edward Watkin. Photo: F. A. Young. Music: Clifton Parker. Cast: Robert Newton, Bobby Driscoll, Basil Sidney, Finlay Currie, Geoffrey Wilkinson, Denis O'Dea, Walter Fitzgerald, Ralph Truman.

Treasure Island (1972). Prod: National General/Harry Alan Towers. Dir: John Hough. Scr: Wolf Mankowitz, O. W. Jeeves (Orson Welles). Photo: Cicilio Paniagua. Music: Natal Massara. Cast: Orson Welles, Kim Burfield, Lionel Stander, Walter Slezak, Rik Battaglia, Maria Rohm, Jean Lefevbre.

Little Lord Fauntleroy (1936). Prod: United Artists/David O. Selznick. Dir: John Cromwell. Scr: Hugh Walpole. Cast: C. Aubrey Smith, Freddie Bartholomew, Dolores Costello Barrymore, Henry Stephenson, Guy Kibbee, Mickey Rooney.

Little Lord Fauntleroy (1980). Prod: Norman Rosemont. Dir: Jack Gold. Scr: Blanche Hanalis. Cast: Sir Alec Guinness, Ricky Schroder, Colin Blakely, Connie Booth, Eric Porter.

Kidnapped (1971). Prod: American International/Frderick Brugger. Dir: Delbert Mann. Scr: Jack Pullman. Photo: Paul Beeson. Music: Roy Budd. Cast: Michael Caine, Trevor Howard, Lawrence Douglas, Jack Hawkins, Donald Pleasance, Vivien Heilbron, Gordon Jackson.

The Wizard Of Oz (1939). Prod: MGM/Mervyn LeRoy. Dir: Victor Fleming. Scr: Noel Langley, Florence Ryerson, Edgar Allan Woolf. Photo: Harold Rosson. Music: Herbert Stothart, E. Y. Harburg, Harold Arlen. Cast: Judy Garland, Frank Morgan, Ray Bolger, Bert Lahr, Jack Haley, Margaret Hamilton, Charley Grapewin, Clara Blandick, Billie Burke.

Kim (1951). Prod: MGM. Dir: Victor Saville. Scr: Leon Gordon, Helen Deutsch, Richard Schayer. Photo: William Skall. Music: Andre Previn. Cast: Errol Flynn, Dean Stockwell, Paul Lukas, Robert Douglas, Cecil Kellaway, Reginald Owen.

The Railway Children (1971). Prod: Universal. Dir & Scr: Lionel Jeffries. Photo: Arthur Ibbetson. Music: Johnny Douglas. Cast: Dinah Sheridan, Jenny Agutter, Bernard Gribbens, William Mervyn, Sally Thomsett, Gary Warren, Allan Cuthbertson, Peter Bromilow, Gordon Whiting.

The Secret Garden (1949). Prod: MGM/Clarence Brown. Dir: Fred Wilcox. Scr: Robert Ardrey. Photo: Ray June. Music: Bronislau Kaper. Cast: Margaret O'Brien, Brian Roper, Dean Stockwell, Herbert Marshall, Gladys Cooper, Elsa Lanchester, Reginald Owen, Aubrey Mather.

The Hobbit (1977—Anim). Prod & Dir: Arthur Rankin, Jr., Jules Bass. Scr: Romeo Muller. Music: Maury Laws. Lyrics: Jules Bass. Voices: Orson Bean, John Huston, Otto Preminger, Hans Conreid, Cyril Richard, Richard Boone.

The Little Prince (1974). Prod: Paramount/Stanley Donen. Dir: Stanley Donen. Scr & Lyrics: Alan J. Lerner. Photo: Christopher Challis. Music: Frederick Loewe. Cast: Richard Kiley, Steven Warner, Bob Fosse, Gene Wilder, Joss Ackland, Clive Reville, Victor Spinetti, Donna McKechnie, Graham Crowden.

Pippi Longstocking (1969). Prod: Nort-Art (Sweden)/Constantin Films (Germany). Dir: Olle Hellblom. Scr: Astrid Lindgren. Photo: Kalle Bergholm. Music: Georg Riedel. Cast: Inger Nilsson, Maria Persson, Par Sundberg, Beppe Wolgen, Margot Trooger.

The Lion, the Witch and the Wardrobe (1979—Anim). Prod: David Connell. Dir: Bill Melendez. Scr: David D. Connell, Bill Melendez. Music: Michael J. Lewis. Voices: Dick Vosborough, Rachel Warren, Victor Spinetti, Don Parker, Liz Proud, Beth Porter.

Charlotte's Web (1973—Anim). Prod: William Hanna, Joseph Barbera. Dir: Charles Nichols, Iwao Takamoto. Scr: Earl Hamner,

Jr. Music & Lyrics: Richard M. Sherman, Robert B. Sherman. Voices: Debbie Reynolds, Henry Gibson, Paul Lynde, Martha Scott, Agnes Moorhead. Narrator: Rex Allen.

Island Of The Blue Dolphins (1964). Prod: Universal/Robert B. Radnitz. Dir: James B. Clark. Scr: Ted Sherdeman, Jane Klove. Photo: Leo Tover. Music: Paul Sawtell. Cast: Celia Kaye, Carlos Romero, George Kennedy, Junior, the Manchester and Kashai Tribes of the Poma Nation.

Willy Wonka And The Chocolate Factory (1971). Prod: Paramount/ David L. Wolper, Stan Margulies. Dir: Mel Stuart. Scr: Roald Dahl. Photo: Arthur Ibbetson. Music: Walter Scharf, Leslie Bricusse. Lyrics: Anthony Newley. Cast: Gene Wilder, Jack Albertson, Peter Ostrum, Michael Bollner, Ursula Reit, Denise Mickerson, Leonard Stone, Roy Kinnear, Julie Dawn Cole, Paris Themmen.

Chitty Chitty Bang Bang (1968). Prod: United Artists. Dir: Ken Hughes. Scr: Roald Dahl, Ken Hughes. Photo: Christopher Challis. Music: Irwin Kostal. Songs: Richard M. Sherman, Robert B. Sherman. Cast: Dick Van Dyke, Sally Ann Howes, Lionel Jefries, Adrian Hall, Heather Ripley, Gert Frobe, Anna Quayle, Benny Hill, Robert Helpmann.

From The Mixed-Up Files Of Mrs. Basil E. Frankweiler (1973). Prod: Cinema V/Charles G. Mortimer. Dir: Fielder Cook. Scr: Blanche Hanalis. Photo: Victor J. Kemper. Music: Donald Devor. Cast: Ingrid Bergman, Sally Prager, Johnny Doran, George Rose, Richard Mulligan, Madeline Kahn. Reissued as *The Hideaways*.

Sounder (1972). Prod: 20th Century-Fox/Robert B. Radnitz. Dir: Martin Ritt. Scr: Lonne Elder III. Photo: John Alonzo. Music: Taj Mahal. Cast: Cicely Tyson, Paul Winfield, Kevin Hooks, Carmen Matthews, Taj Mahal, Janet MacLachlin, James Best.

Watership Down (1978—Anim). Prod: Avco-Embassy/Martin Rosen. Dir & Scr: Martin Rosen. Voices: John Hurt, Richard Briers, Roy Kinnear, Ralph Richardson, Denholm Elliot, Zero Mostel.

A Hero Ain't Nothin' But A Sandwich (1978). Prod: New World Pictures/Robert B. Radnitz. Dir: Ralph Nelson. Scr: Alice Childress. Photo: Frank Stanley. Music: Tom McIntosh. Cast: Cicely Tyson, Paul Winfield, Larry B. Scott, Helen Martin, Glynn Turman, David Groh, Kevin Hooks, Harold Sylvester, Kenneth (Joey) Green.

SELECTED FILMOGRAPHY

Film Adaptations of Children's Novels

The following compilation is meant as a better than representative but by no means exhaustive list of film adaptations of children's novels. The inclusions, or exclusions, in some cases are admittedly open to opinion as to their categorization as children's books, or as deserving the company of reputed literary "classics." However, of those works cited, it was felt that since no such filmography at present exists, a free interpretation in the selection of these titles could better suit a greater percentage of interested readers. Also, while every effort has been made to accommodate every filmed version of each novel. many, particularly from the pre-1920 silent era, are quite obscure and hence may have been herein ignored. With regard to international adaptations, limited source materials and a rapidly expanding foreign industry, in the area of the animated feature in particular, make a complete listing extremely difficult to achieve.

Those considering film rental should note that while this information is current as of publication, the rental industry so fluctuates that a timely double-checking of agency holdings is recommended. A film appearing with no rental source is not necessarily unavailable for viewing; it may have been released to the agencies after this volume went to press or, the limited references for rental sources may have somehow failed to include its distributors.

Readers desiring further information on the filmed adaptations of children's fiction are directed to: A.G.S. Enser's *Filmed Books and Plays, 1928–1974*, London: Andre Deutsch, 1975; Richard B. Dimmitt's, *A Title Guide to the Talkies* (2 vols.), Metuchen, NJ: Scarecrow Press, 1970, 1971, 1973, with supplements by Andrew A. Aros, *A Title Guide to the Talkies, 1964–1974*, Metuchen: Scarecrow Press, 1977; D. Richard Baer's *The Film Buff's Checklist of Motion Pictures (1912–1979)*, Hollywood: Hollywood Film Archive, 1979; and Dennis La Beau's, *Theatre, Film And Television Biographies Master Index*, Detroit: Gale Research, 1979.

Author—Title	Film Version: Title (if changed), Production Company, Release Date Director (d)	Rental Source(s)
ADAMS, Richard (1920–)		
Watership Down (1972)	AVCO/Embassy, 1978– animated (d) Martin Rosen	FNC
ALCOTT, Louisa May (1832–1888)		
Little Men (1871)	Mascot, 1934 (d) Phil Rosen	BUD, CFM, FCE
	RKO, 1940 (d) Norman Z. McLeod	ALB, BUD, IVY, MOG, ROA, TMC, VCI, WHO
Little Women (1868)	Brady, 1918—silent (d) Harley Knowles	—
	RKO, 1933 (d) George Cukor	FNC
	MGM, 1949 (d) Mervyn LeRoy	MGM
	TV, 1978 (d) David Lowell Rich	—
ARMSTRONG, William H. (1914–)		
Sounder (1969)	20th Century-Fox, 1972 (d) Martin Ritt	FNC
	Part 2, Sounder Gamma III, 1976 (d) William A. Graham	CWF, ICS, MOD, SWA, WCF, WHO
BABBITT, Natalie (1932–)		
Tuck Everlasting (1975)	Robert Nesslin Productions, 1976 (d) Frederick King Keller	ERF
BAGNOLD, Enid (1889–1981)		
National Velvet (1930)	MGM, 1944 (d) Clarence Brown	MGM

Author—Title	Film Version: Title (if changed), Production Company, Release Date Director (d)	Rental Source(s)
	International Velvet MGM, 1978 (d) Bryan Forbes	MGM
BAUM, L. Frank (1856–1919)		
The Wonderful Wizard of Oz (1900)	*The Wizard of Oz* Chadwick Pictures, 1925— silent (d) Larry Semon	BUD, EMG, KPF, SEL
	The Wizard of Oz MGM, 1939 (d) Victor Fleming	MGM
	Return to Oz UPA, 1968—animated (d) Norman Prescott	BUD, CCC, CHA, CWF, FNC, ICS, NEW, ROA, SEL, TWY, WCF, WEL, WIL
	Journey Back to Oz EBA, 1973—animated (d) Hal Sutherland	FNC
BURNETT, Frances Hodgson (1849–1924)		
Little Lord Fauntleroy (1886)	United Artists, 1921—silent (d) Alfred E. Green, Jack Pickford	—
	United Artists, 1936 (d) John Cromwell	AIM, ALB, BUD, CFM, FCE, FNC, MOG, ROA, VCI, WEL, WHO
The Little Princess (1905)	20th Century-Fox, 1939 (d) Walter Lang	BUD, CFM, CIE, EMG, FNC, IMA, NCS, NEW, REE, ROA, TWY, VCI, WEL

Author—Title	Film Version: Title (if changed), Production Company, Release Date Director (d)	Rental Source(s)
The Secret Garden (1911)	MGM, 1949 (d) Fred M. Wilcox	MGM
CARROLL, Lewis (1832–1898)		
Alice's Adventures in Wonderland (1865)	Edison, 1910—silent	—
	Alice in Wonderland Nonpareil, 1915—silent (d) W. W. Young	BUD, EMG
	Alice in Wonderland Pathe, 1927—silent	MOG
	Alice in Wonderland Paramount, 1933 (d) Norman Z. McLeod	UNI
	Alice in Wonderland RKO/Disney, 1951— animated (d) Clyde Geronimi	AIM, COU, DIS, FNC, NAT, SWA
	American National, 1972 (d) William Sterling	AIM, BUD, CWF, FNC, JEN, VCI, WCF
CHILDRESS, Alice (1920–)		
A Hero Ain't Nothin' But A Sandwich (1973)	New World, 1978 (d) Ralph Nelson	FNC
CLEAVER, Bill and Vera		
Where the Lilies Bloom (1969)	United Artists, 1974 (d) William A. Graham	MGM
COLLODI, Carlo (1826–1890)		
The Adventures of Pinocchio (1881)	Italy/CAIR, 1936—animated (d) Raoul Verdini	—
	Pinocchio RKO/Disney, 1940— animated (d) Ben Sharpsteen, Hamilton Luske	—

Author—Title	Film Version: Title (if changed), Production Company, Release Date Director (d)	Rental Source(s)
	Pinocchio Childhood, 1969—animated (d) Ron Merk	FNC, ROA, WCF, WHO
	Pinocchio Italy/CCI, 1972—animated (d) Giuliano Cenci	—
DAHL, Roald (1916–)		
Charlie and the Chocolate Factory (1964)	*Willy Wonka . . .* Paramount, 1971 (d) Mel Stuart	FNC
DEFOE, Daniel (1659–1731)		
Robinson Crusoe (1719)	Bison, 1913—silent (d) Otis Turner	—
	Universal, 1917—silent	—
	Universal, 1924—silent	—
	Epic, 1929—silent	FCE
	Guaranteed Pictures, 1936 (d) M. A. Wetherell	—
	The Adventures of . . . United Artists, 1954 (d) Luis Bunuel	ALB, FNC
	Australia/API, 1970— animated (d) Leif Gram	BUD, CWF, ICS, ROA, TWY, WHO
DICKENS, Charles (1812–1870)		
A Christmas Carol (1843)	Essanay, 1908—silent	—
	Edison, 1910—silent	—
	Scrooge Zenith, 1913—silent (d) Leedham Bantock	—
	London Film Company, 1914—silent (d) Harold Shaw	—

257

Author—Title	Film Version: Title (if changed), Production Company, Release Date Director (d)	Rental Source(s)
	Scrooge Master Films, 1922—silent (d) George Wynn	—
	Scrooge British and Colonial, 1923— silent (d) Edwin Greenwood	—
	Scrooge British Sound Films, 1928 (d) Hugh Croise	—
	Scrooge Twickenham, 1935 (d) Henry Edwards	BUC, BUD, FCE, KPF, NEW, SEL, TFC, WEL, WIL
	MGM, 1938 (d) Edward L. Marin	MGM
	Renown, 1951 (d) Brian Desmond Hurst	BUD, CFM, FNC, VCI
	CBS-TV, 1956 (d) Ralph Levy	AIM, BUD, FNC, KPF, LEW, TWY, VCI
	. . . with Mr. Magoo UPA, 1962—animated (d) Abe Levitow	BUD, FNC, ICS, KER, MOD, ROA, TFC, WCF, WEL
	Australia/API, 1970— animated	AIM, BUD, FNC, ICS, MOD
	Scrooge Waterbury, 1971 (d) Ronald Neame	MOD, SWA, TWY
David Copperfield (1849)	Hepworth, 1913—silent (d) Thomas Bentley	—
	Associated Exhibitors, 1923—silent	—

Author—Title	Film Version: Title (if changed), Production Company, Release Date Director (d)	Rental Source(s)
	MGM, 1935 (d) George Cukor	MGM
	20th Century-Fox, 1970 (d) Delbert Mann	—
Great Expectations (1860–61)	Paramount, 1917—silent	—
	Universal, 1934—silent (d) Stuart Walker	UNI
	Universal, 1947 (d) David Lean	BUD, CAL, CON, FNC, IMA, KPF, LCA, MOD, ROA, TWY, WCF, WEL, WHO
	Two Cities, 1974 (d) Joseph Hardy	SWA
Oliver Twist (1837)	Hepworth, 1912—silent (d) Thomas Bentley	—
	Paramount, 1916—silent	—
	Oliver Twist, Jr. 20th Century-Fox, 1921—silent (d) Millard Webb	—
	First National, 1922—silent (d) Frank Lloyd	EMG, KPF, TWY
	Monogram, 1933 (d) William J. Cowan	ALB, BUD, CFM, EMG, FCE
	United Artists, 1948 (d) David Lean	FNC
	Oliver! Columbia, 1968 (d) Carol Reed	ARG, CCC, CWF, FNC, ICS, IMA, JEN, ROA, SEL, SWA, TFC, TWY, VCI, WCF, WHO

Author—Title	Film Version: Title (if changed), Production Company, Release Date Director (d)	Rental Source(s)
The Pickwick Papers (1836)	Vitagraph, 1913—silent (d) Larry Trimble	—
	Renown, 1950 (d) Noel Langley	BUD, KPF, VIC, WHO
DODGE, Mary Mapes (1831–1905)		
Hans Brinker, or The Silver Skates (1865)	*Silver Skates* Monogram, 1943 (d) Leslie Goodwins	AIM, FNC, MOG, ROA, TFC, WHO
	Germany, 1962 (d) Norman Foster	AIM, BUC, CCC, COU, CWF, FNC, LEW, ROA, TWY
FARLEY, Walter (1920–)		
The Black Stallion (1941)	United Artists, 1979 (d) Carroll Ballard	UNI
FLEMING, Ian (1908–1964)		
Chitty Chitty Bang Bang (1964)	United Artists, 1968 (d) Ken Hughes	CWF, MGM, ROA, WCF, WHO
FORBES, Esther (1894–1967)		
Johnny Tremain (1943)	Disney, 1957 (d) Robert Stevenson	AIM, BUC, CCC, CWF, FNC, JEN, MOD, NAT, ROA, SEL, SWA, TFC, TWY
GIPSON, Fred (1908–1973)		
Old Yeller (1956)	Disney, 1957 (d) Robert Stevenson	FNC, SEL
Savage Sam (1962)	Disney, 1963	AIM, BUC,

Author—Title	Film Version: Title (if changed), Production Company, Release Date Director (d)	Rental Source(s)
	(d) Norman Tokar	CCC, COU, CWF, FNC, LEW, NEW, ROA, SWA, TWY
HENRY, Marguerite (1902–)		
Brighty of the Grand Canyon (1953)	Feature Film Corp, 1966 (d) Norman Foster	BUD, CCC, CWF, FNC, JEN, ROA, TFC, TWY, WCF, WHO
Misty of Chincoteague (1947)	*Misty* 20th Century-Fox, 1961 (d) James B. Clark	FNC
HOBAN, Russell (1925–)		
The Mouse and His Child (1967)	Sanrio, 1976—animated (d) Fred Wolf, Charles Swenson	SAN
HUGHES, Thomas (1822–1896)		
Tom Brown's Schooldays (1857)	RKO, 1940 (d) Robert Stevenson	BUD, CFM, CHA, FCE, FNC, IVY, MOG, TMC, VCI, WHO
	United Artists, 1951 (d) Gordon Parry	KPF, UNI, VCI, WHO
JOHNSTON, Annie Fellows (1863–1931)		
The Little Colonel (1895)	20th Century-Fox, 1935 (d) David Butler	FNC
JUSTER, Norton (1929–)		
The Phantom Tollbooth (1961)	MGM, 1970—animated (d) David Monahan, Chuck Jones, Abe Levitow	MGM

Author—Title	Film Version: Title (if changed), Production Company, Release Date Director (d)	Rental Source(s)
KALER, James Otis (1848–1912)		
Toby Tyler, or Ten Weeks With a Circus (1881)	Disney, 1960 (d) Charles Barton	CCC, CWF, FNC, JEN, MOD, ROA, SEL, SWA, TFC, TWY
KASTNER, Erich (1899–1974)		
Emil and the Detectives (1930)	Germany/UFA, 1931 (d) Gerhard Lamprecht	TWF
	Britain, 1935 (d) Milton Rosner	ALB, FCE
	Disney, 1964 (d) Peter Tewksbury	—
Lottie and Lisa (1950)	*The Parent Trap* Disney, 1961 (d) David Swift	CWF, DIS, FNC, FPC, MOD, TWY
KIPLING, Rudyard (1865–1936)		
Captains Courageous (1897)	MGM, 1937 (d) Victor Fleming	MGM
	Norman Rosemont, 1977 (d) Harvey Hunt	—
The Jungle Book (1894)	United Artists, 1942 (d) Zoltan Korda	ARG, BUD, CFM, CWF, EMG, FNC, IMA, JEN, KPF, ROA, SEL, UNI, VCI, WCF, WHO
	Disney, 1967—animated (d) Wolfgang Reitherman	—
Kim (1901)	MGM, 1951 (d) Victor Saville	MGM

Author—Title	Film Version: Title (if changed), Production Company, Release Date Director (d)	Rental Source(s)
KONIGSBURG, E. L. (1930–)		
From the Mixed-Up Files of Mrs. Basil E. Frankweiler (1967)	*The Hideaways* (alternate title) Cinema V, 1973 (d) Fiedler Cook	CCC, FNC
KRUMGOLD, Joseph (1908–1980)		
And Now Miguel (1953)	Universal, 1966 (d) James B. Clark	CWF, SWA, TWY, UNI
LEWIS, C. S. (1898–1963)		
The Lion, the Witch, and the Wardrobe (1950)	CTW/Melendez Productions, 1979 (d) Bill Melendez	ERF
LINDGREN, Astrid (1907–)		
Pippi Goes On Board (1946)	Nord-Art/Constantin, 1971 (d) Olle Hellblom	FNC
Pippi in the South Seas (1948)	Nord-Art/Constantin, 1970 (d) Olle Hellblom	FNC
Pippi Longstocking (1945)	Nord-Art/Constantin, 1969 (d) Olle Hellblom	FNC
	Pippi on the Run Nord-Art/Constantin, 1970 (d) Olle Hellblom	FNC
LOFTING, Hugh (1886–1947)		
The Story of Doctor Dolittle (1920)	*Doctor Dolittle* 20th Century-Fox, 1967 (d) Richard Fleischer	FNC
LONDON, Jack (1876–1916)		
The Call of the Wild (1903)	United Artists, 1935 (d) William A. Wellman	FNC
	MGM, 1972 (d) Ken Annakin	MGM

Author—Title	Film Version: Title (if changed), Production Company, Release Date Director (d)	Rental Source(s)
	Charles Fries Productions, 1976 (d) Jerry Jameson	—
MILNE, Alan Alexander (1882–1956)		
Winnie-The-Pooh (1926)	*The Many Adventures of . . .* Disney, 1977—animated (d) Wolfgang Reitherman	DIS, FNC, MOD, ROA, SWA, TWY
NESBIT, Edith (1858–1924)		
The Railway Children (1906)	Universal/Britain, 1971 (d) Lionel Jeffries	MOD, TWY, UNI
NORTON, Mary (1903–)		
Bedknob and Broomstick (1957)	*Bedknobs and Broomsticks* Disney, 1971 (d) Robert Stevenson	AIM, CCC, CWF, DIS, FNC, FPC, MOD, NAT, ROA, SWA, TWY
The Borrowers (1952)	NBC-TV, 1973 (d) Walter C. Miller	—
O'BRIEN, Robert C. (1918–1973)		
Mrs. Frisby and the Rats of NIMH (1971)	*The Secret of NIMH* MGM-United Artists, 1982— animated (d) Don Bluth	MGM
O'DELL, Scott (1903–)		
Island of the Blue Dolphins (1960)	Universal, 1964 (d) James B. Clark	CWF, TWY, UNI
OUIDA (1839–1908)		
A Dog of Flanders (1872)	RKO, 1935 (d) Edward Sloman	FNC

Author—Title	Film Version: Title (if changed), Production Company, Release Date Director (d)	Rental Source(s)
	20th Century-Fox, 1959 (d) James B. Clark	AIM, ALB, ARG, BUD, CHA, CWF, FNC, MOD, NEW, ROA, SEL, TMC, VCI, WEL, WHO, WIL
PORTER, Eleanor H. (1868–1920)		
Pollyanna (1913)	United Artists, 1920—silent (d) Paul Powell	—
	Disney, 1960 (d) David Swift	AIM, BUC, CCC, COU, CWF, DIS, FNC, MOD, NAT, NEW, ROA, SEL, SWA, TFC, TWY
POTTER, Beatrix (1866–1943)		
The Tale of Peter Rabbit (1902)	*Peter Rabbit and Tales of* *Beatrix Potter* MGM, 1971 (d) Reginald Mills	MGM
PYLE, Howard (1853–1911)		
Men of Iron (1892)	*The Black Shield of* *Falmouth* Universal, 1954 (d) Rudolph Mate	UNI
RANSOME, Arthur (1884–1967)		
Swallows and Amazons (1930)	EMI, 1974 (d) Claude Whatham	—
RAWLINGS, Marjorie Kinnan (1896–1953)		

Author—Title	Film Version: Title (if changed), Production Company, Release Date Director (d)	Rental Source(s)
The Yearling (1938)	MGM, 1946 (d) Clarence Brown	MGM
RAWLS, (Woodrow) Wilson (1913–)		
Where the Red Fern Grows (1961)	Doty/Dayton, 1976 (d) Norman Tokar	CWF, MOD, SWA, WCF
RODGERS, Mary (1931–)		
Freaky Friday (1972)	Disney, 1976 (d) Gary Nelson	DIS, SWA
SAINT-EXUPERY, Antoine de (1900–1944)		
The Little Prince (1943)	Paramount, 1974 (d) Stanley Donen	FNC
SEWELL, Anna (1820–1878)		
Black Beauty (1877)	Vitagraph, 1921—silent	FCE
	Monogram, 1933 (d) Phil Rosen	FCE
	20th Century-Fox, 1946 (d) Max Nosseck	FNC
	The Courage of Black Beauty 20th Century-Fox, 1957 (d) Harold Schuster	FNC
	Paramount, 1971 (d) James Hill	FNC
SHARP, Margery (1905–)		
The Rescuers (1959)	Disney, 1977—animated (d) Wolfgang Reitherman	CCC, CWF, DIS, FNC, JEN, MOD, NEW, ROA, SWA, TFC, TWY

Author—Title	Film Version: Title (if changed), Production Company, Release Date Director (d)	Rental Source(s)
SIDNEY, Margaret (1844–1924)		
Five Little Peppers and How They Grew (1881)	Columbia, 1939 (d) Charles Barton	ARG, BUC, CCC, ICS, MOD
	Five Little Peppers at Home Columbia, 1940 (d) Charles Barton	CCC, ICS, MOD
	Five Little Peppers in Trouble Columbia, 1940 (d) Charles Barton	CHA, ICS, MOD
SPYRI, Johanna (1827–1901)		
Heidi (1884)	20th Century-Fox, 1937 (d) Allan Dwan	FNC
	Switzerland, 1953 (d) Luigi Comencini	BUC, BUD, CCC, FNC, ICS
	NBC-TV, 1968 (d) Delbert Mann	BUD
	Warners/Seven Arts, 1968 (d) Werner Jacobs	ARG, BUD, CHA, CWF, FNC, ICS, MOD, NEW, ROA, SWA, TFC, WCF, WEL
	Heidi and Peter Switzerland, 1955 (d) Franz Schnyder	BUD, FNC
STEINBECK, John (1902–1968)		
The Red Pony (1945)	Republic, 1949 (d) Lewis Milestone	ARG, BUD, CCC, CWF, IVY, KPF,

267

Author—Title	Film Version: Title (if changed), Production Company, Release Date Director (d)	Rental Source(s)
		MOD, ROA, SEL, TWY, WCF, WEL, WHO
	Phoenix/Frederick Brugger, 1974 (d) Robert Totten	BUD, PNX
STEVENSON, Robert Louis (1850–1894)		
The Black Arrow (1889)	Columbia, 1948 (d) Gordon Douglas	BUD, FNC, ICS, WCF, WEL
	Australian, 1972—animated (d) Leif Gram	WCF
Kidnapped (1886)	Edison, 1917—silent (d) Alan Crosland	—
	20th Century-Fox, 1938 (d) Alfred M. Werker	FNC
	Monogram, 1948 (d) William Beaudine	CCC, CIN
	Disney, 1960 (d) Robert Stevenson	AIM, BUC, CCC, COU, CWF, DIS, FNC, FPC, MOD, ROA, SWA, TFC, TWY, WCF, WEL
	American International, 1971 (d) Delbert Mann	ARG, BUD, SWA, VCI, WCF, WHO
	Australian, 1972—animated (d) Leif Gram	BUD, ICS, MOD, SEL, WCF, WHO
The Master of Ballantrae (1889)	Warners, 1953 (d) William Keighley	FNC, SWA, TWY

Author—Title	Film Version: Title (if changed), Production Company, Release Date Director (d)	Rental Source(s)
Treasure Island (1883)	Edison, 1912 (d) J. Searle Dawley	—
	MGM, 1934 (d) Victor Fleming	MGM
	Disney, 1950 (d) Byron Haskin	AIM, BUC, CCC, COU, CWF, DIS, FNC, MOD, NAT, NEW, ROA, SWA, TWY, WHO
	UPA, 1965—animated	FNC, ICS, KER, ROA, SEL, SWA, TFC, WCF, WEL, WIL
	Austrasian, 1970—animated (d) Zoran Janzic	BUD, CWF, ICS, ROA, SEL, SWA, WCF, WHO
	National General, 1972 (d) John Hough	TWY
SWIFT, Jonathan (1667–1745)		
Gulliver's Travels (1726)	*A New Gulliver* USSR, 1935 (d) Alexander Ptushko	—
	Paramount, 1939—animated (d) Dave and Max Fleischer	ARG, BUD, CFM, CWF, EMG, ICS, IMA, IVY, JEN, KPF, NAT, NEW, ROA, SEL, TWY, VCI, WCF, WHO
	The Three Worlds of Gulliver Columbia, 1960	ARG, CCC, CHA, CWF,

Author—Title	Film Version: Title (if changed), Production Company, Release Date Director (d)	Rental Source(s)
	(d) Jack Sher	FNC, FPC, ICS, JEN, KER, KPF, MOD, NAT, NEW, ROA, SEL, SWA, TWY, VCI, WCF, WEL, WHO
	EMI, 1977 (d) Peter Hunt	—
TOLKIEN, J. R. R. (1892–1973)		
The Hobbit (1937)	Rankin/Bass, 1977—animated (d) Arthur Rankin, Jules Bass	XEX
The Lord of the Rings (1954–55)	United Artists, 1978—animated (d) Ralph Bakshi	MGM
TRAVERS, Pamela L. (1906–)		
Mary Poppins (1934)	Disney, 1964 (d) Robert Stevenson	—
TWAIN, Mark (1835–1910)		
The Adventures of Huckleberry Finn (1884)	Morosco/Lasky, 1919—silent (d) William Desmond Taylor	—
	Huckleberry Finn Paramount, 1931 (d) Norman Taurog	CWF, UNI
	MGM, 1939 (d) Richard Thorpe	MGM
	MGM, 1960 (d) Michael Curtiz	MGM

Author—Title	Film Version: Title (if changed), Production Company, Release Date Director (d)	Rental Source(s)
	Huckleberry Finn United Artists, 1974 (d) J. Lee Thompson	CWF, ROA, MGM, WCF, WHO
The Adventures of Tom Sawyer (1876)	Morosco/Lasky, 1917—silent (d) William Desmond Taylor	—
	Tom Sawyer Paramount, 1930 (d) John Cromwell	UNI
	United Artists, 1938 (d) Norman Taurog	AIM, ARG, BUC, BUD, CCC, CWF, FNC, KER, MOD, NEW, ROA, SEL, TWF, TWY, VCI, WCF, WEL, WHO, WIL
	Tom Sawyer United Artists, 1973 (d) Don Taylor	ARG, CWF, MGM, ROA, WCF, WHO
The Prince and the Pauper (1882)	Famous Players/Paramount, 1915 (d) Edwin S. Porter, Hugh Ford	—
	Austria, 1923—silent (d) Alexander Korda	FCE
	Warners, 1937 (d) William Keighley	MGM
	Disney, 1962 (d) Don Chaffey	CCC, CWF, FNC, JEN, MOD, ROA, SEL, SWA, TFC, TWY
	Australia/API, 1970— animated	ICS, MOD, ROA, WCF
Tom Sawyer Detective (1896)	Paramount, 1938 (d) Louis King	UNI

Author—Title	Film Version: Title (if changed), Production Company, Release Date Director (d)	Rental Source(s)
VERNE, Jules (1828–1905)		
From the Earth to the Moon (1865)	Warners, 1958 (d) Byron Haskin	BUD, FNC, JEN, VCI, WHO
Journey to the Center of the Earth (1864)	20th Century-Fox, 1959 (d) Henry Levin	FNC, WHO
Master of the World (1904)	American International, 1961 (d) William Witney	AIM, ARG, BUD, CCC, CHA, FNC, JEN, KER, MOD, SEL, TMC, TWY, VCI, WCF, WEL, WHO, WIL
Mysterious Island (1875)	MGM, 1929 (d) Lucien Hubbard	MGM
	Columbia, 1962 (d) Cy Endfield	ARG, BUC, CCC, CHA, CWF, FNC, ICS, JEN, KPF, LEW, MOD, NAT, ROA, SWA, TFC, TWY, VCI, WCF, WHO
20,000 Leagues Under The Sea (1870)	Universal, 1917—silent (d) Alan Holubar	BUD, IVY, VCI
	Disney, 1954 (d) Richard Fleischer	AIM, CCC, CWF, DIS, FNC, FPC, JEN, MOD, NAT, NEW, ROA, SWA, TFC, TWY
WHITE, E. B. (1899–)		
Charlotte's Web (1952)	Paramount, 1972—animated	FNC

Author—Title	Film Version: Title (if changed), Production Company, Release Date Director (d)	Rental Source(s)
	(d) Charles Nichols, Iwao Takamoto	
WHITE, T. H. (1906–1964)		
The Sword in the Stone (1939)	Disney, 1963—animated (d) Wolfgang Reitherman	—
WYSS, Johann R. (1781–1830)		
The Swiss Family Robinson (1812)	RKO, 1940 (d) Edward Ludwig	BUD, FCE, ICS, MOG
	Disney, 1960 (d) Ken Annakin	CWF, DIS, FNC, MOD, TFC, TWY
	Australia/API, 1972—animated (d) Leif Gram	BUD, CWF, FNC, ICS, MOD, ROA, SEL, SWA, TWY, WCF, WEL, WHO

RENTAL SOURCES FOR FILMS LISTED IN FILMOGRAPHY

AIM
Association Instructional
  Materials
(Association Films)
866 Third Avenue
New York, New York 10022
(212) 736-9693

ALB
Alba House (Don Bosco)
7050 Pinehurst
PO Box 35
Dearborn, Michigan 48126
(313) 582-2033

ARG
Arcus Films
1225 Broadway
New York, New York 10001
(212) 686-2216
  or
3427 Oakcliff Road, N.E.
Atlanta, Georgia 30340
(404) 455-4640

BUC
Buchan Pictures
122 W. Chippewa Street

Buffalo, New York 14202
(716) 853-1805

BUD
Budget Films
4590 Santa Monica Blvd.
Los Angeles, California 90029
(213) 660-0187

CAL
University of California
Extension Media Center
2223 Fulton Street
Berkeley, California 94720
(415) 845-6000

CCC
Cine-Craft Films
1720 N.W. Marshall
Portland, Oregon 97208
(503) 228-7484

CFM
Classic Film Museum
4 Union Square
Dover-Foxcroft, Maine 04426
(207) 564-8371

CHA
Charard Motion Pictures
2110 East 24th Street
Brooklyn, New York 11229
(212) 891-4339

CIE
Cinema Concepts/Cinema Eight
91 Main Street
Chester, Connecticut 06412
(203) 526-9513

CIN
Hurlock Cine-World
13 Arcadia Road
Old Greenwich, Connecticut
  06870
(203) 637-4319

CON
Contemporary/McGraw-Hill
  Films
1221 Avenue of the Americas
New York, New York 10020
(212) 997-6831
  or
828 Custer Avenue
Evanston, Illinois 60202
(312) 869-5010
  or
1714 Stockton Street
San Francisco, California 94133
(415) 362-3115

COU
Cousino Visual Ed. Service
1945 Franklin Avenue
Toledo, Ohio 43624
(419) 246-3691

CWF
Clem Williams Films, Inc.
2240 Noblestown Road

Pittsburgh, Pennsylvania
  15205
(412) 921-5810
  or
5424 West North Avenue
Chicago, Illinois 60639
(312) 637-3322
  or
1277 Spring Street, NW
Atlanta, Georgia 30309
(404) 872-5353
  or
2170 Portsmouth
Houston, Texas 77098
(713) 529-3906
  or
298 Lawrence Avenue
So. San Francisco, California
  94080
(415) 952-5131

DIS
Walt Disney Productions
500 South Buena Vista Street
Burbank, California 91521
(800) 423-2200
  or
666 Busse Highway
Park Ridge, Illinois 60068
(312) 631-8278

EMG
Em Gee Film Library
4931 Gloria Avenue
Encino, California 91316
(213) 981-5506

ERF
Episcopal Radio & TV
  Foundation
3379 Peachtree Road, NE, Suite
  999
Atlanta, Georgia 30326
(404) 233-5419

FCE
Film Classic Exchange
1926 South Vermont Avenue
Los Angeles, California 90007
(213) 731–3854

FNC
Films Incorporated
733 Green Bay Road
Wilmette, Illinois 60091
(312) 256–6600/(800) 323–1406
or
440 Park Avenue South
New York, New York 10016
(212) 889–7910/(800) 223–6246
or
476 Plasamour Drive, NE
Atlanta, Georgia 30324
(404) 873–5101/(800) 241–5530
or
5625 Hollywood Blvd.
Hollywood, California 90028
(213) 466–5481/(800) 421–0612

FPC
Film Presentation Company
1571 Morris Avenue
Union, New Jersey 07083
(201) 688–3311

ICS
Institutional Cinema Inc.
10 First Street
Saugerties, New York 12477
(914) 246–2848

IMA
The Images Film Archive, Inc.
300 Phillips Park Road
Mamaronek, New York 10543
(914) 381–2993/(800) 431–1774

IVY
Ivy Films
165 West 46th Street
New York, New York 10036
(212) 765–3940
or
12636 North Beatrice Street
Los Angeles, California 90066
(213) 390–3602

JEN
Jensen's Cinema 16
4524 Howard Avenue
Western Springs, Illinois 60558
(312) 246–6116

KER
Kerr Film Exchange
3034 Canon Street
San Diego, California 92106
(714) 224–2406

KPF
Kit Parker Films
P.O. Box 227
Carmel Valley, California
93924
(408) 659–3474/(800) 538–5838

LEW
Lewis Film Service
1425 East Central
Wichita, Kansas 67214
(316) 263–6991

MGM
MGM-United Artists
729 Seventh Avenue
New York, New York 10019
(212) 575–4715
or
2180 Yonge Street, Suite 800
Toronto, Ontario M4S 2B9

MOD
Modern Sound Pictures
1402 Howard Street
Omaha, Nebraska 68102
(402) 341–8476

MOG
Mogull's
235 West 46th Street
New York, New York 10036
(212) 757–1414

NAT
National Film Service
14 Glenwood Avenue
Raleigh, North Carolina 27602
(919) 832-3901

NEW
Newman Film Library
400 32nd Street, SE
Grand Rapids, Michigan 49508
(616) 243–3300

PNX
Phoenix Films
470 Park Avenue South
New York, New York 10016
(212) 684–5910

REE
Reel Images
10523 Burbank Blvd., #104
North Hollywood, California
   91601
(213) 762–5341
   or
456 Monroe Turnpike
Monroe, Connecticut 06468
(203) 261–5022

ROA
ROA Films

1696 North Astor Street
Milwaukee, Wisconsin 53202
(414) 271–0861/(800) 558–9015

SAN
Sanrio Communications
1505 Vine Street
Hollywood, California 90028
(213) 462–7248

SEL
Select Film Library
115 West 31st Street
New York, New York 10001
(212) 594–4457

SWA
Swank Motion Pictures
201 South Jefferson Avenue
St. Louis, Missouri 63166
(314) 531–5100
   or
393 Front Street
Hempstead, New York 11550
(516) 538–6500
   or
220 Forbes Road
Braintree, Massachusetts
   02184
(617) 848–8300
   or
7926 Jones Branch Drive
McLean, Virginia 22101
(703) 821-1040
   or
1200 Roosevelt Road
Glen Ellyn, Illinois 60137
(312) 629–9004
   or
4111 Director's Row
Houston, Texas 77092
(713) 683–8222
   or

6767 Forest Lawn Drive
Hollywood, California 90068
(213) 851-6300

TFC
"The" Film Center
938 K Street, NW
Washington, DC 20001
(202) 393-1205

TMC
The Movie Center
57 Baldwin Street
Charlestown, Massachusetts
02129
(617) 242-3456

TWF
Trans-World Films
332 South Michigan Avenue
Chicago, Illinois 60604
(312) 922-1530

TWY
Twyman Films, Inc.
4700 Wadsworth Road
Dayton, Ohio 45414
(513) 276-5941/(800) 543-9594

or
Box 794
Cooper Station, New York
10003
(212) 695-1628
or
2321 West Olive Street
Burbank, California 91506
(213) 843-8052

UNI
Universal 16
445 Park Avenue

New York, New York 10022
(212) 759-7500
or
425 North Michigan Avenue
Chicago, Illinois 60611
(312) 822-0513
or
205 Walton Street, NW
Atlanta, Georgia 30303
(404) 523-5081
or
810 South St. Paul
Dallas, Texas 75201
(214) 741-3164
or
8901 Beverly Blvd.
Los Angeles, California 90048
(213) 550-7461
or
8444 Blvd. St. Laurent
Montreal, Quebec, Canada
(514) 384-4100

VCI
Video Communications, Inc.
6555 East Skelly Drive
Tulsa, Oklahoma 74145
(918) 583-2681

WCF
Westcoast Films
25 Lusk Street
San Francisco, California 94107
(415) 362-4700

WEL
Welling Motion Pictures
454 Meacham Avenue
Elmont, New York 11003
(516) 354-1066

WHO
Wholesome Film Center

20 Melrose Street
Boston, Massachusetts 02116
(617) 426–0155

WIL
Willoughby-Peerless
110 West 32nd Street

New York, New York 10001
(212) 564–1600

XEX
Xerox Films
245 Long Hill Road
Middletown, Connecticut 06457
(203) 347–7251

NOTE: for further information on film rental sources see James L. Limbacher, ed., *Feature Films on 8mm, 16mm, and Videotape,* 6th edition, NY: R.R. Bowker, 1979, and Kathleen Weaver, ed., *Film Programmer's Guide To 16mm Rentals,* 3rd edition, Albany, CA: Reel Research, 1980.

SELECTED BIBLIOGRAPHY

I / *On Film Adaptations of Children's Novels*

Adler, Renata. *A Year in the Dark* [*Chitty Chitty Bang Bang*]. New York: Random House, 1969.

Armes, Roy. *A Critical History of the British Cinema*. New York: Oxford University Press, 1978.

Armstrong, Michael. [*Chitty Chitty Bang Bang*], *Films and Filming*, 15, No. 8 (May 1969), p. 42.

Bart, Peter and Dorothy Bart. "As Told and Sold By Disney," *The New York Times Book Review* (Children's Book Section), (May 9, 1965).

Baum, Frank. "The Oz Film Co.," *Films in Review*, 7 (August-September 1956), pp. 329-333.

Bogdanovich, Peter. *Allan Dwan: The Last Pioneer* [*Heidi* and *Rebecca of Sunnybrook Farm*]. New York: Praeger, 1971.

Boyle, D. "Children's Film: Conspiracy of Mediocrity," *American Librarian*, 8 (May 1977), pp. 267-268.

Burton, Thomas. "Walt Disney's 'Pinocchio'," *Saturday Review of Literature*, 21 (February 17, 1940), p. 17.

Care, R. "Ward Kimball: Animated Versatility," *Millimeter*, 4, Nos. 7-8 (July-August 1976), pp. 18-22, 62.

Carey, Gary. *Cukor and Co.: The Films of George Cukor and His Collaborators* [*Little Women*]. New York: Museum of Modern Art, 1971.

Casper, Joseph Andrew. *The Style of Stanley Donen* [*Little Prince*]. Metuchen, NJ: Scarecrow Press, 1983.

Combs, Richard. [*Railway Children*], *Sight and Sound*, 40, No. 1 (Winter 1970/1971), pp. 51-52.

Culhane, John. "The Last of the 'Nine Old Men,'" [*The Rescuers*], *American Film*, 12, No. 8 (June 1977), pp. 10-16.

Curry, George. *Copperfield '70: The Story of the Making of the Omnibus 20th Century-Fox Film of Charles Dickens' David Copperfield.* New York: Ballantine Books, 1970.

Cutts, John. [*Toby Tyler*], *Films and Filming,* 6, No. 8 (May 1960), pp. 24-25.

Davenport, Tom. "Some Personal Notes on Adapting Folk-Fairy Tales to Film," *Children's Literature,* 9 (1981), pp. 107-115.

Disney, Walt. "How I Cartooned *Alice,*" *Films in Review,* 2 (May 1951), pp. 7-11.

Dunne, John Gregory. *The Studio* [*Doctor Dolittle*]. New York: Farrar, Strauss & Giroux, 1969.

Edera, Bruno. *Full Length Animated Feature Films.* New York: Hastings House, 1977.

Eisenstein, Sergei. "Dickens, Griffith, and the Film Today," *Film Form,* Ed. by Jay Leyda. New York: Harcourt Brace, 1949.

Eyman, Scott. "The Young Turk: Junk-Culture-Junkie Takes On A Hobbit," *Take One,* 6 (November 1978), 34-36, 41.

Film Library Quarterly [special issue on children & films], 9, No. 3 (1976).

Finch, Christopher. *The Art of Walt Disney.* New York: H. N. Abrams, 1975.

Flaherty, Joe. [*Pinocchio*], *Village Voice,* 16, No. 36 (September 9, 1971), pp. 5, 14.

Gaffney, Maureen. "Evaluating Attitude: Analyzing Point of View and Tone in Film Adaptations of Literature," *Children's Literature,* 9 (1981), pp. 116-126.

Garcia-Abrines, Luis. "Rebirth of Buñuel," [*Robinson Crusoe*], *Yale French Studies,* 17 (Summer 1956), pp. 54-66.

Gartley, Lynn, and Elizabeth Leebron. *Walt Disney: A Guide To References And Resources.* Boston: G. K. Hall, 1979.

Gittens, T. "For Children's Eyes: Black Children's Films" [*Sounder, Hero . . .*], *Essence,* 10 (October 1979), pp. 21+.

Goldstein, Ruth M., and Edith Zornow. *Movies For Kids,* Revised Edition. New York: Frederick Ungar, 1980.

——. *The Screen Image Of Youth: Movies About Children And Adolescents.* Metuchen, NJ: Scarecrow Press, 1980.

Gorney, Sondra. "On Children's Cinema: America and Britain," *Hollywood Quarterly,* 3, No. 1 (Fall 1947), pp. 56-62.

Guth, Dorothy, Ed. *The Letters of E. B. White* [*Charlotte's Web*]. New York: Harper and Row, 1976.

Harmetz, Aljean. *The Making of the Wizard of Oz.* New York: Alfred A. Knopf, 1977.

Hollister, Paul. "Walt Disney, Genius at Work," *Atlantic Monthly,* 166 (December 1940), pp. 689-701.

Hulett, Steve. "A Star Is Drawn" [*Pinocchio*], *Film Comment,* 15 (January/February 1979), pp. 13-16.

Kael, Pauline. *Deeper Into Movies* [*Scrooge, Bedknobs and Broomsticks*], Boston: Little, Brown, 1976.

_____. *Reeling* [*Sounder, Little Prince*], Boston: Little, Brown, 1976.

Klein, Michael and Gillian Parker, Eds. *The English Novel and the Movies* [*Robinson Crusoe, David Copperfield, Christmas Carol, Great Expectations*]. New York: Frederick Ungar, 1981.

Lambert, Gavin. "Shadow upon Shadow upon Shadow: Hugh Walpole in Hollywood" [*David Copperfield*], *Sight and Sound,* 23, No. 2 (October/December 1953), pp. 78-82.

Lewin, David. "Why Norman Rosemont Likes To Film The Classics" [*Lord Fauntleroy*], *New York Times* (November 23, 1980), pp. 35D, 40D.

Maltin, Leonard. *The Disney Films.* New York: Crown Publishers, 1973.

_____. "Walt Disney's Films," *Films in Review,* 18 (October 1967), pp. 457-469.

May, Jill P. "Butchering Children's Literature" [*Disney's adaptations*], *Film Library Quarterly,* 11, Nos. 1-2 (1978), pp. 55-62.

McClelland, Doug. *Down The Yellow Brick Road: The Making of The Wizard Of Oz.* New York: Pyramid Publications, 1976.

McGilligan, P. "Clarence Brown: Two Children's Movies" [*The Yearling, National Velvet*], *Focus on Film,* 23 (Winter 1975/1976), pp. 34-35, 40.

Miller, Jonathan. "Another Wonderland," *The New York Times Book Review* (Children's Book Section), (May 7, 1967).

Miller, Mary. [*Kim*], *Films in Review,* 2, No. 1 (January 1951), pp. 41-42.

Nathan, P. S. "Books into Films: Saturday Matinee Plan," *Publishers' Weekly,* 152 (October 25, 1947), p. 2100.

Nelson, Thomas A. "Darkness in the Disney Look," *Literature/Film Quarterly,* 6 (Spring 1978), pp. 2-12.

Parlato, Salvatore J., Jr., Ed. *Films Ex Libris: Literature in 16mm and Video.* Jefferson, NC: McFarland & Co., 1980.

Peary, Gerald, and Roger Shatzkin, Eds. *The Classic American Novel and the Movies* [*Little Women, Tom Sawyer, Prince and the Pauper, Wizard of Oz*]. New York: Frederick Ungar, 1977.

Pipolo, Anthony. [*Railway Children*], *Village Voice,* 16, No. 47 (November 25, 1971), pp. 87-88.

Pratley, Gerald. *The Cinema of David Lean* [*Great Expectations, Oliver Twist*]. New York: A. S. Barnes, 1974.

Radnitz, Robert B. "On Creating Films For Children" [*Island of the Blue Dolphins*], *Horn Book* 40 (August 1964), pp. 415-417.

Rhawn, Flavia. [*Railway Children*], *Films in Review*, 22, No. 10 (December 1971), pp. 638-639.

Rider, David. [*Island of the Blue Dolphins*], *Films and Filming*, 11, No. 10 (July 1965), pp. 31-32.

Roman, Robert C. "Dickens' *A Christmas Carol*," *Films in Review*, 9 (December 1958), pp. 572-574.

———. "Mark Twain on the Screen," *Films in Review*, 12 (January 1961), pp. 20-35.

Rosenbaum, J. "Dream Masters I: Walt Disney," *Film Comment*, 11 (January 1975), pp. 64-69.

Rutherford, Charles S. "A New Dog with an Old Trick: Archetypal Patterns in *Sounder*," *Journal of Popular Film*, 2 (Spring 1973), pp. 155-165.

Sayers, Frances Clarke, and Charles M. Weisenberg. "Walt Disney Accused," *Horn Book*, 40 (December 1965), pp. 602-611.

Schickel, Richard. *The Disney Version*. New York: Simon and Schuster, 1968.

Schindel, Morton. "Children's Literature on Film: Through the Audiovisual Era to the Age of Telecommunications," *Children's Literature*, 9 (1981), pp. 93-107.

———. "Confessions of a Book Fiend: Films and Filmstrips Based on Children's Books," *Library Journal*, 92 (February 15, 1967), pp. 858-859.

———. "Picture Books into Film," *Library Journal*, 84 (January 15, 1959), pp. 224-226.

Seiter, Ellen. "*The Black Stallion*: A Boy and his Horse," *Jump Cut*, 23 (October 1980), pp. 11, 38-39.

Seldes, Gilbert. "Vandals of Hollywood: Why a Good Movie Cannot Be Faithful to the Original Book or Play" [incl. *Treasure Island, David Copperfield, Little Women*], *Saturday Review of Literature*, 14 (October 17, 1936), pp. 3-4, 13-14.

Silver, Alain. "The Untranquil Light: David Lean's *Great Expectations*," *Literature/Film Quarterly*, 2, No. 2 (Spring 1974), pp. 140-152.

Starr, Cecile. "Fiction, Fantasy and Fairy Tales on Film," *House Beautiful*, 98 (October 1956), pp. 212-213+.

Street, Douglas. "An Overview of Filmic Adaptation of Children's Fiction," *Children's Literature Quarterly* 7 (Fall 1982), pp. 13-17.

Tarratt, Margaret. [*Railway Children*], *Films and Filming*, 17, No. 5 (February 1971), pp. 51-52.

Tupper, Lucy. "Dickens on the Screen," *Films in Review*, 10 (March 1959), pp. 142-152.

Viguers, Ruth Hill. "Not Recommended," *Horn Book*, 39 (February 1963), pp. 76-79.

Wilms, D. "Status of Children's Books and Films," *Education Digest,* 45 (November 1979), pp. 50-52.

Windeler, Robert. *The Films of Shirley Temple.* New York: Citadel Press, 1978.

Wood, Robin. "Images of Childhood," in *Personal Views: Explorations in Film.* London: Gordon Fraser, 1976.

Wright, Basil. *The Long View.* New York: Alfred A. Knopf, 1974.

Zambrano, Anna Laura. *Dickens and Film.* New York: Gorden, 1976.

————. *Great Expectations*: Dickens and David Lean," *Literature/ Film Quarterly,* 2, No. 2 (Spring 1974), pp. 154-161.

II / *On Film and Literature*

Admussen, Richard L., Edward J. Gallagher and Lubbe Levin. "Novel into Film: An Experimental Course," *Literature/Film Quarterly,* 6, No. 1 (Winter 1978), pp. 66-72.

Agate, James. *Around Cinema*; rpt. New York: The Arno Press, 1972.

Armes, Roy. *Film and Reality.* Baltimore: Penguin Books, 1974.

Bates, H. F. "When the Cinemagoer Complains That—'It Isn't Like the Book'—Who's to Blame?" *Films and Filming,* 5, No. 8 (May 1959), p. 7.

Bauer, Leda V. "The Movies Tackle Literature," *American Mercury,* 14 (July 1928), pp. 288-294.

Bluestone, George. *Novels into Film.* Berkeley: University of California Press, 1957.

————. "Word to Image: The Problem of the Filmed Novel," *Quarterly of Film, Radio and Television,* 11, No. 2 (Winter 1956), pp. 171-180.

Bodeen, DeWitt. "The Adapting Art," *Films in Review,* 14 (June/July 1963), pp. 349-356.

Burton, Thomas. "Books into Pictures," *Saturday Review of Literature* (March 30, 1940), p. 20; (April 13, 1940), p. 21; (May 11, 1940), p. 21; June 8, 1940), p. 21.

Butcher, M. "Look First upon the Picture; Books into Film" *Wiseman Review,* 238 (Spring 1964), pp. 55-64.

Caughie, John, Ed. *Theories of Authorship: A Reader.* London: Routledge & Kegan Paul, 1981.

Chatman, Seymour. *Story and Discourse: Narrative Structure in Fiction and Film.* Ithaca, NY: Cornell University Press, 1978.

————. "What Novels Can Do That Films Can't (and Vice Versa)," *Critical Inquiry,* 7 (Autumn 1980), pp. 121-141.

Cohen, Keith. *Fiction and Film: The Dynamics of Exchange.* New Haven: Yale University Press, 1979.

Conger, Syndy and Janice Welsch, Eds. *Narrative Strategies: Essays in Film and Prose Fiction.* Macomb: Western Illinois University Press, 1981.

Durgnat, Raymond. "The Mongrel Muse," *Films and Feeling.* Cambridge, MA: M.I.T. Press, 1971, pp. 13-30.

Edel, Leon. "Novel and Camera," in *The Theory of the Novel: New Essays.* Ed., John Halperin. New York: Oxford University Press, 1974, pp. 177-188.

Eidsvik, Charles. "Soft Edges: The Art of Literature, the Medium of Film," *Literature/Film Quarterly,* 2, No. 1 (Winter 1974), pp. 16-21.

_____. "Toward a 'Politique des Adaptations,'" *Literature/Film Quarterly* 3, No. 3 (Summer 1973), pp. 255-263.

Enser, A. G. S. *Filmed Books and Plays: A List of Books and Plays From Which Films Have Been Made, 1928-1974.* London: Andre Deutsch, 1975.

Fadiman, William. "But Compared to the Original," *Films and Filming,* 11, No. 5 (February 1965), pp. 21-23.

_____. "The Great Hollywood Book-Hunt," *Saturday Review,* 43 (September 17, 1960), pp. 27-30+.

Fell, John L. *Film and the Narrative Tradition.* Norman: University of Oklahoma Press, 1974.

_____. "Vladimir Propp in Hollywood," *Film Quarterly,* 30, No. 3 (Spring 1977), pp. 19-28.

Geduld, Harry M., Ed. *Authors on Film.* Bloomington: Indiana University Press, 1972.

_____. and Ronald Gottesman. "Adaptation [Annotated Bibliography]," in *Guidebook to Film.* New York: Holt, Rinehart, 1972, pp. 30-35.

Godfrey, Lionel. "It Wasn't Like That in the Book," *Films and Filming,* 13, No. 7 (April 1967), pp. 12-16.

Holmes, Winifred. "The New Renaissance," *Sight and Sound,* 5, No. 18 (Summer 1936), pp. 7-9.

Holt, P. "Books into Movies," *Publishers' Weekly,* 219 (April 3, 1981), pp. 28-30+; (June 5, 1981), pp. 34-37.

_____. "Turning Best Sellers into Movies: A Sometime Success Story," *Publishers' Weekly,* 216 (October 22, 1979), pp. 36+.

Horton, Andrew and Joan Magretta, Eds. *Modern European Filmmakers and the Art of Adaptation.* New York: Frederick Ungar, 1981.

Hulseberg, Richard A. "Novels and Films: A Limited Inquiry," *Literature/Film Quarterly,* 6, No. 1 (Winter 1978), pp. 57-65.

Jay, Herman. "Hollywood and American Literature: The American Novel on the Screen," *English Journal,* 66 (January 1977), pp. 82-86.

Jinks, William. *The Celluloid Literature: Film in the Humanities.* Riverside, NJ: Glencoe Press, 1971.

Kawin, Bruce F. *Telling It Again and Again: Repetition in Literature and Film.* Ithaca, NY: Cornell University Press, 1972.

Kittredge, William and Steven M. Krauzer. *Stories into Film.* New York: Harper and Row, 1979.

Koch, Stephen. "Fiction and Film: A Study for New Sources," *The Saturday Review* (December 27, 1969), pp. 12-14.

Marcus, Fred H., Ed. *Film and Literature: Contrasts in Media.* Scranton, PA: Chandler Publishers, 1971.

Mason, Ronald. "The Film of the Book," *Film,* 16 (March/April 1958), pp. 18-20.

McConnell, Frank D. *The Spoken Seen: Film and the Romantic Imagination.* Baltimore: Johns Hopkins Press, 1975.

———. *Storytelling and Mythmaking: Images from Film and Literature.* New York: Oxford University Press, 1979.

Messenger, James R. "I Think I Liked the Book Better: Nineteen Novelists Look At the Film Version of Their Work," *Literature/Film Quarterly,* 6, No. 2 (Spring 1978), pp. 125-134.

Miller, Gabriel, Ed. *Screening The Novel.* New York: Frederick Ungar, 1980.

Monaco, James. *How to Read a Film.* New York: Oxford University Press, 1977.

Murray, Edward. *The Cinematic Imagination: Writers and the Motion Pictures.* New York: Frederick Ungar, 1972.

Nicoll, Allardyce. "Literature and the Film," *English Journal,* 26 (January 1937), pp. 1-9.

Peary, Gerald and Roger Shatzkin, Eds. *The Modern American Novel and the Movies.* New York: Frederick Ungar, 1979.

Probst, Robert E. "Visual to Verbal," *English Journal,* 61, No. 1 (January 1972), pp. 71-75.

Richardson, Robert. *Literature and Film.* Bloomington: Indiana University Press, 1969.

Roud, Richard. "Novel Novel; Fable Fable?" *Sight and Sound,* 31, No. 2 (Spring 1962), pp. 84-88.

Ruhe, Edward. "Film: The 'Literary' Approach," *Literature/Film Quarterly,* 1, No. 1 (January 1973), pp. 76-83.

Schneider, Harold W. "Literature and Film: Making Out Some Boundaries," *Literature/Film Quarterly,* 3, No. 1 (Winter 1975), pp. 30-44.

Spiegel, Alan. *Fiction and the Camera Eye: Visual Consciousness in Film and the Modern Novel.* Charlottesville: University of Virginia Press, 1975.

Symposium, 27, No. 2 (1973). Issue devoted to film/literature relationships.

Thorp, Margaret. "The Motion Picture and the Novel," *American Quarterly,* 3, No. 3 (1951), pp. 195-203.

Vale, Eugene. *The Technique of Screenplay Writing.* New York: Grosset and Dunlap, 1972.

Wagner, Geoffrey. *The Novel and the Cinema.* Rutherford, NJ: Fairleigh Dickinson University Press, 1975.

Winston, Douglas G. *The Screenplay As Literature.* Rutherford, NJ: Fairleigh Dickinson University Press, 1973.

III / *General Entries*

Agee, James. *Agee on Film.* Boston: Beacon Press, 1964.

Armour, Robert A. *Film: A Reference Guide.* Westport, CT: Greenwood Press, 1980.

Babbitt, Natalie. "How Can We Write Children's Books If We Don't Know Anything About Children?" *Publishers' Weekly,* 200 (July 1971), pp. 64-66.

Bader, Barbara. "Notable Booklists," *Wilson Library Bulletin,* 46 (March 1972), pp. 589+.

Batty, Linda, Ed. *Retrospective Index to Film Periodicals, 1930-1971.* New York: R. R. Bowker, 1975.

Bean, Keith. "A Letter to Oliver Bell," *Sight and Sound,* 12, No. 46 (1943), pp. 35-39.

Cameron, Eleanor. *The Green and Burning Tree: On the Writing and Enjoyment of Children's Books.* Boston: Little, Brown, 1969.

Crist, Judith. *The Private Eye, The Cowboy and the Very Naked Girl: The Movies from Cleo to Clyde.* Chicago: Holt, Rinehart, 1968.

Crouch, Marcus. *The Nesbit Tradition: The Children's Novel in England, 1945-1970.* Totowa, NJ: Rowman and Littlefield, 1972.

Denby, David, Ed. *Awake in the Dark: An Anthology of American Film Criticism, 1915 to the Present.* New York: Vintage, 1977.

Deutelbaum, Marshall. "Film Archives: Unexplored Territory," in *Society & Children's Literature,* Ed., James H. Fraser. Boston: David R. Godine Publisher, 1978.

Durgnat, Raymond. "The Great British Phantasmagoria," *Film Comment,* 13, No. 3 (May/June 1977), pp. 48-53.

Edgar, Patricia. *Children and Screen Violence.* Lawrence, ME: University of Queensland Press, 1977.

Egoff, Sheila, et. al., Eds. *Only Connect: Readings On Children's Literature,* Second Edition. New York: Oxford University Press, 1980.

Eisner, Lotte. "Children's Films at Lido," *Film Culture*, 2, No. 4 (1956), pp. 31-32.

Everson, William K. *The Art of W. C. Fields*. New York: Bobbs-Merrill, 1967.

Fenwick, Sara. "Which Will Fade, Which Endure? American Children's Classics," *Wilson Library Bulletin*, 47 (October 1972), pp. 178-185.

Field, Mary. "Children and the Entertainment Film," *Sight and Sound*, 15, No. 58 (Summer 1946), pp. 46-47.

———. "Children's Entertainment Films: Good Company," *Sight and Sound*, 20 (Summer 1951), pp. 59-60.

Field, Mary, Maud Miller and Roger Manvell. *The Boy's and Girl's Book of Films and Television*. New York: Roy Publishers, 1961.

Gaffney, Maureen, Ed. *More Films Kids Like: A Catalog of Short Films for Children*. Chicago: American Library Association, 1977.

Geduld, Harry M., Ed. *Film Makers on Film Making*. Bloomington: Indiana University Press, 1967.

Gow, Gordon. *Hollywood in the Fifties*. New York: A. S. Barnes, 1971.

Greene, Ellin and Madalynne Schoenfeld. *A Multimedia Approach To Children's Literature*, Second Edition. Chicago: American Library Association, 1977.

Halas, John. *Visual Scripting*. New York: Hastings House, 1976.

Halliwell, Leslie, Ed. *Halliwell's Film Guide*, Second Edition. New York: Charles Scribner's, 1979.

Haviland, Virginia, Ed. *Children and Literature: Views and Reviews*. Glenview, IL: Scott, Foresman, 1973.

Higham, Charles and Joel Greenburg. *Hollywood in the Forties*. New York: A. S. Barnes, 1968.

Hills, Janet. "Children's Films," *Sight and Sound*, 21, No. 4 (April/June 1952), pp. 179-181, 185.

Hoffer, Eric. *The Temper of Our Time*. New York: Harper and Row, 1967.

Hoffer, Thomas W., Ed. *Animation: A Reference Guide*. Westport, CT: Greenwood Press, 1982.

Holman, L. Bruce. *Puppet Animation in the Cinema: History and Technique*. New York: A. S. Barnes, 1975.

Hürlimann, Bettina. *Three Centuries of Children's Books in Europe*. Cleveland: World Publishing Co., 1968.

Jacobs, Lewis. *The Emergence of Film Art*. New York: Hopkinson and Blake, 1969.

———. *The Movies as Medium*. New York: Farrar, Straus & Giroux, 1970.

_____. *The Rise of the American Film.* New York: Teacher's College Press, 1968.

Jordan, Alice M. and Paul Heins. "Children's Classics," Fifth Edition. Boston: *Horn Book* Press, 1976.

Kael, Pauline. *Going Steady.* Boston: Little, Brown, 1970.

_____. *I Lost It At The Movies.* Boston: Little, Brown, 1965.

_____. *Kiss Kiss Bang Bang.* Boston: Little, Brown, 1968.

_____. *When The Lights Go Down.* New York: Holt, Rinehart, Winston, 1980.

Kauffmann, Stanley. *Figures of Light: Film Criticism and Comment.* New York: Harper & Row, 1971.

_____. *Living Images: Film Comment and Criticism.* New York: Harper & Row, 1975.

_____. *A World on Film.* New York: Harper & Row, 1966.

Koszarski, Richard, Ed. *Hollywood Directors 1914-1940.* New York: Oxford University Press, 1976.

Kroll, Sidney. "Making Movies," *Take One,* 4, No. 7 (December 1974), pp. 37-39.

Lambert, Gavin. *On Cukor.* New York: Putnam, 1972.

Lee, Walt and Bill Warren, Eds. *Reference Guide to Fantastic Films, Science Fiction, Fantasy, and Horror.* 3 vols. Los Angeles: Chelsea Press, 1973.

MacCann, Richard Dyer, Ed. *Film: A Montage of Theories.* New York: E. P. Dutton, 1966.

Madsen, Axel. *The New Hollywood: American Movies in the Seventies.* New York: Crowell, 1975.

Maltin, Leonard. *Of Mice and Magic: A History of American Animated Cartoons.* New York: McGraw-Hill, 1980.

_____, Ed. *TV Movies,* Revised (1981-82) Edition. New York: New American Library, 1982.

Manvell, Roger. "Giving Life to the Fantastic: A History of the Cartoon Films," *Films and Filming,* 3, No. 2 (November 1956), pp. 7-9, 13.

_____ and Lewis Jacobs, Eds. *The International Film Encyclopedia.* New York: Crown Publishers, 1972.

Martin, Andre. "Animated Cinema: The Way Forward," *Sight and Sound,* 28, No. 2 (Spring 1959), pp. 80-85.

Meigs, Cornelia, Anne Thaxter Eaton, et. al. *A Critical History of Children's Literature,* Revised Edition. New York: Macmillan, 1969.

Miller, H. "Feature Films for Children," *Wilson Library Bulletin,* 45 (February 1971), pp. 560-571.

Patterson, Lindsay, Ed. *Black Films and Film-Makers: A Comprehensive Anthology from Stereotype to Superhero.* New York: Dodd, Mead, 1975.

Peary, Danny and Gerald Peary. *The American Animated Cartoon: A Critical Anthology.* New York: E. P. Dutton, 1980.

Pellowski, Anne. "Children's Cinema: International Dilemma or Delight?" *Film Library Quarterly,* 2, No. 4 (Fall 1969), pp. 5-11.

Perry, George. *The Great British Picture Show: From the Nineties to the Seventies.* New York: Hill and Wang, 1974.

Phillips, Gene D. *The Movie Makers: Artists in An Industry.* Chicago: Nelson-Hall, 1973.

Rice, Susan, Ed. *Films Kids Like: A Catalog of Short Films for Children.* Chicago: American Library Association, 1973.

Rovin, Jeff. *The Fabulous Fantasy Films.* New York: A. S. Barnes, 1977.

Rubbo, Michael. "Love and Life in Children's Films," *Take One,* 1, No. 7 (1967), pp. 20-22.

Sarris, Andrew. *The American Cinema: Directors and Directions, 1929-1968.* New York: E. P. Dutton, 1968.

Simon, John. *Private Screenings.* New York: Macmillan, 1967.

Sklar, Robert. *Movie-Made America.* New York: Random House, 1975.

Steinbrunner, Chris and Burt Goldblatt. *Cinema of the Fantastic.* New York: Saturday Review Press, 1972.

Stephenson, Ralph. *The Animated Film.* New York: A. S. Barnes, 1973.

Street, Douglas. "Movies Kids Like: Current Trends in Juvenile Taste in Cinema," *Children's Literature Quarterly,* 7 (Spring, 1982), pp. 12-15.

Taylor, John Russell. *Directors and Directions: Cinema for the Seventies.* New York: Hill and Wang, 1975.

Tuska, Jon, Ed. *Close Up: The Contract Director.* Metuchen, NJ: Scarecrow Press, 1976.

——. *Close Up: The Hollywood Director.* Metuchen, NJ: Scarecrow Press, 1978.

UNESCO. *The Influence of the Cinema on Children and Adolescents.* Westport, CT: Greenwood Press, 1961.

Index